THE GOOD LIFE

Alternatives in Ethics

▼▼▼

BURTON F. PORTER
WESTERN NEW ENGLAND COLLEGE

ARDSLEY HOUSE, PUBLISHERS, INC.
NEW YORK, NY

Address orders and editorial
correspondence to:
Ardsley House, Publishers, Inc.
320 Central Park West
New York, NY 10025

Library of Congress Cataloging in Publication Data

Porter, Burton Frederick.
  The good life.

  Includes bibliographies, glossary, and index.
  1. Ethics   I. Title.
BJ1012.P67   170   78-31491

ISBN: 1-880157-15-2

Printed in the United States of America

10 9 8 7 6 5 4 3 2 1

To Barbara and Sarah

Other Books by Burton F. Porter

RELIGION AND REASON.   New York: St. Martin's Press, 1993.

REASONS FOR LIVING.   New York: Macmillan Publ. Co., 1988.

PERSONAL PHILOSOPHY.   New York: Harcourt Brace, 1976.

PHILOSOPHY: A LITERARY AND CONCEPTUAL APPROACH.
New York: Harcourt Brace, 1974, rev. eds. 1980, 1995.

DEITY AND MORALITY.   London: Allen and Unwin, New York:
Humanities Press, 1968.

CONTENTS

2 THE RIGHT AND THE GOOD 35

CONTENTS

PREFACE

eople today have an unprecedented degree of freedom in deciding how they want to live, but this freedom of choice comes at a time of widespread uncertainty as to which way of life is best. The two are related, for freedom generates uncertainty as we realize the range of possibilities and the amount of responsibility we bear for the life we select; but our confusion goes beyond that. Deciding how to live is a problem today in ways that would not have seriously troubled our ancestors. The contours of an individual's life used to be more narrowly defined, social and religious expectations held people more firmly within acceptable limits, and there were clear standards as to what constituted a worthwhile (and a worthless) existence. However, as we approach the end of the twentieth century, the traditional sources of knowledge have lost their authority, and people are left in a state of perplexity and anxiety, without center or direction. We have enormous latitude to choose whatever life we want, but we are not sure what life we want to choose.

This analysis of our contemporary condition has become commonplace, although the solutions that have been proposed are highly disappointing. We cannot return to the old certainties as though the intervening historical developments had not taken place any more than we can go home again and be children. Therefore, suggestions of this nature can only induce nostalgia and lead ultimately to escapism. Likewise, surrendering our freedom is unsatisfactory whether we do it in the name of totalitarianism, the corporate organization, Islam, or fundamentalist Western religion. We value our self-respect and freedom far too much to accept a monolithic system without adequate proof, even though by doing this, we would be relieved of the burden of individual responsibility.

In our present historical situation, the only justifiable course open to us is to consider the various life alternatives that exist, in an independent and critical way, and thereby arrive at some viable purpose for our own lives. This book has been written to help the reader in this search—not to provide ready answers but to highlight possible directions. Although the book will be used primarily as a text in ethics courses, the ideas that it contains should not be treated as academic material to be assimilated in the manner of mathematical formulas. Rather, the reader should "mix his blood" with the conceptions of the good life that are presented, and sincerely attempt to decide which is most defensible and fulfilling. For we are dealing with one of the most personal and fundamental questions of existence, namely, what is the best way for our lives to be lived.

The book contains eleven chapters, each of which deals with a major area in ethics. The chapters are further subdivided into sections and subsections to facilitate readability. Each chapter concludes with a recapitulation of the major ideas presented and with review questions. An afterword sums up the major theories involved in the two basic problems of ethics, determinism and relativism, and invites the students to formulate their own theories of the good life. A glossary of the most important terms is included for reference.

► **ACKNOWLEDGMENTS.** I wish to express my appreciation to Ms. Ann Guyotte for her assistance in the preparation of the manuscript. She carried out this project, as she has all others, with accuracy, discernment, and unfailing cheerfulness.

I would also like to thank Richard Bett of Johns Hopkins University and Edward Sandowski of the University of Oklahoma, both of whom reviewed the entire manuscript of this Second Edition and offered many useful suggestions. I also appreciate the careful work of Lester Strong, who copyedited the manuscript and Howard Johnson, who designed the book. Finally, I would like to thank the editorial staff of Ardsley House for their intelligent guidance throughout the project.

THE NATURE OF ETHICS

P eople are not content merely to live; they feel impelled to evaluate their existence and to determine whether they are living well or badly. They try to judge the value of the goals they are pursuing and the broad purposes that motivate their actions. They want to know whether their conduct toward others is right and reasonable or whether they are being unjust, unfair, or in some way morally blameworthy. They want to justify themselves to themselves, and be assured that their life choices are not only good but are pursued in ways that are ethically right.

In short, people reflect upon their lives throughout the living of them, and measure their conduct against an ideal that strikes them with the force of an external standard. To some this is God; to others it is conscience; to still others it represents a higher self that draws them forward beyond the self of any given moment. Whatever the name assigned to this power, it operates at times of deliberation and introspection, and distinguishes human from animal life. For animals may be conscious and the higher species even self-aware and capable of reason and symbolization at some level, but they cannot feel remorse at having ruined their lives or satisfaction at having fulfilled their potentialities. No animals experience a sense of integrity, regret, penitence, innocence, or self-reproach.

There are, then, ongoing internal dialogues within human beings that can also become interpersonal conflicts when values are at variance and generate basic disagreement. People are concerned with defending the principles they hold, either to others or themselves, summoning good reasons to support their commitments. That is, they feel the necessity to enter into the realm of ethical discussion, and attempt to establish strong grounds for maintaining the values fundamental to their lives.

But how is it possible for values to be justified? Disputes about scientific facts can be very difficult to settle, but one can use independent empirical tests which help confirm or refute claims about the physical world. The proof takes the form of the reaction of gases, the color of litmus paper, or the appearance of organisms under a microscope. But how can one resolve the question of whether filial devotion or personal development is more important, or whether loyalty transcends the value of honesty? It may seem that ethical disputes cannot be resolved in any objective way but merely reflect differences in taste and attitude between people. Perhaps values, by their very nature, are impossible to verify, and the ethical positions people take only show the societal or parental norms they have assimilated. When a person says "Promises should be kept," this may be only an autobiographical comment which reveals more about the psychology of the person than about the nature of promises.

Such a conclusion is extremely tempting when one is faced with the difficulties of justifying values but it does not hold up well under scrutiny; in a sense, it is not a conclusion at all but a throwing up of one's hands, a cry of exasperation. People who say that value claims cannot be established usually mean that they are baffled as to how to validate value judgments. But not knowing how to justify values is not the same as knowing that values cannot be justified.

It is certainly true that ethical problems are not solved in empirical ways, that is, by means of the types of observation and experimentation common to physical science; nevertheless standards do exist for determining which ethical ideals and practices are more likely to be correct. Although scientific empiricism is not the principal method used in ethics, that does not mean no criteria are available to separate better and worse values or that all ethical judgments simply reflect our sociopsychological background.

THE STANDARD OF REASONABLENESS

The standard most often employed in ethics is that of reasonableness whereby that theory which is most in accord with reason is judged to be true. More specifically, the standard of reasonableness means that an ethical theory must (1) be consistent within itself and with regard to its implications, (2) take the relevant facts into consideration and not contradict those facts, and (3) provide the most probable interpretation of human experience. Each of these criteria requires elaboration.

▶ CONSISTENCY. It would be inconsistent and therefore invalid to claim, for example, that all events occur according to a divine providence which rules the universe *and* to maintain that people have responsibility for their lives. Such a position has been taken at various points in intellectual history by theologians such as Martin Luther (1483–1546), Sören Kierkegaard (1813–1855), and St. Augustine (354–430)[1] who tried to explain away the inconsistency by calling it a mystery. But it seems to be more of an evasion,

---

1. See M. Luther, *The Bondage of the Will*, trans. H. Cole (Grand Rapids: William Eirdmans, 1931), Sec. XXV, pp. 72–74, Sec. XXVI, pp. 76–79; see also S. Kierkegaard, *Fear and Trembling* and *The Sickness Unto Death*, trans. W. Lowrie (New York: Doubleday and Co., 1954), passim; and St. Augustine, *The City of God*, trans. M. Dods (Buffalo: 1887), Vol. I, p. 391.

a retreat into obscurantism in an attempt to explain the inexplicable. If all events are preordained, this must include human actions as well, and people would not, therefore, be responsible for their behavior. When a person cannot do other than he or she did, then that individual has no freedom of choice and cannot be held personally accountable for what has been done. "I could not help it" is a complete excuse, placing a person beyond all liability for his or her actions.

The inconsistency therefore invalidates the theory as it stands, and this example represents the type of muddled thinking that should be avoided if we are to arrive at a sound philosophic position. One cannot logically give credence to the incredible any more than one can doubt the indubitable.

Parenthetically it should be stated that no inconsistency exists in maintaining (as Christian theology does) that God *foresees* all human choices but human beings are nevertheless free to choose. In other words, people are only denied freedom and responsibility for their actions if what they do is foreordained, not just foreseen. The point may be made clear by an analogy: If you know people well, you know their characteristic choices, that is, the choices they consistently make. But that does not imply they must decide as they do; it only means that you know they will not decide differently. The fact that you can accurately predict how people will act does not imply that their behavior is forced.

Foreseeing, then, does not mean the absence of freedom for it is simply predicting what people will do, not what they must do. The person *would* not do otherwise but that does not mean they *could* not do otherwise. Therefore, Christian theology is consistent in saying that foreknowledge does not imply the absence of choice. The theologian asserts that God, in his omniscience, knows how we will act, yet the decision is ours. Human beings are responsible for their actions even though God knows in advance every action they will choose.

The point of these examples is that consistency is a prime requisite in building an acceptable theory. To hold people responsible for their behavior is inconsistent with a belief in a predetermined universe but consistent with the view that God foresees all events. If we were to build an ethic around a religious system, then this distinction would have to be kept in mind.

▶ **THE NONCONTRADICTION OF FACTS**. To illustrate the second point, that the relevant facts must be taken into consideration and not contradicted, let us take an idea from ancient philosophy. The Greek philosopher Plato (c. 427–347 B.C.) held as part of his ethical theory that virtue is knowledge. This cryptic phrase has been variously interpreted, but one meaning is that moral behavior is the result of knowledge concerning the nature of goodness, and wrong acts can be attributed to ignorance about the good. It was Plato's view that no one who knows what is good would deliberately do what is bad. All wrongdoing, therefore, is due to people mistaking what is good, rather like a child who foolishly eats too much dessert not realizing that a stomachache will follow. With wisdom, one naturally makes sensible and worthwhile choices. Moral education, then, is a prerequisite for moral behavior, for whoever knows the good will automatically act in accordance with it.

Plato may be forgiven for what seems to our post-Freudian mentalities to be a naive assumption, but a modern thinker who failed to consider the findings of psychoanalysis could hardly escape criticism. That is, if a modern theory claimed that people always act rationally, in accordance with what they know to be good for others or themselves, it would be condemned as superficial and inadequate. For Freud and others have shown us that people will act in irrational and destructive ways even after they realize the wrong they are doing. Out of frustration, guilt, compulsion, fear, aggression, success, anxiety, and so forth people will repeatedly commit harmful acts despite their knowledge of good and bad. In fact, the concepts of guilt and sin presuppose an awareness by the person of his or her wrongdoing, and moralists have expended a great deal of energy attempting to fortify not the weak-minded but the weak-willed against temptation. Even among the Greeks the concept of *akrasia* existed, and it was defined by Aristotle as knowing what one ought to do but not doing it. Plato himself referred to it as the conflict of reason with other "parts of the soul," but by and large neglected to integrate the concept into his overall theory.

In brief, the relevant facts about human psychology are largely neglected, and that undermines the claim that virtue is knowledge. Plato did not pay proper attention to the phenomenon where one's principles are stronger than one's character. Any ethical theory that fails to consider factors of this degree of significance can be criticized as having a serious gap; sins of omission can be as important as sins of commission.

Saying that relevant facts must be taken into account does not mean that facts form the *basis* for values. Rather, facts can influence value judgments, usually by illuminating their implications or consequences. In the subsequent discussion on ethics and science and on the naturalistic fallacy, the prohibition against deriving value from facts is made clear.

▶ **THE PROBABILITY OF INTERPRETATION**. An example of the third criterion, that a theory must offer the most probable interpretation of human experience, can be found in the doctrine of a retributive universe.

People sometimes feel that their wrongdoings are known and punished by a hidden but just power governing the world. Usually this power is identified as God but it need not be; an impersonal moral force or a mechanical system of rewards and punishments could also be thought responsible for all human joy and suffering as in the Hindu and Buddhist concept of karma. Whatever the attribution, people may believe that they reap what they sow, that when disaster strikes it is the result of some transgression on their part. "What have I done to deserve this?" is a familiar cry when sickness occurs or when people find themselves the victim of some natural catastrophe. It is the cry of Job in the Bible, an upright and God-fearing man who suffered a multitude of misfortunes, and the cry of all those who feel themselves oppressed by calamities and try to discover the sins that have brought such punishment down upon their head.[2] We say, "Why me?" and by that phrase we mean not only to search our own souls but the soul of the universe, wondering whether fairness and justice exist and whether our pain is deserved.

But at this point, when we question the justification for our suffering, we can be led to doubt the entire idea of the universe

---

2. Even the fact of our mortality may make us wonder what crime we have committed to deserve a sentence of death. The Biblical story of the Fall trades upon this type of thinking, offering an explanation for death in terms of the sin of Adam and Eve, which all of humankind inherited. Also included would be the belief that Christ died for our sins, and through belief in him we can gain eternal life.

functioning in a retributive way. For the scheme of rewards and punishments is strangely askew, so much so that a scheme of this kind does not seem to be operating at all. People who are essentially good can experience one tragedy after another while some awful people enjoy amazing luck, getting through life virtually unscathed. Not only is the distribution of suffering askew but the degree of suffering does not correspond to the severity of people's offenses. In a court of law we may strive for justice but in the natural world the punishment rarely fits the crime.

Simply stated, the universe is not necessarily fair, at least this side of the grave. Human experience does not support the notion that immoral people are visited with natural evils in their earthly life and moral people are blessed with happiness. The rain seems to fall on the just and the unjust alike.

A more probable interpretation as to why certain people are the victims of a catastrophe is that they happen to be at the place on earth where the event occurs, whether the event is a hurricane, an earthquake, or a volcanic eruption. Similarly, the reason why some people contract poliomyelitis or leukemia has to do with micro-scopic forms of life that happen to be present in their bodies. It does not seem to correlate at all with the moral characters of those indi-viduals. To think otherwise would be an unreasonable position, aris-ing perhaps from our desire for justice but not borne out by experience or logic.

▶ **THE IMPLICATIONS OF THE STANDARD OF REA-SONABLENESS**. These three criteria, then, constitute the stand-ard of reasonableness that an ethical theory must satisfy if it is to be taken seriously. This means that the mode of ethical justification certainly differs from that of scientific verification but not in being subjective; it is an equally external and rational matter. Therefore, one person's opinion is not necessarily as good as another's, for, as we have seen, ethical theories vary in the degree to which they are rationally defensible. As Voltaire remarked, "Men will continue to commit atrocities as long as they continue to believe absurdities"; reason can help us avoid the absurd ideas.

From the foregoing it should not be inferred, of course, that science does not operate rationally as well as empirically. In fact, we label a field as science not because of its subject matter but because of its rigorous method of dealing with empirical phenomena. Both astronomy and astrology are concerned with the stars but only one is a science; the same is true of alchemy and chemistry. It is scientific method that distinguishes science, and that is a highly rational activity involving the formulation of a hypothesis, intelligent experimentation, observation, and statistical analysis, and the testing of the predictive power of the hypothesis.

JUSTIFYING THE USE OF REASON

It could be objected here that the standard of reasonableness used by ethics, in all of its individual criteria, depends upon an acceptance of reason as the yardstick for measuring truth, and that such an acceptance is biased and arbitrary. Why should reason be awarded pride of place in deciding truth and falsity?

This charge appears plausible but is really rather odd because it uses reason in questioning the reliance upon reason. In actuality, it presupposes the necessity for reasonable argumentation by attacking reason rationally. The individual who refuses to reason about reason is in a stronger position, but few people are satisfied with a refutation consisting of silence or slaps as in Zen Buddhism. And the moment one enters into rational debate about the validity of reason one gives the game away, for one reaffirms rationality in the very act of denying it.

Usually a criticism is launched against reason whenever a person dislikes the conclusion to which he or she is forced by a rational argument. But this is rather like kicking over the chessboard when one's opponent says checkmate. Or as one philosopher puts it, when reason goes against people, they then tend to go against reason.

In all fairness it should be pointed out that although one cannot rationally argue against the use of reason, it may be equally absurd to argue in favor of reason by marshaling rational arguments to support that choice. For one is then begging the question, that is, presupposing the efficacy of reason, which is precisely the point at issue. But here we have reached our ultimate "epistemological" level, our fundamental position as to how reliable knowledge is obtained. And if, at this level, we accept the primacy of reason, then no further appeal can be made to verify our decision. One cannot support reason by referring to its reasonableness, and if one refers to any other type of proof, such as intuition or experience, then reason is no longer being considered as the basic means of knowing.

But although calling reason reasonable does not really lend support, it is preferable to the self-contradiction that is involved in attacking reason rationally. Furthermore, there are considerations that justify our rejecting the nonrational approach, the main one being the implications that are involved.

If we reject reason as a standard, we could then readily indulge our wishes, whims, and passions, unrestrained by considerations of fairness, logicality, coherence, or even sanity. We could convict innocent people of capital crimes because we disliked their appearance; believe that inanimate objects possess spirits and are willful in their behavior; eat sawdust for nourishment and salt to allay our thirst; accept a political system that calls slavery freedom; and maintain that an object is both large and small, rough and smooth, wet and dry, and red and green all over. Once we abandon the authority of reason, there is no criterion for separating good sense from nonsense, and the irrationality or meaninglessness of a theory would not deter us from accepting it. The potential for deception and harm in such an approach is overwhelming, and constitutes strong evidence against it. For if the implications of a position are unacceptable, this reflects upon the worth of the position itself. It does not seem justified, then, to cut the rational ground from under our feet but rather to use the standard of reasonableness as a way of ascertaining truth. Perhaps "the heart has its reasons,"[3] but we need our minds to determine whether it has good reasons.

3. B. Pascal, *Thoughts*, trans. W. F. Trotter (New York: P. F. Collier, 1910), Sec. IV, No. 277: "The heart has its reasons which reason does not know." (*"Le coeur a ses raisons que la raison ne connait pas."*)

ETHICS AND SCIENCE

In the field of ethics, reason is especially valuable because, as was previously stated, the empirical method used by science is largely irrelevant in deciding ethical issues. In fact, ethics operates in a sphere which is distinct from science in several respects, and the difference is worth exploring.

Not only do the two differ in methodology, but science is essentially a descriptive and explanatory discipline, whereas ethics is concerned with evaluation and prescription. That is, science deals with the material world, and, through the use of observation and experimentation, attempts to describe and explain the factual aspects of that world. Ethics inhabits a far more subtle realm: that of moral evaluation. It is not so much interested in what is the case as with what should be the case, not the area of factual assertions but that of value judgments. That is not to say that scientists do not make implicit or explicit value judgments (or that ethicists never employ descriptions), but that as scientists, doing so is not within their realm.

For example, chemists can tell us that strychnine kills people and streptomycin cures certain diseases, but they cannot tell us whether to use the strychnine or the streptomycin. *Qua* chemists, they are disqualified from judging the moral question involved in, say, assassinating a tyrant; their expertise extends only to the behavior of chemical substances. In the same way, sociologists can determine whether the high divorce rate in the United States is due primarily to the decline of religion and the consequent loss of belief in the sanctity of marriage, but they cannot, as sociologists, make any moral judgment as to whether marriage itself is worth preserving. In other words, they can provide an explanation of the causes, function, and structure of the institution but not an evaluation of whether marriage is a contribution or an impediment to the good life. Even if the sociologist were to point out that the marital relationship lends stability and security to human existence, that still would not tell us whether marriage is worthwhile, for the values of stability and security remain to be judged—perhaps against considerations of personal growth, openness, and freedom. On a question of this kind sociologists are necessarily mute, confined as they are to descriptions of social institutions and social relationships. It is the ethicists who have the area of value judgments as their province.

Not only are the physical and social sciences barred from the realm of evaluation but ethics, in making evaluations, is basically unconcerned with scientific facts about the world. For value judgments are not founded upon factual information. Ethics may refer to facts in drawing out the implications of a theory or in showing the relation between actual and ideal behavior, but it does not use facts as the basis for any system of values.

Facts are actually irrelevant in determining values. How people actually behave does not affect the question of how they ought to behave; it neither adds nor detracts from any ideal of human conduct. And how the world operates is beside the point in deciding which principles we ought to hold; it leaves the question of right and wrong fundamentally untouched. The following two examples should help clarify this point.

▸ **PSYCHOLOGICAL EGOISM**. The doctrine of *psychological egoism* maintains that human beings are so constituted that they tend to act in terms of their self-interest. In support of this position, the egoist points to the pleasure principle described by Sigmund Freud (1856–1939) according to which people generally seek the immediate satisfaction of their desires and immediate relief from pain and discomfort. It is simply the nature of the beast, the egoist claims, for people to pursue satisfaction for themselves and avoid any personal discomfort. This means that people will always place their own interests above those of others, and behave selfishly rather than altruistically. Whenever people have a choice between helping others and helping themselves, they will naturally choose themselves first.

To the psychological egoist, then, altruism is either extremely rare or altogether a myth because, upon analysis, every supposedly unselfish act can be found to be motivated by selfish concerns. People may pretend to others or to themselves that their actions are founded on noble purposes and humanitarian ideals but these are simply disguises for self-seeking. They may even perform actions that are helpful to others but only as a means of benefiting themselves, for if helping another person should conflict with one's personal advantage then that behavior soon ceases. People are only generous in cases where helping others and helping themselves happen to coincide, which shows that, at bottom, they have been selfish all along, performing altruistic actions for egoistic reasons.

To the objection that military heroes are admired for their unselfish bravery and dedication to their country, the psychological egoist answers that heroes are characteristically people who desire personal distinction, advancement, and fame; self-aggrandizement is the motive behind their actions. And if one should point to acts of philanthropy, the psychological egoist explains these away by showing how humanitarians usually want public acclaim for their generosity; they do not cast their bread upon the waters. Philanthropists are also said to want the feeling of self-satisfaction at knowing they have been good, and to have a sense of superiority over the needy people they have helped. Even martyrdom is accounted for by the egoist as an act designed to secure posthumous recognition by society, perhaps canonization as a saint. The martyr would rather live a brief, spectacular life, climaxed by a superb moment of glory, than have the long, uneventful, and unrecognized life of the average citizen. His or her martyrdom, therefore, is not for God or humankind but for the perpetuation of his or her name; it is essentially egocentric.

Based upon this psychological interpretation of human nature, the *ethical egoist* then argues that, not only do people usually act for themselves, but they are justified in doing so. The universal fact of selfishness is said to constitute good reason for accepting selfishness as a valid mode of behavior. What *is* the case dictates what *ought* to be the case, showing a model for human conduct in the actual world. In short, the psychological findings are taken as proof of the ethical validity of self-interest.

This argument is often used in business contexts to try to justify immoral actions—whether with regard to insider information and stock scandals, to the production of unsafe products, or to deceptive advertising and warranties. The fact that companies do act for their own advantage and the detriment of others is offered as proof that such practices are acceptable.

It is apparent that this type of reasoning is logically incorrect and grossly misleading. The fact that people may act selfishly is irrelevant to the question of how people ought to behave; in and of itself it does not tell us whether people should act for themselves alone. The fact that people are generally selfish or unselfish is an extraneous consideration in deciding which type of behavior is morally preferable. And that is precisely the point. Scientific descriptions about how people behave cannot furnish the grounds for moral judgments. Not all ethical egoism is based on psychological egoism, but when it is, the logical mistake has been committed of deriving values from facts.

It should also be mentioned that the theory of psychological egoism is an extremely poor one to use as a basis for any conclusions because it is extremely weak in structure. To highlight just one criticism, the psychological egoist dismisses cases of apparent altruism by showing the benefits that the person experienced as a *result* of his or her action. But the fact that people can receive personal rewards for doing something good does not mean that they performed the action for the sake of obtaining those rewards. In the same way, people can feel pride at sacrificing their own interests and helping another human being, but that does not mean they helped someone else in order to feel proud of themselves. The consequences of an action are not necessarily the motives for the action, and in the cases given, the personal satisfaction is most probably a byproduct rather than the motivating force, an effect rather than the end for which the action was done.

To put the point somewhat differently, people perform actions out of desire, including the desire to help others, and not for the benefits expected from the satisfaction of desire. Perhaps people only do what they want to do, but that can include wanting to be generous.

But whether or not psychological egoism presents an accurate analysis of human nature, the important point to notice is that no information about how people do act can help us in deciding how they should act.

▶ **SOCIAL DARWINISM**. Another example of misguided thinking of this type occurs in the ethical doctrine of social Darwinism that is based upon the scientific theory of evolution.

The life sciences now accept as an established principle that there has been a process of natural selection at work throughout biological history whereby those organisms whose particular characteristics rendered them best adapted to their environment were able to survive and perpetuate their species. Those organisms that were maladapted to their environment perished in the struggle for survival so that only fossils now remain to show that they once existed on earth.

Some creatures survived because of their strength or agility, others by virtue of their speed and cunning. Some had defensive adaptations such as armor, quills, or wings, others had sharp teeth or horns or claws. Whatever the particular characteristics, each creature preyed upon others so that there was constant warfare in nature, a continual life-and-death struggle for the available food supply. Only those creatures that happened to possess the qualities demanded by their environments survived and produced offspring. The less favored creatures, which were too weak or inept or vulnerable, were inevitably destroyed.

On the basis of these facts about evolutionary development, it has been argued that nature has shown us a pattern for human behavior. Just as animals in a natural state inexorably follow the law of survival of the fittest, so the human animal should conduct him- or herself according to that governing principle. We must accept the hard code of the natural-selection process whereby the weak perish and the strong survive, rather than artificially sustaining those members of the species who lack the ability to provide for themselves. If people succeed in life, that shows they have the requisite abilities and are fit to live. By the same token, if people fail, then they demonstrate by that failure their unfitness for survival.

We should not, therefore, support the weaklings, the misfits, or the psychological or physical cripples, for they will only transmit the defective strain. They will produce a line of descendants who, raised in a tradition of defeat and carrying genetic weaknesses, will also be unsuccessful in life. The entire race would degenerate if we interfered in the process of natural selection by introducing social measures such as welfare programs for the indigent, health care for the infirm, and retirement programs for the elderly. In a moral sense, it would be wrong, then, to oppose nature's laws and allow the unfit as well as the fit to survive.

The theory of evolutionary ethics is discussed more fully in

Chapter 8, but for our present purposes the significant aspect of the theory is its erroneous attempt to deduce a value system from a description of the natural world. The advocate of evolutionary ethics is arguing that because "survival of the fittest" is the operative principle in nature, therefore it ought to be the prevailing ethic in human society. But as we have seen in discussing the theory of ethical egoism, we cannot logically derive an "ought" from an "is"; because something *is* the case does not mean it *ought* to be the case. Conduct may be judged as right or wrong, praiseworthy or blameworthy, but not on the basis of whether it is actually practiced. Rather, we judge actual conduct, in the human or natural world, according to ethical standards; otherwise the tail is wagging the dog.

In the case of evolutionary ethics, serious questions can be raised about the brutality of allowing the unfortunate members of society to die rather than being compassionate and supportive toward them. But in any case it is illogical to argue that the facts of nature furnish the grounds for values.

THE NATURALISTIC FALLACY

The technical label for the mistake of attempting to derive evaluative conclusions from descriptive premises is the *naturalistic fallacy,* and the discussion of why it is a mistake has been associated principally with the British philosophers David Hume (1711–1776) and G. E. Moore (1873–1958),[4] although the latter gave it an unusually wide meaning. According to the standard version, the naturalistic fallacy is committed whenever an argument asserts that, because of certain facts concerning human behavior or the physical world, certain values therefore follow as a consequence. This is a fallacy in terms of formal logic because the conclusion of a

4. D. Hume, *Treatise of Human Nature* (Oxford, England: Clarendon Press, 1896), p. 469; G. E. Moore, *Principia Ethica* (Cambridge, England: Cambridge University Press, 1959), p. 73.

valid deductive argument cannot contain anything that is not present in the premises. One cannot begin with oranges and reach conclusions about apples. It is a *naturalistic* fallacy because values are said to follow from certain natural facts.

Not all philosophers, of course, accept the naturalistic fallacy as a genuine mistake in thinking; some claim that to call the views of one's opponent a fallacy is merely an ingenious rhetorical device.[5] But the logic is difficult to combat, and there is a definite usefulness in separating the realm of description from that of evaluation. For example, people often make the mistake of assuming that what one desires (descriptive fact) is *ipso facto* desirable (value judgment), and that whatever a person likes is acceptable by virtue of the fact that he or she likes it. But what is desired is not necessarily worth desiring, and what someone likes does not automatically become worthy of being liked. People can pursue the most superficial and loathsome goals, and their pursuit of them does not render the goals worthwhile. In other words, a worthless purpose for living cannot be transformed into a worthwhile one simply by choosing it, any more than something trivial can be made important by taking it seriously. There are better and worse ways of living, and the life of a galley slave, for instance, is pretty dismal even if the galley slave should think differently.

Not only do people desire things that are not worth desiring but, conversely, many desirable things are not generally desired. Good literature, music, and painting, for example are seldom in great demand, but that is not a reflection on the worth of art; it may be an indictment of the public taste.

In brief, the naturalistic fallacy reminds us that no account of what people do has any bearing on what people ought to do. And that brings us back to the point that ethics, which deals with values, cannot be based on science, which is concerned with the description and explanation of phenomena.

Before we leave the topic of the relation between ethics and

---

5. It should be mentioned that some contemporary philosophers believe that the descriptive/evaluative distinction has been overstated; they try to show that values can, in some way, be derived from descriptive facts. See W. D. Hudson, (ed.), *The Is/Ought Question* (New York: Macmillan, 1969); and D. A. Rohatyn, *Naturalism and Deontology* (Paris: Mouton, 1975).

science, it would be useful to differentiate between ethics and psychology (as a social science) in a more specific way.

ETHICS AND PSYCHOLOGY

When psychologists look at behavior they are usually interested in the motivation lying behind it, the basic causal factors that reveal the psychological makeup of the person. They are trying to understand the individual in terms of his or her behavior, and actions are important insofar as they are indicative of the underlying personality. "What made Mary react that way? Why did she respond with such embarrassment or hostility or distress in that situation?" Such questions show the tenor of the psychologist's concern. The fundamental springs of action are of paramount interest.

If the psychologists are Freudian in orientation, they will want to understand the person's mind, the defenses of the ego, the extent to which the superego has repressed the impulses of the id, and so forth. If they are behaviorists, they may deny the person has a mind, and look for the stimulus-response pattern which conditioning has produced; a habitual pattern of behavior, it is assumed, shows the person's basic psychology. In either case, the concern of the psychologist is with the question of why people act as they do.

The ethicist, on the other hand, does not want to know the causes of action but the reasons for action, seeks not the motivation but the justification involved in various forms of behavior. In ethics one looks for good reasons justifying the choice of one mode of conduct over another, and the fact that someone may have been impelled by sadistic tendencies in the performance of some cruel act does not excuse the act. People do not escape blame for blameworthy actions by revealing the psychological forces that prompted them to perform such acts any more than they deserve not to be praised for praiseworthy actions because the psychological reasons behind such behavior can be demonstrated. Unless a person acted under compulsion and could not help but do what he or she did, the ethical judgment should be unaffected by considerations as to the causes involved. In normal circumstances, then, to show the motivation behind action is not to establish good reasons for action; rather, it is ethically irrelevant.

In a case of killing, for example, the psychologist may find that the killer's motivation included rebellion against an oppressive father with whom the victim was identified, the assertion of manliness in the face of anxiety about certain homosexual propensities, the need to combat basic feelings of inadequacy and inferiority, and so forth. However, if we were to attempt to justify the killing ethically as not being a genuine case of murder, we would use arguments such as the following: that the person accidentally fired the gun, or that he was defending himself against an unjust attack (a plea of self-defense), or that he was ordered to shoot by someone who held his wife and children hostage. It is the second set of factors, not the first, that could exonerate the person from a charge of murder.

By this example we can see that the ethicist analyzes action without regard to psychological considerations, and that questions about the moral nature of actions are not answered in terms of what prompted a person to act as he or she did. Ethics and psychology, therefore, do not have the same subject matter by any means. As the American philosopher William James (1842–1910) put it: "... the only logical position is to judge an idea not according to its motivation but according to its content.... By their fruits ye shall know them, not by their roots."[6]

THE GENETIC FALLACY

To evaluate conduct in terms of its origins is, in fact, to commit a logical error that has been variously labeled the genetic fallacy, the biographical fallacy, or even, when a person's personality is being criticized, an *argumentum ad hominem* (argument to the

6. W. James, *Varieties of Religious Experience* (New York: Longmans Green, 1923), p. 20. Cf. the entire discussion in Lecture I.

person). Like the naturalistic fallacy, it is the confusion of fact and value but, more specifically, it is the mistake of judging an idea or an action in terms of its source. Examples of this fallacy would be to dismiss the system of Freudian psychology because of Freud's use of cocaine, to ridicule the philosophy of Friedrich Nietzsche (1844–1900) because he may have been insane when he wrote some of his books, or to reject the movement to free Ireland because Parnell was an adulterer. The fallacy would also be committed if we *approved* of actions or ideas because we admired the person behind them, accepting vegetarianism because we respected Gandhi, or believing in Christian Science because of the charisma of Mary Baker Eddy.

It takes only a moment's reflection, however, to realize that the authority of an individual does not establish the worth of what he or she says; rather it is the worth of what is said that establishes the authority of the person. The quality of an idea is what counts, and that is judged in terms of its intrinsic value irrespective of where it originated. "Who said it?" is irrelevant in forming an evaluation; "What was said?" is all that matters.

Relating this to our discussion of psychology and ethics, since we do not evaluate moral issues in terms of their source, then psychology, which deals with the springs of behavior, cannot be identified with ethics, which is concerned with evaluation.

ETHICS AND RELIGION

Another field which is often erroneously identified with ethics is that of religion, and the difference between the two should also be made clear.

Religion obviously differs from ethics in that it deals with beliefs and practices related to the holy or transcendent and especially faith in a supernatural being; but this is not the area of confusion. Frequently people make the mistake of thinking that ethical positions must ultimately be based on religious convictions, that religion is the foundation of ethics. This is a time-honored notion and widely prevalent, but its truth is questionable.

▶ **MEDIEVAL AND MODERN VIEWS**. Historically, philosophy as a whole has been considered at times to be conscripted in the service of religion, and ethics along with it. This view was especially prevalent during the Middle Ages when philosophy was thought "the handmaid of theology," and philosophic reasoning was used whenever possible to demonstrate the truths which, it was believed, had been imparted by God through scripture, miracles, and divine revelation. But whenever philosophy conflicted with revealed truth, it was philosophy that had to give way, for primacy could not be awarded to the fallible intellect when God's word was available as the basic source of knowledge. If reason and faith collided, then so much the worse for reason; Athens must not take precedence over Jerusalem. Philosophy could lend support to theology, as St. Thomas Aquinas (1225?–1274) showed in his famous five proofs for the existence of God,[7] but it could not challenge church dogma with critical arguments.

But the Middle Ages were not (broadly) labeled the "Dark Ages" without some justification, and the contemporary view is that philosophy is independent of theology and need not function to confirm allegedly revealed points of doctrine. Philosophic reasoning is now employed by the religious to separate apparent from authentic revelations, to differentiate between the valuable parts of scripture and those which are the product of superstition and primitive science, and to decide which of the competing interpretations of God's will is closest to the truth. (As we pointed out earlier, even if God is considered to be infallible, we can never assume that we are interpreting his will infallibly.) Philosophic reasoning is also used by the nonreligious as an analytic instrument to probe the foundations of belief and as a means of supporting skepticism. Just as Socrates (469?–399 B.C.) maintained that the unexamined life is not worth living, we can also say that the unexamined faith is not worth holding. If a religion can withstand critical examination, then we may be justified in accepting it, but if it fails to meet critical standards, then perhaps the faith, not the philosophy, should be called into question.

---

7. St. Thomas Aquinas, *Summa Theologica* (London: Burns, Oates and Washbourne, 1927–1935), Part I, Question 2, Article 3.

▶ **PLATO'S** *EUTHYPHRO*. Ethics has gained its independence from religion together with the rest of philosophy and is usually declared autonomous today. The specific reason for the liberation of ethics can be explained by referring to a logical distinction made prior to the Middle Ages. It occurs in a Platonic dialogue called the *Euthyphro,* and is uncovered by Socrates during one of his customary inquiries into the nature of a basic idea. All of Plato's writings are cast in dialogue form, in which Socrates (469–399 B.C.) is almost always the principal spokesman (and usually gets the better of the argument). In this particular dialogue Socrates is questioning a man named Euthyphro in order to educe from him a sound definition of piety. Socrates professes to be interested in knowing the true nature of piety so that he can defend himself against charges of impiety that have been brought against him by certain citizens in the city-state of Athens. Euthyphro appears to be the person to ask, Socrates tells him, because he is bringing legal charges against his own father for causing the death of a slave. Anyone who can accuse his father of impiety before a court of law, Socrates reasons, must surely know what pious action consists of, and Socrates could do no better than to become his disciple.

Euthyphro rises to the bait and declares, "... what all the gods love is pious and holy, and the opposite which they all hate, impious."[8] But Socrates finds this definition unsatisfactory and replies, "The point which I should first wish to understand is whether the pious or holy is beloved by the gods because it is holy, or holy because it is beloved of the gods."[9] In other words, Socrates asks whether God approves of actions because they are intrinsically right or whether actions become right by virtue of the fact that they are approved by God.

This distinction may appear trivial and pedantic but it carries enormous consequences. For if one affirms the first and says that God loves conduct that is right in itself, then morality is independent of religion; rightness and wrongness do not depend upon God's approval and disapproval. If, however, one affirms the second, then God is declared the creator of morals, and conduct becomes

---

8. Plato, *Euthyphro,* in *The Dialogues of Plato,* trans. B. Jowett (New York: Random House, 1920), Vol. I, p. 391.
9. Ibid.

right only insofar as it is valued by God. On this reading, morality is derived from religion, for it is God who confers value upon actions.

In the dialogue, Socrates forces Euthyphro to admit that the pious is loved by God because it is pious, not pious because it is loved. God cannot imbue conduct with rightness but can only recognize its inherent moral quality. He cannot, for example, make cruelty praiseworthy by approving of it or compassion blameworthy by condemning it. Even though he is God, he is precluded from changing or inverting moral values; he can only condone actions that are right by their very nature and prohibit actions that are innately wrong.

▶ <u>GOD AND ETHICS</u>. Religion, therefore, does not furnish the basis for ethics. Even if religion entirely disappeared from the earth and the concept of God along with it, there could still be ethical principles. Right conduct would remain right regardless of whether God existed. The decline of religion, then, need not entail any corresponding decline in moral behavior. There may be a psychological connection between ethics and religion (because of the association in people's minds) but no logical connection exists.

As Brand Blanshard has put it:

> . . . the conviction that the ultimate ground for duty is the will of God . . . is questionable. It is questionable, first, because it implies, regarding Deity, that he does what he does, not because it is right but because he wants to, which imputes to him a character below our own; and secondly, because it implies that if he willed that we should commit murder, that would make it right, which seems clearly untrue. The moral law is an immutable and objective law, which holds because the good is really good and the bad, bad; and only a morality so based is safe. The person who accepts it because it is the will of God will all too naturally conclude, if he loses his belief, that he has lost all reason for morality also.[10]

10. B. Blanshard, "Morality and Politics," in *Ethics and Society*, ed. R. T. deGeorge (New York: Doubleday, 1966), p. 19.

A common objection to the preceding argument is that if God is the Creator, as he is considered to be within traditional Western religion, then he also created moral values and can change them if he so chooses. God *would* not make cruelty right and compassion wrong, but that is not to say he *could* not do so. As the supreme being who brought heaven and earth into existence, he is also responsible for the moral standards of the human race.

But theologians never assume that God can do everything. He cannot, for example, both forgive sinners and not forgive sinners, perform miracles and fail to perform miracles, create the world and not create the world simultaneously. He could erase his actions and begin again but each fresh start would involve him in the same limitation. In short, God cannot do what is logically self-contradictory; nevertheless, he is still considered to be omnipotent.

This is the answer, incidentally, to the old philosophic chestnut of whether an almighty God can create a rock so large that he cannot lift it. Replying yes or no is equally unsatisfactory here, but one escapes the dilemma by realizing that even God cannot perform self-contradictory actions; he is constrained by what is logically possible.

Just as God can be limited by logic, he can also be limited in his capability to dictate moral values. The fact that he cannot make awful actions into virtuous ones by divine decree does not militate against his divinity. Therefore, even if one believes in God, one can still maintain that ethics is independent of religion.[11]

ETHICS AS A BRANCH OF PHILOSOPHY

Having described the scope of ethical concerns and differentiated the subject matter from both science and religion, it is appropriate now to show the relation between ethics and other areas of philosophy. For ethics is a branch of philosophy along with

11. See B. F. Porter, *Deity and Morality* (New York: Humanities Press, 1968), especially pp. 44ff.; see also K. Nielsen, "Some Remarks on the Independence of Morality from Religion," *Mind*, Vol. LXX, No. 278 (April, 1961), pp. 175–186.

metaphysics, epistemology, logic, and aesthetics, and it involves each of these, for the fabric of philosophy is an interweaving of these threads. Therefore, to understand ethics more fully we will need to explore the nature of these fields and how they interrelate with ethical concerns.

▶ **METAPHYSICS**. *Metaphysics,* which lies at the core of philosophy, takes as its subject matter the study of the nature of reality—its essential character, processes, and order. To Aristotle (384–322 B.C.) metaphysics is a single, comprehensive study of what is fundamental to all existence, and he categorized everything as a substance or a quality or a quantity or a relation.[12] This approach (although not necessarily this classification) may be taken as paradigmatic of the metaphysician's concerns. Metaphysicians want to comprehend the basic nature of the real, its ultimate truths, first principles, underlying essence. They speculate on whether self and object, form and matter, cause and reason, space and time are in some way realities as opposed to mere appearances, and they try to diagram the universe as it is in actuality. They inquire into the mode of being of mind, number, infinity, spirit, or God, and even question the powers and capacity of human beings to understand reality either piecemeal or as a whole. David Hume and Immanuel Kant (1724–1804), for example, regarded the primary task of metaphysics as the determination of its own limits.

The metaphysician also wants to discover whether the universe possesses an end or purpose toward which it is destined—an ultimate aim such as a Day of Judgment or the maximum evolutionary development of all forms of existence. Metaphysicians ask if there is any meaning inherent in the universe or whether all events occur by chance—including the occurrences of human life on earth. Are people a natural part of the material and mechanical order without any spiritual entity such as a soul animating their bodies, or does the external universe resemble the internal psyche of human beings, with consciousness, a will, and unfolding ideals? When one

12. Aristotle, *Categoriae,* in *The Basic Works of Aristotle,* ed. R. McKeon (New York: Random House, 1941), pp. 8–28.

asks questions of this type one is engaged in metaphysical speculation.

Ethics involves itself in metaphysics when issues are raised concerning the ontological status of values, that is, the place of values in the overall scheme of reality. Do certain purposes in living have an objective foundation, and are certain principles grounded in the universe itself? If, for example, we choose to live in accordance with nature, following the rhythm of its seasons, harmonizing our spirit with its tranquility, reducing our activities to simple movements for the satisfaction of elemental needs, are we then linking ourselves to the cosmos in some fundamental way? If we choose to develop our potentialities to the utmost, striving to realize our ideal selves and become all that we can be, is this in keeping with the basic function that human life is intended to serve? And when we defend the worth of freedom, compassion, justice, and honesty, are these natural and universal values, objectively defensible and real? Does the universe contain intrinsic rules of right and wrong that can be found and followed or is it devoid of values, containing only physical matter, brute facts? Has the universe a moral dimension as part of its metaphysical reality or do human beings invest the universe with principles and purposes through their freely chosen commitments, creating values rather than discovering them?

One can see by these questions how ethics and metaphysics are necessarily intertwined. Whenever one begins wondering why certain types of actions and ways of life are preferable to others, one is inevitably led to reflect on their relation to the metaphysical scheme of things.

▶ **EPISTEMOLOGY**. When one reflects not on the nature of reality but on the means for gaining reliable knowledge of reality, then one is involved in a second branch of philosophy called *epistemology*. Epistemologists are not so much concerned with what we know as with how we know. They want to determine how genuine knowledge may be obtained, and how to differentiate between certainties, possibilities, assumptions, hypotheses, guesses, convictions, and self-evident truths. They want to know how one verifies historical statements, scientific laws, aesthetic judgments, mathematical propositions, and religious beliefs, and whether sense perception, reason, or intuitive awareness is the most trustworthy means of knowing the world.

Normally one is only concerned with the content of knowledge, not with its basis; but occasions can arise when *how* one knows becomes an important issue. To take an exotic example, suppose we are traveling in the desert and see what appears to be a body of water in the distance at a place off our route where, according to our knowledge of geology, there should not be any water. We then must decide whether to trust our senses which tell us there is water at that site or our reason which tells us there is not, and if we are dying of thirst it will be a critical matter whether we conclude that seeing is believing or call the phenomenon a mirage. Furthermore, our decision in these circumstances cannot be avoided; it is, in the phrase of William James, a "forced option." We must decide one way or the other because not deciding would itself be deciding: We would, in effect, be choosing reason and continuing the line of our march. Therefore, we have to rely on either the evidence of our senses or our rational judgment; an epistemological choice is unavoidable.

Obviously, not all decisions in epistemology are matters of life and death, but the point of the example is that we must establish reliable criteria for knowledge or we will have no way of deciding what is actuality and what is appearance. Conflicts do occur between the various means of knowing that make the epistemological issue manifest and insistent, and force us to come to terms with the question of how we are to determine what is real.

The connection between epistemology and ethics is quite obvious, for in order to assert that certain values are worthwhile, one is eventually led to explain how one knows this to be so. That is, whenever one claims priority for particular ethical standards and modes of conduct, one must substantiate that claim, not only in terms of a moral justification but also according to some epistemological verification. Every ethic must have its epistemic base, otherwise value assertions have only the status of prejudices, wishes, or dogmas. One cannot reply, "It is self-evident," when asked for the authority behind an ethical judgment, for that may mean only that it is evident to oneself.

How do we know, for example, that the preservation of life is morally preferable to the taking of life? Presumably we cannot use our senses and see that life is better than death. We can only perceive the characteristics of the two states; as with the wind, we see the results but not the thing itself. Do we reason, then, that consciousness is superior to unconsciousness? But that judgment hardly seems to be a rational truth in the manner of "parallel lines never meet" (in Euclidean geometry), "bachelors are unmarried males," or "the square of the hypotenuse of a right triangle is equal to the sum of the squares of the other two sides." Is it, therefore, a matter of intuitive awareness whereby we experience an immediate appreciation of the value of life over death? But intuitions are notoriously changeable and vary enormously between individuals. How can something so fickle, subjective, and unverifiable be taken as the foundation of moral knowledge? Can we depend upon an authority such as parental wisdom, a sacred book, or the weight of tradition? No, because we establish someone or something as an authority according to certain criteria of reliability, and those criteria must be decided first and are the very ones here in question.

Many of these objections can be met, but they are being raised here to show some of the difficulties involved in establishing an epistemological foundation for ethics. It was argued previously that we use a criterion of reasonableness in dealing with moral issues, and that perhaps a "moral sense" or intuitive awareness plays a part in achieving moral knowledge, particularly of first principles in ethics. But the point is that some epistemological standard must be found to serve as the basis of any ethical theory.

▶ **LOGIC.** A third branch of philosophy with which ethics is integrally related is that of *logic,* and the connection is, again, quite apparent. In order to develop our ethical ideals in a systematic and rigorous way, we must employ the rules of logic; otherwise we will have a mass of notions that may be inconsistent or mutually contradictory.

Logic is the study of the laws of inference or the theory of proof. Correct reasoning is its chief concern, and it does not matter what is being reasoned about or even whether the conclusions of an argument are true. The logician is only interested in the form of rational argumentation, that a system of thought be valid in its chain of inference.

The logician's work is both positive and negative. He or she wants to elucidate the procedures for valid argument and to detect fallacies in reasoning, such as claiming that if "nothing is better than a good doctor," and "a bad doctor is better than nothing," then "a bad doctor is better than a good doctor." The logical mistake, of course, consists in an ambiguity in the term "nothing." The first statement, which is called the major premise of the syllogism, can be paraphrased as "there is not anything which surpasses a good doctor," whereas the second statement, or the minor premise, translates to "a bad doctor is better than none at all." Once this ambiguity is made clear, the conclusion can be seen not to follow from the premises.

In constructing valid arguments there are rules of formal reasoning that must be used, and they apply to both induction and deduction. In inductive logic one reasons from the particular to the general, so that if one observes a substantial number of green plants and finds that each one forms starch in the presence of light, one logically infers that green plants in general form starch in the presence of light. The degree of probability of the conclusion depends upon the adequacy of the survey; if the generalization is based upon the observation of two cases, it is naturally much weaker than if several thousand cases from different geographic locations are taken into account. Randomness and stratification are also significant factors. In deductive logic one reasons from the general to the particular, beginning, for example, with the proposition that "all fish have gills" and arguing that if "marlin are fish" then "marlin have gills."

Ethics, like all other disciplines, must adhere to logical standards in developing its systems of ideas. It is possible to reach sound conclusions using an illogical argument, but then the conclusions are true by chance and not by logic. For example, one could argue that since dancing makes people happy, and only U.S. citizens can become President, therefore the earth turns on its axis. The conclusion happens to be true but only by chance; there is no rational connection between the statements that makes the conclusion true. If an argument follows the rules of logical thinking, it is much more likely that a correct conclusion will be reached because the reasoning is systematic. In fact, if the premises of a deductive argument are true and the form of the syllogism is valid, then the conclusion is necessarily true. It is advantageous, therefore, for anyone interested in building a viable theory of ethics to pay attention to the validity of the reasoning process.

▶ **AESTHETICS**. *Aesthetics* is the fourth branch of philosophy and it is very often grouped with ethics under the common heading of value theory or axiology. For aesthetics deals mainly with the determination of standards of judging art (and natural objects), and many of the same questions can be raised about the value of a work and the value of an action or ideal. One can ask, for example, whether there exists an objective basis for evaluation (the question, in art, of whether beauty is in the eye of the beholder), and to what extent our aesthetic judgments reflect our society's tastes. Another common question relates to the degree to which a person can pursue his or her individual interests apart from the obligations which are owed to society at large. Can artists, for example, in clear conscience, foster art for art's sake without considering the moral impact to their vision on humankind?

As this last question indicates, aesthetics and ethics also touch on the issue of obscenity. Some philosophers feel that a genuine work of art, by its very nature, cannot be obscene since beauty and goodness are one. For art to be beautiful and degrading would be an internal contradiction. However, others believe that, beauty apart, a work of art can be aesthetically effective but morally corrupt, seducing society to self-debasement by its sensual and emotive force; the writings of Jean Genet (1910–1986) and the Marquis de Sade (1740–1814), for example, have sometimes been placed in this category.[13] And if genuine works of art can be corrupting, then the moral question of censorship arises. Should that which is obscene be prohibited, or should people be allowed the freedom to demean themselves if they so choose (provided, of course, that they do not inflict

---

13. Works of art do not have to be beautiful in order to be aesthetically attractive, and in the present century most artists do not strive for the attainment of beauty. A work of art can be moving, witty, profound, disturbing, uplifting, and so forth instead of being lovely or picturesque.

the demeaning experience on others)? Which takes precedence in the case of obscene art: the moral dimension or the aesthetic? Is it more important for people to have access to the art or to be protected from the obscenity?

One attempt that has been made to evade the problem is to claim that although art may be obscene, it should be available to the public because it does no real damage; no one was ever harmed by a book, it is argued. But if art never harms people, then it never helps them either; it is irrelevant to life and does not affect people's attitudes or behavior one way or the other. That claim is obviously false and certainly would not be maintained by anyone who takes art seriously. Most artists assume that what they create has some influence on society; otherwise they would stop creating. It would be the rare exception for an artist to work only for himself, sculpting in the morning and destroying the stone at night, writing one moment and burning the pages the next. Artists generally want to affect others by their art and believe that they can in fact do so. The view that art does have an influence seems closer to the truth, and this influence can be for good or ill. Therefore the question of censorship for the sake of the public welfare is a real one.

One final point of contact between ethics and aesthetics might be mentioned. From time to time a proposal has been made to judge the quality of a person's life in terms of its aesthetic character. According to this approach, what is done is not nearly so important as how it is done; the style of an action is significant, not its content—its manner, not its matter. If a person lives in charming ways, with great spirit and grace and poise, if he or she has a harmonious personality and sensitivity to others and to the variety and depth of experience, then it becomes almost irrelevant whether this particular action rather than that has been chosen. It is the way the person's life is conducted that counts, not the particular conduct, for all actions that flow from such a person are imbued with beauty.

There are serious problems in accepting this theory, of course, when one considers whether graceful assassins are exonerated because of their style. Nevertheless it holds considerable appeal and deserves mention as an identification of aesthetics and ethics. The aesthetically refined life is here offered as the standard of excellence. In a sense we have returned to the idea that what is beautiful is good, not only in art but in a human life which has become a work of art.

▶ **POLITICAL PHILOSOPHY**. Metaphysics, epistemology, logic, and aesthetics each has a place in the construction of ethical theories, and these four areas together with ethics make up the main fields of philosophy.

But brief mention should also be made of *political philosophy* which, although not one of the five principal areas of philosophy, is nevertheless important and intimately connected with ethics. Broadly defined, political philosophy deals with theories concerning the ideal form of government, with the nature and purpose of the state, and with the ultimate justification of its authority over individuals. In speculating on how the state should be constituted so as to bring about the maximum good for its citizens, the political philosopher relies upon a base of ethics to determine what the good life might be, both individually and collectively. Aristotle, for example, conceived of his *Nicomachean Ethics* as a necessary complement to his *Politics*; they were in fact, two halves of a single work. And Plato in *The Republic* began with a discussion of virtue and justice in the individual, then developed his famous theory of the just state as a natural analogue. To Plato, the state is the individual "writ large," and the nature and ideal functioning of the one directly corresponds to that of the other. Although most philosophers would not identify the state and the individual quite so closely, there is certainly a logical connection between the two, and anyone concerned with the welfare of human beings would want to understand which political structure would promote that well-being to the greatest extent. Conversely, in order to form a theory of a political utopia, one must first know what it is that constitutes human welfare. Thus political philosophy and ethics are necessarily interrelated.

▶ **THE SCOPE OF ETHICS**. *Ethics* itself has been defined throughout the chapter, but it might be useful to describe its scope more precisely. As a branch of philosophy, ethics consists of an inquiry into the nature of the right and the good. *Right* refers to actions, conduct, and behavior, and here the ethicist is concerned with the morality of acts such as promise-keeping, suicide, truth-telling, and stealing, and concepts such as self-deception, integrity, exploitation, and compassion. This part of ethics also deals with duties and obligations, the relations between "right" and "ought," means and ends, excuses and responsibility. *Good,* on the other hand, applies to the ends, goals, or purposes of existence, the fundamental reasons for living rather than to particular portions of conduct. One refers to someone having lived well or poorly, having led a worthwhile life or a worthless one, and it is in this sense that the ethicist or moral philosopher considers the question of the good life. What goals should people pursue in order to lead personally successful lives? What constitutes a valid reason for living, and what purposes should motivate people overall in their life choices?

It is the latter part of ethics which forms the subject matter of this book. We are almost exclusively concerned here with the examination and evaluation of the various theories of the good life offered by moral philosophers, the alternative proposals and complementary conceptions as to the purpose of human existence. Questions of right are only dealt with insofar as they contribute to our understanding and evaluation of some life purpose.

The problem of the good life is not, of course, the exclusive domain of professional theorists, for everyone speculates on the best way to live. But moral philosophers tend to explore the question more systematically and rigorously, with a knowledge of the various theories that have been proposed throughout human history. They bring to the issue a certain expertise in assessing rival claims and in developing a personal system of thought. Therefore, their findings are more worthy of attention and consideration than the haphazard ideas one is likely to find in most people's minds.

At the same time, because of the universality of the issues involved, we can identify with the moral philosophers' theories and appreciate their efforts. These theories are not beyond us, and we too want to assess the meaning and value placed upon the various lives people live, the basic aims and principles around which human activities are organized. We are equally involved in the search for the best way to live. It is more than an academic matter, therefore, to investigate what some outstanding minds have thought to be good reasons for being in the world.

RECAPITULATION

In this chapter we discussed how people generally reflect on the purpose of their lives and wonder whether their ideals of a worthwhile life can ever be substantiated. We said that, in ethics as contrasted with science, we can only rely upon a standard of reasonableness in determining the soundness of a theory. Then we developed the three criteria of reasonableness with examples of the application of each. The validity of reason is presupposed as the yardstick for determining truth, and the problems with that assumption were explored.

Ethics was then differentiated from science in other respects than methodology, and two major examples were provided to illustrate the differences; in this connection, the naturalistic fallacy was described and its relevance explained. The particular distinction between ethics and psychology as a social science was subsequently drawn and the genetic fallacy was invoked to clarify the distinction further. Ethics was then shown to be separate and independent of religion, and reference was made to Plato's *Euthyphro* to explain the logical basis of its autonomy.

The relation between ethics and the other branches of philosophy was described, including metaphysics, epistemology, logic, aesthetics, and political philosophy, and the chapter ended with an exposition of ethics in its two principal forms: the study of the right and the good. In this book our main concern is with the various theories as to what constitutes the good life.

▼ ▼ ▼

REVIEW QUESTIONS

1. *Explain the standard of reasonableness with illustrations of the three criteria that comprise it.*

2. *Differentiate between ethics and science. How does the naturalistic fallacy confuse the two realms?*

3. *Differentiate between ethics and religion. What does Socrates mean by asking whether "the pious or holy is beloved by the gods because it is holy, or holy because it is beloved of the gods"?*

4. *Explain the nature of the branch of philosophy called metaphysics; compare and contrast it with epistemology.*

5. *Discuss the relation between aesthetics and ethics. Can a work of art be both beautiful and immoral—a masterpiece and an obscene work—simultaneously?*

2

THE RIGHT AND
THE GOOD

he vast majority of this book is concerned with the good, but in this chapter we will also spend some time discussing the right. For the two are intertwined, and we cannot be indifferent to what is right in determining what is good.

RIGHTNESS

As was mentioned previously, *right* refers to actions that are ethically correct, usually in terms of specifiable rules of conduct. Philosophers might, for example, defend the rightness of honoring commitments or respecting the sanctity of life, and argue

35

against treating people as means rather than as ends in themselves. Or they might condemn acts of murder, theft, and adultery, and endorse principles such as paying one's debts, being just and generous, or acting in accordance with social responsibilities.

Religion too has its sets of right principles and moral laws, from the Code of Hammurabi in Mesopotamia (1800 B.C.) and the Eightfold Path of Buddhism (c. 520 B.C.) to the Ten Commandments and the Sermon on the Mount. (Usually the "thou shalt nots" dominate the list and greatly outnumber the "thou shalts," which is unfortunate since prohibitions can create a taste for that which they prohibit and, from a psychological standpoint, they are of limited effectiveness in curbing behavior; positive reinforcement does far more to alter conduct than forbidding people certain actions.)

▶ **THE DIFFICULTY IN FINDING ACCEPTABLE GENERAL PRINCIPLES.** When we begin analyzing "the right," one of the problems that forcibly strikes us is the difficulty in finding any principle that survives critical examination. As was noted, it might be right to honor commitments and to respect the sanctity of life. But some commitments should never be made, such as committing ourselves to a person who is destructive toward us or committing ourselves to a life of crime. In such cases, it would be wrong to maintain our commitments and to finish what we started, to "stay the course." With regard to the sanctity of life, we do not seem to treat life as sacrosanct when we kill in defense of our country. (Not long after Moses fetched the Ten Commandments down from Mt. Sinai, he was, in fact, engaged in a bloody war; yet the Fifth Commandment says, "Thou shalt not kill.") Furthermore, many people feel that capital punishment can be a just response to certain crimes, for instance, espionage, murder, and terrorism; and acts such as mercy killing can be thought courageous and humane as in the case of a patient who is suffering through the last stages of an excruciating, incurable, terminal disease and who begs for death. In these cases, killing might well be regarded not as a moral wrong but as a moral obligation.

In light of the numerous exceptions that immediately spring to mind, it seems extremely difficult to defend any principle as being right. We are told that promises should be kept, but surely not the promise to return a package entrusted to us for safekeeping when we realize that it contains heroin or counterfeit currency or a terrorist's bomb. We may believe that stealing is wrong, but if we are starving because of an unjust social system, then stealing food may become justified. For a spy it is obligatory and even a patriotic duty to steal enemy secrets. Or we may have been raised to think that violence is evil, but in a political situation where the worst people hold the best people in a state of subjection and cannot be deposed by peaceful means, then a good argument could be made for fomenting a violent revolution. We may also accept honesty as a value, but would not want to practice it if a woman has a weak heart and the truth would kill her, or if a man with a smoking gun in his hand and a wild look in his eye should ask us which way his wife went. Here we would have a moral duty to lie, and to do so as convincingly as possible.

There seem to be problems with every conceivable value, including the seven classic virtues of prudence, fortitude, temperance, justice, faith, hope, and charity. Is it impossible, then, to find any principles to believe in, any actions that are ethically defensible?

▶ **FORMULATING CORRECT PRINCIPLES**. Let us review the situation. The difficulties that we were experiencing came about because we assumed that exceptions overturn principles. But in point of fact exceptions reinforce principles. That is, if we discover some cases contrary to what we believe is generally right, then our belief is supported by the fact that there are only a few contrary cases; in general, the belief is seen to hold true. Thus, the fact that the principles of being honest, preserving life, maintaining trust, and so forth all have exceptions in no way invalidates them, but rather verifies their general soundness.

If the contrary cases should outnumber the supporting ones, then, of course, we would have to rethink our general principle— but not when the contrary cases are a small minority. In addition, if the principle is thought to be an absolute law, then exceptions would overturn it, for laws are undermined by exceptions as, for example, the law of gravity would be by the discovery of weightless mountains on earth. But if we treat our principles as general rules, or what is technically termed *prima facie obligations* (apparent or obvious duties), then the contrary cases can be seen for what they are: unusual instances which, by virtue of being usual, support the rightness of our general principles.

One additional point should be made in this connection. If, for example, we should violate our principles of preserving life and kill an incurably ill elderly cancer patient, we are not then saying that killing is right but only that in some cases it may be permissible. Killing is still wrong and preserving life is still right, but we are temporarily suspending our adherence to that principle for the sake of some overriding consideration. Therefore, people who say that killing is sometimes right are being imprecise in their speech or muddled in their thinking. Killing always remains wrong, but may be allowable in certain circumstances and, in fact, ought to be practiced in those cases.

RIGHT AND OUGHT

This last thought introduces a further distinction in ethics between "right" and "ought." Broadly speaking, we assume that whatever is right ought to be done and, conversely, that an act ought to be done because it is right. It would be odd, therefore, to say to a person, "I know that I told you this act is right, but why did you think you ought to do it?" Or stated differently, commending would seem to imply recommending; if we commend certain conduct, then it would appear normal to recommend that people emulate it.

However, right and ought are not inseparable. Sometimes several things are right but we ought to do just one, not all of them. And as we have seen, the preservation of life is right but sometimes it ought not to be done. Keeping promises is right but there are circumstances in which we ought not to follow this principle. In short, we are faced with the paradox that sometimes we ought to do what is wrong and ought not to do what is right. We then must undertake the burden of proving or justifying why the exception should be made—perhaps in terms of a higher obligation.

This paradox is worth noticing but not dwelling upon, for our previous discussion about exceptions to principles indicates why a disparity occasionally exists between right and ought, although by and large a congruence pertains between them. That is, whenever we judge an action to be right, we can also expect that it ought to be done. Right and ought should be seen as separable but intrinsically related elements.[1]

EVALUATING THE MORAL NATURE OF ACTIONS

Another problem with regard to the right, in addition to the establishment of principles and to a minor degree the adjustment of right and good, pertains to the way in which the moral nature of actions is evaluated. In the history of ethics, three approaches can be identified, and they have been labeled *intentionalism, teleologism,* and *formalism.*

▶ INTENTIONALISM

The Importance of Motives. According to the intentionalist view, conduct should be evaluated in terms of the intention (or motive) of the moral agent.[2] The consequences of action, it is argued, often fall outside the power of the person and cannot necessarily be foreseen; every act spreads ripples and ends in mystery, that is, in unknown future events. But the agent is in control of his or her

---

1. See the discussion on "right," "ought," and imperatives in R. M. Hare, *The Language of Morals* (Fair Lawn, NJ: Oxford University Press, 1952), Chapters 10 and 11.
2. Sometimes motive and intention are differentiated rather than being treated as synonymous, and when they are, "intention" refers to the engaging of our conscious will, while "motive" indicates the desire that makes us want to will something.

own intentions, and that is what should be judged. If a person has commendable intentions in performing an act, then the act can be judged as praiseworthy regardless of whether it happens to turn out badly. In the same way, if someone has evil intentions, then the act is blameworthy even if by some chance occurrence the results prove to be beneficial. If you intend to lie but tell the truth by accident, you have still committed a moral wrong; the fact that you told the truth is beside the point. What matters is that people have a good will, that their heart be in the right place.

For example, if someone borrows your car and subsequently has a terrible accident, you may feel partly responsible and blame yourself for the disaster: "If only I hadn't lent him my car. . . ." But the intentionalist would say that you are praiseworthy in this situation, not blameworthy. Although the person would not have had the accident if you had not loaned him your car, you are not responsible for what you could not foresee. But you can be praised for being generous and responding to someone's needs. You did the right thing but it happened to result in tragedy. Because your intentions were good, your conduct is commendable, and the unforeseen consequences of your action are morally irrelevant.

Avoidable and Unavoidable Ignorance. Quite obviously, in some cases ignorance about the results of action is avoidable, and in those cases where we could have known that unfortunate consequences would follow yet persisted in our action we might be blamed;[3] then the knowledge of the consequences may have formed part of our intention. But where our ignorance of the future outcome of our action is unavoidable, then only the intention behind our action matters in assessing its moral worth and not the unexpected results.

Incidentally, Aristotle (384–322 B.C.) analyzed the question of ignorance vis-à-vis responsibility and concluded that people can be excused if the ignorance involved is unavoidable. For example, you

---

3. Whether or not we are blameworthy depends upon the degree of wrong in the consequence we intend or allow. If we merely foresee but do not intend some harmful result in an essentially worthwhile act, then most Catholic moralists would call the act right. If, for example, in trying to save the life of a baby, the mother is allowed to die this is an unwilled, foreseen side effect and therefore permissible in Catholic ethics. The mother is not being killed but rather the baby is being saved.

could not have foreseen that someone traveling to your house at your invitation would be struck by lightning; your ignorance is unavoidable because it was impossible for you to predict that occurrence. However, it is not a viable excuse for a doctor to claim immunity from responsibility for malpractice on the grounds that he or she did not know the latest treatment for a disease; the doctor could have kept up with the current literature and his or her ignorance is thus avoidable. The same point applies to the disclaimer "I did not know the gun was loaded." That is clearly a case of avoidable ignorance.

Aristotle did find excusable one class of actions done through avoidable ignorance and that is when people *could* have gained certain knowledge but there was no compelling reason why they *should* have done so. For example, although a cleaning woman could go through all discarded papers to make sure nothing valuable has been thrown away, there is no reason why she should do so. It is not part of her job, and while her ignorance about the value of the documents is avoidable, it is not blameworthy.

The intentionalist is mainly concerned with cases of unavoidable ignorance and in stressing that the unforeseen results of action are not what determines their moral character. It is the intention of the person that counts, not the consequences of conduct; for that intention is wholly within the person's control and is the most important element in the moral equation.

Earnestness of Purpose. To the intentionalist, the concept of intention does not mean the wish, inclination, or vague hope that some state of affairs be brought about, but the earnest striving to accomplish a moral purpose. It is the empty wish that people have in mind when they say that the way to hell is paved with good intentions, and certainly we would not want to exonerate people from responsibility simply because they hoped that something else would happen. An honest and active attempt must be made, otherwise the person's intentions cannot be judged as genuine; that is, an intention should be something that moves us to act. But when people do try to the best of their ability, and earnestly desire to effect some worthwhile end, then, the intentionalist claims, we can say that what they did was right regardless of how it turns out. As Immanuel Kant (1724–1804), the celebrated German philosopher, stated: "A good will is good not because of what it performs or effects, not by its aptness for the attainment of some proposed end, but simply by virtue of the volition, that is, it is good in itself. . . . Even if it should happen that, owing to a special disfavor of fortune, or the niggardly provision of a stepmotherly nature, this will should wholly lack power to accomplish its purpose, if with its greatest efforts it should yet achieve nothing, and there should remain only the good will . . . then, like a jewel, it would shine by its own light, as a thing which has its whole value in itself."[4]

Theoretical Problems. Kant's statement is a moving one and very persuasive; nevertheless the intentionalist theory is fraught with theoretical problems. One criticism maintains that intentionalism does not evaluate the moral nature of actions at all but only the character of the person performing the actions. The "good will" that Kant prizes, for instance, is that of the person since actions do not possess a will, good or bad. And although people may be praised for what they intended to do, that is not the same as saying that they performed praiseworthy actions. The intention of the agent is separate from the nature of the act and cannot be used to impart a moral quality to it. If someone with the intention of feeding the poor were to poison them painlessly instead, one cannot commend that action because of the good will of the poisoner; at best one could only excuse him or her for the wrong that was done.

It would be odd, then, to have a theory of moral evaluation that has no bearing on action but only judges the actor. Furthermore, critics have pointed out that intentions are extremely difficult to determine. One can see what people actually do, but their inner motives are a matter of conjecture, even when they make some verbal claim as to what is moving them to act. Intentions lie behind overt action and are intangible and elusive, a function of the person's mind, and what a person has in mind can be difficult to know.

One way, of course, of determining people's intentions is by observing their actions, but the intentionalist drives a wedge between the two by saying there can be good motives and bad actions and the former are what counts. This implies that people's motives

---

4. Immanuel Kant, *Foundations of the Metaphysics of Morals* (Chicago: Chicago University Press, 1950), Chapter I. Kant is really saying that a right action is one which is done because it is right, that is, from a sense of obligation to obey the moral law.

are not necessarily established by their conduct, and leaves the question open as to how those motives are to be determined. If we cannot tell what people think by what they do, then how are we to know their thoughts and when their intentions are good?

A further problem with intentionalism occurs when it takes on the form it does in Christianity and asserts that sinning in thought is the same as sinning in deed—that coveting thy neighbor's wife (or husband) is as bad as committing adultery.

One can see why intentionalists might be led to adopt this position, for they do not want the act or its consequences to serve as the basis for moral judgment, and to see right and wrong as lying in the thought alone is a very pure form of intentionalism. But a problem with this position, in addition to the two already described, is that avoiding thoughts is an impossible task. Our actions are within our power and, to a considerable extent, our intentions also, but how is it possible not to allow ourselves certain thoughts? We can dismiss shameful ideas that produce a conflict between our evil wishes and our principles, but not to think certain things is virtually impossible. The situation is very like the game of telling children that there is a treasure hidden in the garden but it can only be found if they do not think of a white rabbit while they are hunting for it. The children then cannot help but think of a white rabbit because they must remember the very thing they are supposed to forget. That is, they have to think of that which they are not supposed to think about.

The point is that one cannot tell oneself not to have certain ideas, feelings, memories, etc., and thereby banish them from one's mind. And if people cannot help what they think, then it makes no sense to blame them for their thoughts.

▶ TELEOLOGISM

The Importance of Outcomes. Because of these criticisms some moral philosophers have adopted an alternative theory called *teleologism* or consequentialism, which asserts that actions should be judged not by the thoughts or intentions of the agent but by their results or consequences. The teleologist believes that the outcome is the most important consideration in the moral evaluation of actions for the following reasons.

Intentionalism, according to the teleologist, not only assesses the goodness of the person rather than the rightness of the act, and is hidden and unknowable rather than extant and perceivable, but in addition, it is entirely inconsequential to morality. What someone actually accomplishes is the relevant factor, not what the person intended to achieve. If, for example, a program of political action were motivated by a sincere desire to benefit the public but, in fact, produced widespread misery, we could not regard the action as morally commendable. Or if an act begins in benevolence but ends in violence, then the act is wrong and no amount of explanation as to the purity of the person's intentions can make it right.

A comparison with the conduct of murder cases in American law will make the teleologist's position clearer. When one person unintentionally kills another, as in a car accident or by knocking a flower pot off a ledge which strikes a passerby on the street below, the person is tried for third-degree murder or manslaughter (the nomenclature varies between states). If the court finds that the person's actions did cause the death of another, then the charge is substantiated regardless of the fact that the killing was not motivated by any malicious intention. Because the act was not done "with malice aforethought," the sentence is usually commuted and the defendant goes free, but the important point to notice is that the court finds a crime has been committed, that something wrong has been done. The agent may be absolved of responsibility but the consequences of the person's action make the act itself morally reprehensible in the eyes of the law.

This is precisely what the teleologist claims. The moral judgment of the action is determined by the results, and the intention behind the action can only function to free the agent from blame; it cannot establish the moral character of the act itself.

Problems with Teleologism. Teleologism, then, seems to be a more tough-minded and empirical theory which uses observable results for moral evaluations. In the words of John Stuart Mill (1806–1873), the English utilitarian philosopher, it values "only the dry and hard consideration of the consequences of actions."[5]

---

5. J. S. Mill, *Utilitarianism* (New York: Bobbs Merrill, 1971), p. 26.

But even though the teleological approach appears to be strongly defensible and in keeping with legal thinking and common sense, there are certain criticisms that are difficult to meet. For one thing, the results of actions are sometimes outside the control of the agent (as the intentionalist points out), and it would be odd to have the uncontrollable ramifications of an action reflect on the act itself. That is, it seems illogical that a morally correct action could be made wrong by an unanticipated train of events, and questions of control aside, it appears unfounded to judge an act by consequences that are distinct from the act being judged. In terms of the moral quality of the act, it seems as irrelevant as the agent's intention. A more reasonable position might be to say that the nature of an action remains the same regardless of subsequent happenings, its moral character being unaffected by what follows from it. The compassionate gesture of helping an older person with heavy baggage catch a train does not become wrong if the train is later derailed and the person is injured; it is a right action that had unfortunate consequences. In the same way, generous giving to charity is not negated if the funds are diverted to some corrupt political organization. As an act of sacrifice and compassion, it still remains commendable.

Another weakness in the teleological theory is that concentration on the consequences of action as the moral determinant implies that the ends can justify the means. That is, if as the teleologist argues the results are what count, then we need not be squeamish about the morality of actions that produce good results. Whatever is done, no matter how vile, is purified by the worth of the outcome, so that any sort of action, even those usually termed immoral, could be justified by the teleologist so long as it resulted in some beneficial end. Cheating or deceiving people, exploiting their ignorance or credibility, manipulating their desires, invading their privacy, being unjust or unfair could all be endorsed in the interest of the final result.

For example, the Soviet government under Stalin's leadership imprisoned and executed millions of people in a ruthless "purge" aimed at ridding the country of undesirable elements and consolidating the gains of communism. Many of the people who were summarily tried and convicted were not actually guilty of the crimes with which they were charged, but guilt or innocence was not the significant factor. The point was to have mass arrests and "show trials" in which examples were made of prominent people to serve as an awful warning to others not to deviate from Stalinist ideas. The effect on the Russian society was what mattered to the government, not whether justice had been done. So long as it was thought that the nation benefited in terms of having the ideals of communism further advanced, then practically any means could be tolerated—including false convictions, torture, and legal murder.[6]

Whenever too great a disparity exists between means and ends, then the moral integrity of an action is placed in jeopardy. To wage war for the sake of preserving peace, to kill murderers as a deterrent to murder, to preserve justice by unjustly convicting someone who is a threat to the system of justice—all of these paradoxes create a moral tension that is deeply disturbing. And these paradoxical situations can only occur when we operate teleologically, looking toward some ultimate good and accepting awful means to that end. It is a basic flaw inherent in the teleological approach that it would allow such a division to open up, permitting wrong action to occur provided it produces a good result; the good outcome can be erroneously assumed to make the wrong act right.

We might say that intentionalism is too far ahead of action and teleologism too far behind for either to be used as the criterion of morality. The intentionalist is really judging the person's character and the teleologist is concerned with the aftereffects of action; neither is addressing the act itself.

► FORMALISM

The Nature of the Act Itself. This leads to the third approach to moral evaluation, that of *formalism* or deontologism. Formalism has the advantage of focusing on conduct or action, not on the preceding motive or the subsequent result, and uses as its standard the moral nature of the act itself. If an action is intrinsically correct, then the intention and the consequences do not matter; the act is still right. To the formalist, the act is what should be judged and other factors are beside the point. Helping others, for example,

---

6. See R. H. S. Crossman, *The God That Failed* (New York: Harper, 1950). The essay by Arthur Koestler is especially relevant.

might be regarded as ethically correct and, if it were, then no external considerations could make it wrong. The fact that the help later proved to be harmful so that the people were worse off than before would make no difference in the moral equation. Likewise, if people help others with the intention of thereby helping themselves, that fact is morally inconsequential. A correct action remains correct even if it turns out badly and even if the right thing is done for the wrong reasons.

The formalist usually accepts the *objectivist* theory of ethics whereby certain acts are considered intrinsically right regardless of societal norms. Paying one's debts, for example, might be considered objectively valuable even if one's society thought otherwise. The act itself is sometimes difficult to separate from motives or results, but insofar as it is separable, it should be treated as the main element. And if certain acts are right in themselves, then they should be practiced everywhere and at all times. If paying one's debts is right in the United States in the twentieth century, then it is equally right elsewhere in the world at any period in history. In short, that which is intrinsically right is morally obligatory for everyone; an act cannot be right for one person without being right for all.

Problems with Formalism. Although formalism is an attractive theory in many respects and avoids some of the principal defects of the other two theories, it has problems of its own. Oddly enough, the chief weakness of this position consists in its ignoring the virtues of teleologism and, to a certain extent, those of intentionalism also in its concern to avoid the vices of these theories. It throws out the baby with the bath water. To judge actions solely in terms of their nature without regard to the reasons behind them or their consequences can produce some monstrous moral conclusions.

For example, it is not praiseworthy but blameworthy to tell a dying person that he was a financial success in life but a failure as a human being even though that may be the truth. The consequences of truth-telling in this instance are extremely injurious, and we cannot conclude that because telling the truth is right, the act is commendable. It is pointless and cruel to be honest here and the action cannot be praised because of its formal correctness. In the abstract, truth-telling may be right, but as an action in particular circumstances it may be the wrong thing to do. That is, being honest in this case is not praiseworthy since it results in suffering, and we cannot ignore consequences of this kind in assessing the morality of action.

More precisely, the formalist's principal mistake is to assume that if *X* is right, then it ought to be done, that its rightness validates any action done in terms of it. John Wesley stated, "I would not tell a willful lie to save the souls of the whole world," and Immanuel Kant said that if a sentence of death were just it should be carried out today even if the world were known to be ending tomorrow.[7] This type of formalistic thinking, which dismisses consideration of the effect of actions, appears blind and maintains principles at the expense of people.

In terms of our discussion of "right" and "ought," the formalist assumes that whatever is right ought to be done (*bonum faciendum*), and that an action is always commendable if it is right in itself. But sometimes we ought not to perform an action even though it is right, and that refusal comes from considering the consequences. If an action will be harmful, then, despite its rightness, we ought not to do it. We cannot morally approve of the execution of a criminal in the above case even if this person should die, for without a world to benefit by the example the death would be largely drained of meaning.

DIFFERENCES BETWEEN FORMALISM AND TELEOLOGISM

Formalism, then, is by no means the clear answer to the question of how actions should be evaluated, although it does occupy a strong position in ethical theory. The major rival theories are, in fact, formalism and teleologism, with intentionalism either

---

7. Immanuel Kant made this claim, and his ethical position, while embracing both intentionalism and formalism, stands in strong opposition to teleologism.

dismissed as dealing with the moral agent rather than the moral action or subsumed under one of the other two categories. That is, intentionalism can be considered a species of formalism if it is viewed as emphasizing the intention to perform an act because of its moral nature, or as a kind of teleologism because of its emphasis on intending to achieve a worthwhile end, some ultimate purpose.

The difference between these two principal approaches, the formalist and the teleologist, can be more finely drawn by reference to a distinction in the theory of penology between retributive and utilitarian justice.

▶ **RETRIBUTIVE JUSTICE**. The reasoning behind the incarceration of a convicted criminal can be either formalistic or teleological in character. On formalistic grounds, the criminal is given a particular sentence relative to the enormity of the crime committed. Certain acts, it is thought, deserve certain punishments as just retribution. By and large, perjury and fraud, for example, should be lightly punished while armed robbery and kidnapping deserve heavier sentences. If people are imprisoned thirty years for a trivial offense, common sense says they have been unjustly treated; when the punishment fits the crime, in the sense of being proportional to it, then we consider that justice has been done. We say, "A debt to society has been paid," or "The criminal received his just deserts," or "He got what he had coming," or "The scales of justice have been balanced." There is the feeling that justice means a fair equation between crime and punishment (or virtue and reward) so that people get what they deserve.

In a cosmic sense, it is as though the natural order of the universe had been restored to an equilibrium, and this, incidentally, is the foundation of the Old Testament idea of an eye for an eye and a tooth for a tooth, which was thought to be just in the sight of God. By this the ancient Hebrews did not mean literally returning offenses exactly *in kind* so that robbers should be robbed or rapists raped, but responding to crimes *in proportion* to their evil nature or to a degree commensurate with their seriousness. It was a measure-for-measure morality rather than the belief that wrongdoers should have the same wrong done to them in retaliation.

Technically, this approach is termed *retributivist*, for it takes fair retribution as the hallmark of justice. There is no thought of the effect that the punishment might produce upon the person or society but only the rightness of the punishment in relation to the offense that has been committed. It is backward-looking not forward-looking, because particular kinds and degrees of punishment are thought appropriate in response to previous crimes. Because John has done *X* therefore he should receive *Y*, not in order to reform him but to give him what he deserves. There is a formalistic rightness in giving a person his due.

▶ **UTILITARIAN JUSTICE**. On teleological grounds, or what is called a *utilitarian* theory of justice, a criminal is punished in order to bring about certain consequences.[8] Principally, the punishment is designed to reform and rehabilitate the offender so that he or she will not repeat the offense. The severity of the punishment which is meted out does not depend on the nature of the crime but on what is needed to change the person's future conduct.[9] The punishment is also aimed at deterring others from committing similar crimes by showing what could happen to them if they did likewise. An example is made of the offender which, it is assumed, will have the effect of forestalling any unlawful behavior that others might be contemplating. In addition to reform, rehabilitation, and deterrence, criminals are jailed so that society will be protected from them, and when they are again considered safe risks, they are released or paroled. Until then, they are disabled and rendered harmless. In pronouncing the original sentence, the judge tries to consider the time needed to effect a criminal's reform and rehabilitation as well as the harshness necessary as a deterrent to others; the judge's overall aim is to safeguard society.

The punishment is thus not apportioned to the crime but to the effect that is desired; the crime itself only serves as an index of

8. This utilitarian view of punishment should not be confused with the theory of utilitarianism discussed in Chapter 5, which advocates providing the greatest amount of happiness for the greatest number of people. They are distinct but related theories, and both would advocate this view of punishment.
9. To reform someone means to ensure that he or she will not commit the offense again. To rehabilitate means to provide that individual with the means to lead a law-abiding life.

the need for punishment and of the severity of the sentence that is required. Since it is forward-looking rather than backward-looking, it has a teleological character; the main concern is the consequences of the action taken.

▶ **DIFFERENCES BETWEEN RETRIBUTIVE AND UTIL-ITARIAN THEORIES OF JUSTICE.** If, then, a bank robber is sentenced to ten years in prison because that is considered appropriate to the crime of grand larceny, a retributive theory of justice is being applied that is formalistic in nature. If, however, the ten-year sentence is handed down because that is thought to be the length of time needed to reform and rehabilitate the criminal, to protect society, and to deter potential criminals, then a utilitarian theory is operative with teleologism as its ethical foundation.

The debate between the retributivist and the utilitarian is ongoing and it would be extraneous to our purposes to pursue it extensively. One point might be worth noting, however. Although the utilitarian theory appears to be more liberal, enlightened, and humane, and retributivism seems based on revenge and thus more primitive, nevertheless the utilitarian approach has an inherent weakness: namely, it can be used to justify punishing people who have not committed any crime. For if a psychological profile shows that someone appears in need of reform (perhaps to prevent him or her from committing a crime), and society would profit from the example, then that person could be sent to jail regardless of the fact that he or she is innocent of any wrongdoing. The retributivist theory may be too close to the idea of vengeance to make us comfortable but at least it ties punishment to the actual commission of an offense; because someone is guilty of unlawful conduct, the retributivist says, therefore certain punitive measures are appropriate. In utilitarianism, punishment need not be connected to any crime, and this makes it potentially dangerous.

In any case, the difference between formalistic and teleological thinking is evident. Formalism asserts that certain acts are right; a ten-year sentence is the appropriate and just response to grand larceny (to use the previous example). Teleologism maintains that the consequences of action are what matter. If a ten-year sentence will produce the desirable effect, then that sentence is justified. The formalist concentrates on the nature of the action in assessing the morality of conduct and the teleologist judges the results.

Each individual who reflects on the basis for moral evaluation must weigh these two approaches to determine which is preferable. Ideally we would want a blend of the two but conflicts can arise between them; they can stand in opposition to each other. Then we must decide which should take precedence in our evaluation of moral conduct: the nature of the act or its consequences.

As one can see, decisions about the right are more complex than one would initially suppose. Not only is it difficult to identify general principles that are ethically defensible but we must also decide whether to judge actions in terms of the intentionalist, formalist, or teleological theory. We have to determine *what* is right and *why*, with good reasons supporting our conclusions.

THE GOOD

▶ **GOALS AND THE GOOD**. Good, in contrast to right, is applied to worthwhile goals in living, the ethically desirable aim or end of existence to which people should aspire. It refers to the basic meaning beneath human choices and the ultimate reason for living—or dying. For as Albert Camus (1913–1960) reminded us, what one is willing to die for is essentially what one lives for. Whatever is posited as being of fundamental importance in life, the pivotal purpose around which human activities are organized, constitutes a person's conception of the good.

We are able to speak about various lives being good or bad because they are lived by people who do it well or badly but we cannot refer to objects as morally good or bad. Objects are value-neutral; they have no ethical quality in themselves. Our moral judgments regarding objects has to do with the use to which they are put. An axe can be used to chop down trees for homes or violins or it can be wielded by an executioner to chop off people's heads. A buoy can save lives by marking a safe channel or cause the loss of lives if a boat should collide with it and capsize. Nuclear energy can be used for constructive purposes or as a horrible weapon in war. The examples are endless, but the point is that *things* are neither good nor bad, and people make a mistake when they judge an object morally. Alcohol and drugs cannot be categorically condemned as evil; it all depends on how they are used. And there is nothing obscene about sex in and of itself, although there are ways in which sex can be made obscene.

The only legitimate use of "good" in reference to objects is a nonmoral usage as when we speak about a good watch, a good tree, a good dinner. These are obviously descriptive not evaluative uses of the term "good"; we mean that the objects function efficiently or are excellent in the particular qualities of their type. We are not morally praising the watch, the tree, or the dinner. In its customary employment in ethics "good" applies to a worthwhile purpose for living, as in "a good life."

To some people happiness is the goal of existence, the ultimate purpose that motivates their activities. To others, pleasure is what should be sought, with pleasure defined as physical and sensual rather than the mental and spiritual states of happiness. Or the realization of potentialities may be taken as the ideal, or following the model of nature, or doing one's duty to God or humankind, or maximizing the experience of existence itself. There are numerous possibilities, which are not necessarily alternatives, for a philosophy of the good can incorporate several conceptions within itself—provided they are not mutually exclusive.

► **HEDONISM**. Each of these definitions of the good must be examined for the purpose of elucidating its claims and evaluating its strengths and weaknesses. For example, the common goal of happiness, or what is technically called the *theory of hedonism*, must be carefully defined for it can be conceived in different ways. We must, for example, decide whether happiness should be sought for ourselves alone or for humanity in general, with our personal happiness counting as only one among the claims of humankind. In addition, we must confront the problem called the *hedonistic paradox*, which points up the self-defeating character of having happiness as a life purpose. For happiness does not seem to be the kind of state that can be pursued directly; rather, it appears to come about as a byproduct of the pursuit of some other aim. If we actively try to be happy, the chances are that we will be frustrated in the attempt precisely because we are striving so deliberately, but if we seek some other purpose in living we are more likely to find that we have led a happy life as a consequence. To try to grasp happiness directly is like putting on a light to see the nature of darkness, or trying to reach the horizon when the horizon line moves as we do. If we are to attain happiness at all, it must be done obliquely or indirectly rather than as a goal that we consciously aim to achieve.

If the hedonistic paradox is a valid criticism (and not all philosophers regard it as such), then it would be odd to recommend that people pursue happiness as their goal, for by doing this we would probably be condemning them to unhappiness. The paradox consists in having a life purpose that cannot be pursued or recommended.

Equally vexing problems plague every conception of the good. It is, therefore, no easy matter to decide which theory is worthy of acceptance as our own purpose in living. The various definitions of the good are not elaborated here since the bulk of the book deals with that issue. When the discussion is completed, hopefully we will have formed a much clearer idea as to what constitutes a justifiable reason for living.

THE RIGHT VERSUS THE GOOD

▶ **WHEN THE RIGHT AND THE GOOD CONFLICT.** Ideally, what is right and what is good should be in a harmonious relationship such that the good can be achieved by doing what is right. But sometimes a disparity exists between the two, and this creates an interesting moral tension.

Suppose, for example, that a woman's goal in life is the attainment of happiness, and she also believes in the value of honesty, which includes not giving a false impression by omitting the truth. However, she finds herself in a situation where to disclose the truth about her past will result in her losing a man whom she regards as essential to her happiness. Perhaps she lived as a prostitute for several years and the man would find that intolerable. In these circumstances she cannot both be honest and attain happiness; either she must forgo doing what is right or sacrifice what she regards as good.

One can always argue that if the man really loves her it will not matter, or that giving up this man does not necessarily mean that she will never be happy. But in our hypothetical case the probability is that the woman would lose the man if she told the truth and that she would not find happiness in the future. Which, then, should she choose: her principles or her purpose?

Our initial response would probably be to advocate the good of happiness over the rightness of honesty. It is the broader, more inclusive goal which gives direction to our existence. But to generalize that choice would be to favor the sacrifice of principles whenever they conflicted with what we want out of life. If lying, stealing, and cheating were necessary in order to achieve our purpose, then those actions would become acceptable on the grounds that the good takes precedence over the right.

Or consider the case of a young man who wants nothing more than to enjoy himself, maximizing the amount of pleasure in his life from whatever sources it can be obtained. He wants the voluptuous pleasure of lovemaking, the sense satisfaction of eating, drinking, and music, the physical enjoyment of the beach, the heightened sensations of the drug world. His only interest is the free life of bodily pleasure, and the more pleasure he experiences the better he considers his life to be.

However, the young man's mother suddenly becomes an invalid as a result of a stroke and needs his constant care at home. For financial or other reasons no one else can be obtained to nurse her adequately besides him, and her emotional stability seems to depend on his concern, attentiveness, and presence. The young man believes he has an obligation to look after his mother but he also feels that a good life for himself could only be one of sensuous enjoyment. Staying at home would not allow him the opportunities to gain the pleasure he needs, yet because his mother is dependent upon him she would suffer considerably and probably deteriorate physically if he led the life he seeks. In this situation, the young man has the choice of either pursuing the type of existence he considers good or meeting his moral obligations to care for his mother. He cannot both achieve a good life and do what is right.

Again, we could argue that the mother may not need the son so desperately, or that the young man may not have chosen an ideal conception of the good life. But in arguing this way we are changing the given conditions of the example; we are evading the choice between good and right rather than confronting it.

In assessing the case as presented, our judgment is complicated by the fact that doing what is right benefits the other person, the mother, and doing what is good benefits the young man who is deciding the moral issue. Therefore, considerations of altruism and egoism are involved as well as the priority of good or right; pursuit of the good is here an egoistic choice, and the right entails altruism.

From a moral point of view, then, we might be inclined to recommend doing what is right. Unlike the previous case, where our initial impulse was to award priority to the good, here we may feel that principles of right take precedence—principles such as the duty of children to care for their parents in their old age (repaying them for what the children were given in their youth), or caring for those we love who are sick and dependent upon us, or not allowing the innocent to suffer when we can alleviate their distress. But to generalize that judgment would be to say that doing the right thing is morally preferable to doing the good, especially what is only good for ourselves. This appears to be unjustifiably severe; for although self-sacrifice may be noble, there must be an excellent reason to give up our chosen lives. And to decide in favor of right conduct over a good life (however construed) seems austere, short-sighted, cramped, and cold. In brief, it would be odd to believe so firmly in following principles that we let our chance at life slip by.[10]

▶ **A POSSIBLE SOLUTION**. We are back to square one, wondering whether the right or the good is superior. The problem

10. For an excellent dramatization of the conflict between good and right read J. Anouilh, *Antigone*, trans. L. Galantiere (London: Methuen, 1960).

will not be definitively solved here for it is an ongoing philosophic debate, and at this point it is sufficient to recognize the ethical dilemma. But one possible way out is to arrange our principles in a hierarchy of importance placing, say, the preservation of life over truth-telling, and respecting persons over promise-keeping. We might then say that, in general, we should act to realize our ultimate goal in life but that this pursuit can be overridden by the moral necessity to perform certain actions high on our list of values. For example, if our overall purpose were to live passively, avoiding anxiety and maintaining our poise and equanimity, this type of life might have to give way before the moral need to defend someone from attack. Or if we sought self-realization as our goal in life, that might be less important than respecting the rights of another person to be treated as a human being and not to be used as an object for the realization of our sensual self.

Using this approach we might conclude that, in our previous examples, the young man should care for his mother because a life of pleasure cannot be obtained at the expense of a loved one's health. However, the former prostitute does not have to be honest about her past because truth-telling is not so valuable that it should be allowed to destroy a person's happiness.

In other words, one can have a justifiable preference for the overall good that one wants to achieve in life while deferring to some high-order principle of right as having priority in certain circumstances. There are bound to be difficult cases in which we are not sure whether a principle is sufficiently important to merit sacrificing the good; but such cases need not destroy the overall approach to resolving conflicts. The fact of twilight does not make it impossible to differentiate between night and day. Insofar as possible we should strive to reconcile our conduct and our goals so that they are not in fundamental opposition.

In our subsequent discussion about worthwhile purposes in life, we must bear in mind that the decision about the good cannot be made in a vacuum. Questions about what is right are also relevant and constitute important factors in our ethical deliberations about the good life.

THE ABORTION
CONTROVERSY

Before ending this topic, we should touch on one of the most difficult moral problems today—a moral dilemma that dramatically points up a conflict between the right and the good. This is the abortion controversy that has effectively divided the nation and caused anguish to millions of people.

From our perspective, the pro-life faction believes in certain basic principles that should not be overridden: the sanctity of life, the wrongness of taking innocent life, and the special obligation we have to protect the helpless. The pro-life advocates usually maintain that it would be sinful to reject life, which is a precious gift from God, for we are not the arbiters of life and death but the servants of God's will.

They further assert that even if life must sometimes be taken, it is only in cases where the persons are guilty of some terrible offense. Capital punishment might be justifiable for murderers, especially serial killers, or in the case of aggravated murders where the victims were brutalized as well. Or killing might be necessary in war when the other side is the aggressor, threatening our homes, families, or nation. However, taking the life of a fetus or unborn child is unjustified because the fetus has committed no crime and is not guilty of any wrongdoing. Here, killing is murder since there is no provocation or threat; the fetus or baby is entirely innocent as well as helpless. It would be wrong, therefore, to have an abortion.

The pro-choice advocates, on the other hand, while attributing value to having a choice, stress the good that would be produced by allowing women to have an abortion. Family planning could take place, the world-population problem would be alleviated, and those children who were born would be wanted. Men and women could decide when to have a baby, and the babies would be properly cared for with adequate physical and psychological preparation.

Furthermore, women would not be forced to bear children that were the result of rape or incest, nor would they undergo the trauma of raising a child who resembles the father in such cases. They would not have to give birth to genetically defective children or be subject to the pain, expense, and practical difficulties that such a child brings.

In short, pro-life advocates emphasize that preserving life is the right thing to do, whereas pro-choice advocates maintain that abortion can promote good for the woman, the family, and society. Viewed from this standpoint, the abortion controversy concerns whether the right or the good should have priority.

RECAPITULATION

We first discussed the difficulties involved in establishing principles as being right, and analyzed the place of exceptions in the determination of those principles. The relation between "right" and "ought" was then described in the light of these difficulties. We offered a critical analysis of intentionalism, teleologism, and formalism as the three ways of evaluating the moral nature of action; under intentionalism, reference was made to Aristotle's explanation of responsibility and ignorance. Following an assessment of the strengths and weaknesses of each theory, the two principal ones of formalism and teleologism were further explicated in terms of the retributivist and the utilitarian approaches to penology.

A discussion of the good then followed, which distinguished between the moral and nonmoral uses of good. Various possibilities were mentioned as to what a valuable purpose in living might be, and the theory of hedonism was elaborated to some extent.

Then the relationship between right and good was explored, with particular examples given in which each could be considered as having priority, although the good was said to have greater importance overall. A way of reconciling conflicts between the two was suggested, and the chapter ended by underscoring that ethical reflection on the overall in life must not neglect considerations of what is right. Abortion was viewed as a contemporary example of the right-good conflict.

1. *Explain the difference between right and good. Would the two always coincide or could they be at variance?*

2. *Discuss the question of whether an action that is right should always be done.*

3. *Present an example of the different ways in which an intentionalist, a formalist, and a teleologist would judge the same moral issue.*

4. *Explain how the retributive theory of justice is deontological (formalistic) in character, whereas the utilitarian theory of justice is teleological in nature.*

5. *Why is it that people can be judged good or bad, but objects cannot be regarded that way? Are there exceptions, as in the case of guns, drugs, or nuclear power?*

3

THE PROBLEM OF DETERMINISM

I n attempting to establish values, either of right conduct or good ends, one soon confronts two theories that have been problematic for ethics since its inception: determinism and relativism. These theories present a problem because each in its own way casts doubt on the authenticity of ethics; each opposes the assumption that genuine values can be supported.

The determinist claims that all of our thoughts and actions, including those of an ethical nature, are the result of forces beyond our control. There are laws of nature that govern all events, including personal ones, and they admit of no exceptions. We think and act the way we do as a direct consequence of external factors, and all of our moral values can be traced to some combination of these determinants. It is an illusion, therefore, to believe that we can arrive at sound values after due deliberation or that we can freely choose to act in accordance with our ethical judgments. According to determinism it is also a mistake to preach or recommend any values, for doing so presupposes people's ability to freely change their minds and behave differently. As Immanuel Kant said "ought implies can." There is no point in telling people that they *ought* to do something unless they *can* do it. Determinism here denies that people can do what they are told they ought to do; they lack free will and are unable to purify their characters or mend their ways.

Relativists are equally challenging in their theory, for they maintain that values do not possess any objective moral quality but are relative to the person or group from which they emanate. What is right in one society is wrong in another, and what Mary may praise, John may condemn. Nothing can be said to have intrinsic worth, but rather each group of individuals establishes values relative to itself. These values are not arguable since right and wrong and good and bad mean different things to different people, and whatever is thought valuable is valuable to the group that believes it to be so; no objective standard exists against which it can be measured.

Each of these positions must be carefully examined because of their powerful effect on all theories of ethics, and although we have touched on them previously[1] it is now necessary to undertake a critical analysis to see if they are genuine threats or paper tigers. In this chapter we undertake the examination of determinism. In Chapter 4 we will turn to relativism.

THE ILLUSION OF FREEDOM

Determinism maintains that all ideas, attitudes, and values are the necessary products of antecedent and external forces. Our allegedly independent decisions in favor of one set of beliefs over another or for a particular mode of conduct are only the con-

---

1. The problems of determinism and relativism were mentioned at the beginning of the book in discussing how ethical theories may be justified, and reference was made to them again in developing the objectivist aspect of formalism.

sequences of causal factors external to ourselves. Equally illusory is the assumption that we are free to act in accordance with our ethical ideals. To the determinist, all of our actions are inevitable responses to given conditions, the strict effects of prior causes. People cannot do other than they do and are not responsible for their actions; consequently, neither praise nor blame is appropriate.

Opposed to the determinist view is that of the libertarians, who affirm the freedom of the will. They believe that human beings are in control of their lives, and that their decisions proceed from themselves as autonomous entities. Libertarians do not assert that all ideas and actions are free, since people can be unconsciously manipulated and controlled, but they do say that human beings possess free will and have the potential to think and act freely. Determinists, on the other hand, deny free will and maintain that choices are never self-initiated; to the determinist, free will is an egotistical illusion.

HARD AND SOFT DETERMINISM

A technical distinction that is usually made within philosophy between *hard and soft determinism* can be useful to our understanding of the determinist position. *Hard determinists* maintain that since all of our actions are caused by either physiological events in the brain (neural impulses) or mental events (such as early experiences which have produced certain desires) we cannot be said to have free will. To speak of freedom and personal responsibility when all of our actions are part of a causal chain makes no sense. *Soft determinists* hold that although all of our actions are caused and could not be other than they are (given the existent factors) nevertheless individuals are important as factors in the causal chain. It was the nature of the individual plus the circumstances that caused a given action to occur.

Both forms of determinism deny free will, but the soft determinist admits the role of self as a causal agent, and assigns praise or blame to individuals as a way of affecting future behavior (although not holding anyone responsible for past behavior). On this reading, the universe is a system of physical laws embracing all things, including human beings, and the libertarian notion of an uncaused choice is impossible. People, however, are agents in the causal sequence.

The distinction between hard and soft determinism, while important in certain contexts, is not crucial to our present discussion, which is concerned with determinism in the broad sense. For our purposes, the determinist is one who denies the ability of any individual to intervene freely in the causal chain of events, and consequently denies that anyone is responsible for what occurs. The libertarian, in contrast to the determinist, affirms both concepts, postulating an autonomous self and holding people generally responsible for their actions.

PREDETERMINISM

The older form of determinism, called *predeterminism*, is the view that destiny or fate rules all events in the natural world, including people's lives. Predeterminism is sometimes linked to a belief in God as the author of the Book of Fate, or it can be founded on a general religious conception of the universe as permeated with spiritual forces which control the movement of stars and people and nations. In any case, the predeterminist affirms a fatalistic view in which every happening is attributed to a cosmic power which predestines its occurrence, and human beings are thought simply to respond to the inevitable events that are their lot in life; they have no choice in the matter. It is not just that events are foreseen, in which case free will might be present, but that they are wholly predetermined.

Arabs use the term "*kismet*" and believe that whatever occurs is preordained; "*inchallah*," they say, meaning "it is Allah's will." The ancient Greeks called it *moira*, which was not the will of the gods but a more encompassing destiny embracing the lives of both mortal and immortal beings; the Greek gods too were governed by fate. Among the Greek dramatists, Sophocles and Euripides especially dealt with the ways in which the machinery of fate operates to bring about some inexorable, tragic end; Oedipus, for example, cannot escape from fulfilling the prophecy that he would one day murder his father and marry his mother. And because the events are pre-destined, they can be foreseen by the seer Tiresias in the same way that Hebrew prophets could foretell disaster. The Romans too accepted predestination as part of their dominant philosophy of Stoicism; they thought that practicing fortitude and equanimity in the face of inevitable tragedy was the wisest way to live. The Spanish say "*que sera sera,*" "what will be, will be," and mean that the future is as fixed as the past. The French have the expression "*c'était écrit,*" which literally translates to "this was written," and the Germans speak about *seinem Schicksal entgegengehen,* or "going to one's fate." Almost every nation has the doctrine of predeterminism as part of its cultural heritage—although considerable differences exist in the degrees to which the theory is adhered to today.

Most Western people have now abandoned predeterminism and regard it merely as an interesting historical curiosity. We only feel sympathy for fatalistic views when events are out of our control or when we try to escape responsibility for our actions and need some psychological defense against anxiety. For example, people who smoke heavily might claim that if they were meant to die at forty they will die at that time and smoking cigarettes will not make any difference. Or a soldier on a battlefield might feel that if "his number is up," then he will be killed, but otherwise he will be safe even in a hail of bullets. In both types of cases, we might be inclined to revert to a belief in predeterminism. Nevertheless our customary attitude today is to reject it as a general description of the way in which the universe operates. Predeterminism is largely an archaic view which has not been refuted so much as abandoned. Not all theories in intellectual history die as a result of philosophic attack; some die of neglect.

The following passage from Shakespeare's *King Lear* might be a fitting epitaph:

▼ ▼ ▼
This is the excellent foppery of the world, that when we are sick in fortune, often the surfeits of our own behaviour, we make guilty of our disasters the sun, the moon, and the stars; as if

we were villains on necessity; fools by heavenly compulsion; knaves, thieves, and treachers, by spherical predominance; drunkards, liars, and adulterers, by an enforc'd obedience of planetary influences; and all that we are evil in, by a divine thrusting on—an admirable evasion of whoremaster man, to lay his goatish disposition to the charge of a star![2]

▲ ▲ ▲

CONTEMPORARY DETERMINISM

The contemporary form of determinism has a social scientific character as opposed to the cosmic overtones of predeterminism. The modern determinist maintains that people's character, conduct, ideas, attitudes, and so forth are the product of hereditary and environmental factors. We think and act as we do because of our genetic inheritance as well as the various social, psychological, political, educational, cultural, and economic forces that play upon us. According to the contemporary determinist, we harbor the illusion that we are free to decide in favor of one alternative or the other but in actuality all of our decisions are made for us. For example, if a student opts to attend college, it may seem to be a free choice in that he or she was able to choose otherwise; but the determinist would say that, upon analysis, various external factors can be seen to be responsible for the decision. The expectations and socioeconomic level of the student's parents would have played a major role, as would peer pressure, prior educational experiences, the temperament and intelligence that the student inherited, the psychological need to achieve, and so forth. These are the operative elements that caused the decision; it was not a voluntary act of choosing the option of going to college. The student could not do anything else.

2. W. Shakespeare, *King Lear*, in *William Shakespeare: The Complete Works*, ed. Peter Alexander (New York: Random House, 1952), Act. 1, Scene 2, p. 1078.

The determinist is here denying that human beings possess free will, which is different from the denial that freedom exists. To have freedom means to be able to effect what one wills. To possess free will means to have the ability to will something freely. People in jail are in circumstances that constrict their freedom but they still might be said to be in control of their decisions and thus to have free will. In the same way, if a political regime restricts people's civil liberties, their freedom has been limited but their free will remains unaffected. However, the determinist rejects the idea that people have free will, and claims that it is a mistake to think that people can autonomously decide which beliefs and behavior they will choose. According to this view, all our decisions are the result of determinants beyond our control, and though conventional wisdom may say that we are the masters of our fate and the captains of our souls, that is simply an outmoded mythology; cool and objective scientific analysis proves otherwise.

The social scientific determinist when called upon to specify the factors behind people's thoughts and deeds will usually draw up a list of determinants including many or all of the following: genetic endowment, climate and geography, social and cultural influences, and psychological factors. We consider each of these here.

▶ **GENETIC ENDOWMENT.** The chemical, anatomical, and physiological characteristics that we inherit make a considerable difference in the kind of person we become. These traits include skeletal structure, nervous system, glandular activity, gender, height, coloring, mental capacity (that is, the complexity of one's cerebral cortex), sense organs and internal organs, secondary sexual characteristics, chemical metabolism, and so forth. It also includes body type or physique which, according to the classification by W. H. Sheldon, can be divided into ectomorph, a slender, angular, fragile, light body build; endomorph, a round, soft body with a tendency toward fat; and mesomorph, a muscular, large-boned type of body.[3]

Accordingly, an ectomorphic female with a short, slight build,

---

3. See W. H. Sheldon, *The Varieties of Human Physique* (New York: Harper and Brothers, 1940).

an underactive thyroid and sluggish metabolism (resulting in a low level of energy), poor motor coordination, and high intelligence is extremely unlikely to become a professional football player. In the same way, someone with an endomorphic male body, having slow reflexes, a low intelligence quotient, and poor eyesight, has a slim chance of becoming an astronaut. Not only would these individuals be barred from the respective fields by the existing standards but, more importantly, the choice would not be a viable one for them. They simply would not choose to do anything contrary to their bodily capabilities and in that sense their biology would dictate their destiny. Only those fields compatible with their biological selves would hold any appeal, which means that their "decisions" would be made by their physical natures, not by they themselves.

▶ **CLIMATE AND GEOGRAPHY**. The influence of climatic and geographical factors upon people's personalities and activities is generally recognized by laypeople and scholars alike, and in recent years historians have been taking a closer look at their effects. In this they are following the seminal theory of Arnold Toynbee (1889–1975), who maintained that people in cool climates are characteristically serious and industrious, and have highly developed social, economic, and political systems; everyone tends to be brisk, organized, and efficient. In warm climates, on the other hand, there is a tendency for people to be phlegmatic, to value pleasure over accomplishment, to live sensuously rather than intellectually, and to be lighthearted and less organized (One may think, perhaps, of North America as opposed to South America, Germany as compared to Italy, or northern France in relation to southern France.)

Toynbee, in fact, proposed as a theory of history that the world's work is done by people in the northern temperate zone, and that the main contributions to civilization have come from the northern latitudes of Asia, Europe, and America.[4] The climate cannot be too harsh, for arctic conditions can stifle progress, but an equatorial

---

4. A. Toynbee, *A Study of History* (New York: Oxford University Press, 1935). Toynbee believed that societies succeed or fail depending upon their response to the challenges of the environment.

climate, on the other hand, does not offer enough challenge. According to Toynbee, soft conditions produce soft people, while hardy conditions are needed to produce hardy souls who are stimulated to achieve for themselves and their society. The latter transform stumbling blocks into stepping stones, having just enough opposition to mobilize their will and energy.[5]

Other climatic conditions can operate in a like manner: A rainy climate inclines people toward indoor activities, a sunny climate induces them to enjoy more of an outdoor life. Hot, humid conditions produce torpor, whereas cool, dry weather is invigorating and results in spirited action.

It has been similarly proposed that the geographical area in which one lives partly determines the kind of person one becomes. People in mountainous regions are said to be more independent and self-reliant, quiet, strong, and introspective, whereas those in the plains tend to be more gregarious, extroverted, and mutually dependent. People in landlocked areas are allegedly inclined toward isolationism, conservatism, and ingrown attitudes; those living along the seacoast are thought to be more open-minded, sophisticated, and liberal in their thinking.

In analyzing the effects of climate and geography, determinists are not stereotyping and declaring that every person, say, from

---

5. One proposed explanation given by theologians for the existence of natural evil and human suffering in a world governed by a benevolent God trades upon these facts of psychology. That is, theologians will sometimes argue that human development depends upon there being obstacles to struggle against. If the world were a paradise, they say, people would not be challenged and their character would not have the stimulus to improve over a lifetime. God provides sufficient incentives on earth in the form of disease, illness, volcanic eruptions, floods, earthquakes, tigers, scorpions, deserts, jungles, and so forth for the human race to develop medicine, engineering, science, and all the other means of controlling the environment. In addition, combating these evils encourages individuals to build strength of character.

The problem, of course, in maintaining this view is that obstacles and suffering do not always build character (or civilization); suffering, in fact, tends to demean more people than it elevates. Also, a good character can be developed without suffering. People can find enough incentives in struggling upward to attain higher levels of good; they do not need to experience the bad in order to improve themselves. Therefore, if the suffering that natural evil engenders is not strictly necessary to human development, and is, in fact, largely harmful, then its existence is incompatible with God's love for humankind. A benevolent God would not allow or introduce pointless natural evil into the human environment.

Brazil is apathetic and lethargic; rather they are only generalizing and perceiving differences in national character between peoples living under different climatic and geographical conditions, and they are saying that these differences show the influence of climate and geography on people's personalities and choices.

Whatever nation one inhabits, then, will unconsciously affect one by its size, shape, outline, and location, as well as by its climate and weather. Also operative are such social geographical factors as density of population, age distribution, male-to-female ratio, and principal occupations. A pastoral or agricultural people is different from a people that is the product of a modern postindustrial society.

▸ **SOCIETY AND CULTURE.** No one lives in a vacuum or a hermetically sealed box; rather, each person is part of an identifiable social group with particular beliefs, traditions, and language, and common interests and institutions, artifacts and activities, patterns of behavior and standards of conduct. This means that the society in which a person lives determines the range of ideas and actions that will appear as viable options to that person.

For example, someone raised in India as a Hindu, speaking Urdu and living in a rural village with a long tradition of passivity, would probably not consider becoming an entrepreneur and following the Protestant ethic. Similarly, a person brought up as an Irish Catholic in Dublin in a working-class environment with blue-collar values would hardly be tempted to retreat to the desert and follow Mohammed. What one regards as a real choice is severely limited by one's cultural background. As the anthropologist Ruth Benedict wrote:

> No man ever looks at the world with pristine eyes. He sees it edited by a definite set of customs and institutions and ways of thinking. . . . The life history of the individual is first and foremost an accommodation to the patterns and standards traditionally handed down in this community. From the moment of his birth the customs into which he is born shape his experience and behavior. By the time he can talk, he is the little creature of his culture, and by the time he is grown and able to take part in its activities, its habits are his habits, its beliefs

his beliefs, its impossibilities his impossibilities. Every child that is born into his group will share them with him, and no child born into one on the opposite side of the globe can ever achieve the thousandth part.[6]

Thus each individual is culturally determined in such factors as dress, concept of beauty, recreation, ornamentation, moral code, religion, temperament, political convictions, speech, family concept, and so forth. There are also secondary effects such as those emanating from language, for all languages possess built-in values and attitudes toward the world that will shape the minds of their users. Certain ideas that would be temptations of thought in English are almost unthinkable in Chinese. A theory has been proposed, in fact, called the *Sapir-Whorf hypothesis,* which maintains that language determines thought much more than thought determines language.[7] Ludwig Wittgenstein (1889–1951), one of the founders of the contemporary philosophic movement of linguistic analysis, claimed that language traps us into making intellectual mistakes; the task of philosophy, he believed, is to show "the fly the way out of the fly-bottle."[8] That is, philosophy should help us escape from the conceptual confusions to which language makes us prone. In both theories the effect of language upon thought is being underscored.

The effects of education should also be mentioned in this context because that too is part of the social baggage we carry with us. It makes a considerable difference whether one attends a village school in Afghanistan or a lycée in Paris, or if one is a graduate of a major American university or a technical training school in Nairobi. One's informal education is also formative, for the books and magazines one reads, the films, videos, and television programs one watches, the friends and relatives one listens to all affect the type of individual one becomes. (It has been remarked that if a

6. R. Benedict, *Patterns of Culture* (London: Routledge and Sons, 1935), pp. 2–3; see also A. Montagu, *The Biosocial Nature of Man* (New York: Grove Press, 1956), pp. 74–76.
7. See E. Sapir, *Culture, Language and Personality* (Berkeley: University of California Press, 1970).
8. For an exposition of this idea, see A. Flew (ed.), *Logic and Language,* Vol. II (Oxford: Basil Blackwell, 1961), especially the papers by G. Ryle, F. Waismann, J. Austin, and J. O. Urmson.

man's wife is unfaithful and he has been reading "machismo" authors his tendency will be to seek blood revenge, but if his reading has consisted of Proust and Henry James he will invite the man over for cocktails and talk it over.)

Thus culture and society, together with biological factors, climate, and geography help to determine people's identity and conduct. The determinist is not stating anything revolutionary here but reminding us that the effect of a person's social environment and upbringing cannot be denied.[9]

▶ **PSYCHOLOGY**. Several schools of psychology lend support to the determinist position, the most notable being that of *behaviorism*, which is associated with the names Ivan Pavlov (1849–1936), J. B. Watson (1878–1958), and B. F. Skinner (1904–1990).[10] The behavioral psychologist sees human conduct in terms of physiological responses to external conditions (stimuli). The human organism responds to stimuli in the environment and is conditioned in its behavior in terms of repeated stimulus-response patterns. In a famous experiment Pavlov conditioned a dog to salivate at the stimulus of a bell that was rung before meals. In the same way people may be conditioned to stop at red lights, clap their hands together at performances, eat their food from plates, help others in trouble, endorse a democratic form of government, and so forth. To understand human psychology, then, we should not study the operations of the will or hidden motives buried in the unconscious but rather the overt structure of habits and abilities that constitutes a person's system of responses.

Within behaviorism, an individual's psychology is nothing but his or her observable behavior and not some mysterious and eva-

9. It should be mentioned that the theory of sociobiology claims that all human behavior is a function of our genes in their drive to perpetuate their group strain. Human organisms are the housing the genes require, and their continued existence is our reason for being. It is as though an egg were using a chicken to produce another egg. See the writings of Edward O. Wilson and Robert Trivers, especially Wilson's book *Sociobiology: The New Synthesis* (Cambridge, MA: Harvard University Press, 1975).
10. See I. Pavlov, *Conditioned Reflexes* (New York: Dover Publications, 1957); J. B. Watson, *Behaviorism* (Chicago: University of Chicago Press, 1930); and B. J. Skinner, *Science and Human Behavior* (New York: Macmillan, 1953), and *Beyond Freedom and Dignity* (New York: Knopf, 1971).

nescent entity called "mind" behind behavior. There is, in fact, no "ghost in the machine," no such thing as the soul, spirit, or even consciousness any more than there are things called emotion, memory, or imagination contained within a mind. Emotion is muscular and glandular activity, memory is the ability to "recall to use," and imagination can only be determined by the visible evidence of its functioning. Even intelligence cannot be regarded as some intangible mental capacity but an index of the ways in which problems are confronted and solved. According to the behaviorist, we should therefore turn away from "mind-gazing" and concentrate on the stimulus-response relationships that characterize people; then we will understand their psychology.

The bearing of this position upon the theory of determinism is not difficult to see. The behaviorist is claiming that our thoughts and actions are nothing but conditioned responses to given stimuli. We do not decide what to think or do after a process of conscious reflection but we are reactive organisms whose behavior is triggered by environmental stimuli; the strongest stimulus wins. People do not voluntarily choose which response they will have among various possibilities or which course of action they will follow in the face of given stimuli but react in the ways their psychology dictates. The same holds true in the sphere of morality. People function as machines do, and one mode of conduct will follow from pressing one button and another from pressing a different button. That is, given one set of stimuli (and a history of responses), one type of moral behavior will result; with different physical stimuli another type of morality will be produced. Once an individual's stimulus-response pattern is known, that individual's behavior, including his or her moral behavior, can be predicted.

THE LIBERTARIAN REBUTTAL

▶ **INFLUENCES VERSUS DETERMINANTS.** The position of social scientific determinism is an extremely strong one, relying on undeniable facts of biology, sociology, and psychology. However, the libertarian who defends free will claims that people still have the freedom to decide between alternatives despite the numerous forces impinging upon them. The libertarian argues that these forces are *influences and not determinants,* and people are always free to choose their influences. Once we are aware of the various forces operative in our lives, these forces are disarmed of power over us; we are then empowered to decide which influences to accept and which to reject. The influences are only determinants when we are unconscious of their existence and the way in which they affect us; once we are aware of them, we can become free of their control.

For example, people raised in a city would be inclined to continue living an urban life, but they need not do so. They could reject these early influences and decide that they would prefer the virtues of country living. Or a person raised in the Roman Catholic faith would be strongly persuaded to remain Catholic, but at some point of reflection he or she could assess the merits of the faith and conclude that atheism or Protestantism or some Eastern religion has greater validity. Someone raised communist could choose capitalism; an atheist might become a believer. In these cases, awareness would ensure that the influences did not become determinants.

People would also be free if they decided in favor of particular influences rather than rejecting them; the significant factor is that a conscious decision be made. For example, individuals raised in cultured homes might choose to continue their involvements with art, music, and literature as part of a satisfying life. In this case, they would not be determined in their decisions even though they were following the values of their backgrounds. So long as individuals are aware of the way in which they are tempted to think and act, they can affirm their customary ways of living, appropriating and owning them as their own.

In this way southerners can decide to resist or yield to the lethargy of a warm climate, mountaineers can be unsocial or not, and mesomorphs can choose whether or not to enter fields that call for physical strength; the last group might, for example, decide to become accountants rather than weight lifters.

As these examples illustrate, libertarians do not deny the importance of climate, psychology, geography, biology, and so forth in their affirmation of a free will position; rather they agree with the social scientist that these influences are present. What the libertarian denies is that these factors determine our behavior, that they necessarily produce our ideas and actions. The libertarian is not being unscientific but rather questioning the logical connection between influences, on the one hand, and thoughts, values, and conduct on the other. If libertarians are unscientific at all, it is by postulating the existence of an autonomous self, free from the causal chain, that is known through introspection and reflection.

Seen from a slightly different perspective, libertarians are criticizing determinists for assuming that actions are nothing but reactions; they claim genuine actions are possible once we know the forces that sway us. A large part of the function of education, therefore, is to make us knowledgeable about these forces operating upon us and thereby to have personally chosen actions rather than a set of reactions. As Erich Fromm put it, "As man approaches maturity he gradually frees himself from instinctive and compulsive behavior and he develops his powers of self-reliance and choice."

From still another vantage point, the libertarian is asserting that there can be *reasons* for actions, not just *causes*. Having reasons implies some process of deliberation whereby a person weighs the conflicting claims and freely decides between the various alternatives. To speak of causes, on the other hand, presupposes a strict mechanical system of cause and effect with no room allowed for self-initiated acts of human beings—acts that are not the result of some prior outside cause. According to libertarianism, people's actions are not necessarily the effects of antecedent causes even though physical matter may operate that way; people can have reasons for what they do. Instinct causes a bird to build a nest but human beings have a purpose in building a home; there is a conscious aim in their doing so, and they could well decide not to do so if they had other goals.

Viewed in this light, criminals cannot claim that, given their disadvantaged backgrounds, they could not help but commit their crimes. Even if they are members of minority groups and suffered discrimination in hiring, housing, and schooling, they do not have to choose a life of crime. Such problems make it more difficult to remain honest but becoming a criminal is not unavoidable.

▶ **THE UNPREDICTABILITY OF HUMAN BEHAVIOR.**
In addition to this group of criticisms the libertarian also charges that the determinist position seems plausible only because it argues backward to prior causes, but the real test of a theory is its ability to

predict future behavior. That is to say, it is easy to declare that Mary did action *X* because of her biological propensities, social background, psychological conditioning, and so forth, since explanations can be found in antecedent conditions for whatever she does. If Mary should become a doctor, the determinist would see the causes in, say, her psychological pattern of concern for others, the milieu of professional people in which she was raised, and her scientific mind. If, however, she should become a business executive, the determinist would see the causal factors as, say, her organizational ability, social and economic class, and the influence of her third cousin twice removed who is a company president. Even if Mary became a high school dropout, turned socialist, and joined a religious cult, the determinist would claim to see this as the inevitable result of prior factors, probably a reaction against her family background, success in school, and the American capitalist values that surrounded her.

But this kind of analysis appears strained; whatever causes are mentioned apply, but they are selected after the fact (*post hoc*) to fit the case. Determinists would be much more impressive in their arguments if they could predict with certainty what Mary will do given her "determinants." Otherwise it seems more reasonable to conclude that, given a set of influences, Mary could choose any combination of them as the dominant ones in her life; that she could, upon maturity, freely decide which aspect of herself she wished to develop. In other words, if human actions are governed by the same mechanistic system as falling stones, then the determinist should be able to predict them with the same degree of certainty. The fact that the determinist cannot do so suggests that the two cases are not alike and that human conduct is of a nonmechanistic character; in short, it suggests that people possess free will.

The determinist's answer to this charge is that, since the scientific study of human behavior is virtually in its infancy, all the factors that determine behavior are not yet known. The social scientist has a certain degree of success in predicting how people will act, and as more knowledge is acquired about the causal determinants of behavior, greater predictability will be achieved. People do act according to natural laws rather than capriciously, and prediction of human behavior will become increasingly accurate as more and more of these laws become known.

But human conduct is of a different kind, the libertarian replies, and the behavior of individuals will never be predictable no matter how much information is acquired about the factors operating upon them. It is not just a matter of gaining greater knowledge of people but of a theoretical difference between people and natural objects. Human beings can come to understand the forces that move them and decide which forces they want to be moved by; people can choose in a way that birds and stones cannot. The libertarian is not saying that human behavior is capricious and independent of all natural laws but that the particular laws that are brought into play are decided by the self-aware person. Therefore, the accurate prediction of human behavior is theoretically impossible and will not come about at some distant point in the future. Regardless of the increase in knowledge about the laws and conditions behind people's behavior there will never be complete predictability because human beings are always free to choose their influences.

▸ **TEMPORAL VERSUS CAUSAL SEQUENCES**. A third objection raised by the libertarian is related to the previous ones but has a specifically logical character. The libertarian accuses the determinist of committing the logical fallacy of *post hoc, ergo propter hoc,* which literally means "after this, therefore caused by this." It is the mistake of assuming that when one event follows another the prior event necessarily caused the subsequent one. For example, the fallacy would be committed if we thought that dancing causes rain because a rain dance preceded a rainstorm, or that day causes night because night follows day. Quite obviously, a temporal sequence is different than a causal one, and a subsequent event is not necessarily a consequent one.

As applied to the determinist thesis, the libertarian argues that prior factors of geography, biology, psychology, and so forth cannot be assumed to be the causes of a person's conduct. The determinist must prove that this temporal sequence is a necessary causal connection such that given conditions *A, B,* and *C,* action *X* must inevitably follow. The determinists have not done this but have shown only that certain conditions preceded a person's action. They have not proven that given these conditions, it would be impossible for a person to act differently, and thus they have not demonstrated a necessary cause-effect relationship.

The burden of proof falls on the determinist to do this; otherwise we are justified in crediting our customary view which is that people are free to kick a stone or not kick a stone, just as they will. That is, if a theory is proposed that contradicts the common-sense view, the proponents are required to prove their point; the onus of proof lies with them rather than on the person who holds a common-sense position. In other words someone cannot say, "All of life is imaginary, a dream in the mind of God. Prove it is not!" Nor can someone state, "The self is an illusion. Prove that you exist!" If life is a dream in the mind of God, this must be established, and if no individual selves exist, then that too must be shown; otherwise we are justified in relying upon our customary assumptions about reality.

Sometimes the extraordinary view is established, as when the earth was shown to be in motion when common sense believed it to be still; but the point is that the unusual view must be established, not the ordinary one. The determinist, then, who claims that all of our actions are really out of our control, must prove that. He or she is required to show that prior factors have forced us to act as we do, that the antecedent conditions are causal determinants, and this has not been established. In the absence of proof of causation we are justified in maintaining the common-sense view that our decisions are free, that prior conditions do not determine our conduct but form the ground for free choice.

▶ **THE INCONSISTENCY OF DETERMINISM**. As a final point the libertarian sees a basic inconsistency in the determinist's position, for if all ideas are the necessary products of prior causes, this must include the idea of determinism. Therefore, those who believe in the determinist position have been determined to do so. They have not freely decided that determinism is a valid theory but simply believe it because they cannot do otherwise. And if that is so, then we need not take their position seriously. It is not an idea judged true or false but an idea the determinist has been determined to believe.

In the same way, if determinists are to be consistent with their position, they must logically maintain that the libertarian has been determined to affirm free will just as they were forced to affirm determinism. Any argument between the two, then, is pointless because each must think as they do. The only reasonable action for the determinist is to remain silent and not argue the virtues of determinism.

However, determinists do try to convince libertarians to change their minds, and in doing so they give the game away. For they thereby presuppose that people are free to think differently regardless of their social upbringing, biology, and so forth, that a good idea could be accepted on its merits, and that people are not determined in what they think. But that is precisely what the determinist has denied. Therefore, the more the determinist tries to convince others of the truth of determinism, the more absurd the position appears. If we become convinced that determinism is true, then determinism cannot be true.

The only rebuttal that determinism offers to this self-contradiction is to say that the argument in favor of determinism can be a determinant forcing us to accept the theory. But the acceptance of a good argument because it is good constitutes a reason, not a cause, and is consonant with the libertarian, not the determinist, model of human behavior. One cannot speak meaningfully of being determined by the superior virtues of a theory but of freely deciding which theory has superior virtues. According to this argument, therefore, if we choose to believe that determinism is right, then determinism must be wrong.

▶ **HUMAN FREEDOM AS ESSENTIAL.** Determinists, then, have not proven their case by any means. Various criticisms can be leveled against their position as we have seen, including the charge that it contradicts itself and is logically impossible to maintain. The libertarian view seems far more acceptable since it is not fraught with logical flaws and is in keeping with our common-sense attitude toward our actions. Although determinism is very much in fashion today among social scientists, it appears much more probable that we are not the products of our society, biological inheritance, psychological background, and so forth. And if we are free in our ideas, attitudes, and behavior, then we cannot claim immunity from responsibility because of the nexus of antecedent conditions. In contemporary terms, the boy raised in a slum need not become a criminal, and the little girl is not unavoidably programmed to be a wife and mother. We are essentially free to choose our own paths, and we bear a burden of personal responsibility for the paths we choose.[11]

RECAPITULATION

We have examined the skeptical position of determinism, first in its earlier form of predeterminism and later in its present version as presented by social scientists. Emphasizing the latter form, we discussed various alleged determinants such as genetic endowment, climate and geography, society and culture, and psychology. Criticisms were then offered of the determinist position in terms of the distinction between influences and determinants, or, from a different perspective, between actions and reactions. Further criticisms centered around the determinist's ploy of arguing backward, not forward, and committing the logical fallacy of *post hoc, ergo propter hoc*. In this latter connection the question of burden of proof was mentioned as counting against the determinist position. Finally, it was pointed out that a basic inconsistency exists within determinism which seriously weakens it as a theory of human behavior.

▼ ▼ ▼

REVIEW QUESTIONS

1. *Differentiate between determinism and predeterminism. Which doctrine is more prevalent in the contemporary age?*

11. For some provocative contemporary discussions of determinism see Thomas Nagel's chapter on freedom in T. Nagel (ed.), *The View From Nowhere* (Oxford, England: Oxford University Press, 1989); and D. Dennett, *Elbow Room: The Varieties of Free Will Worth Wanting* (Cambridge, MA: MIT Press, 1984).

2. *Explain how the individual is affected by genetic endowment and by climate and geography.*

3. *In what way does the behaviorist school of psychology support the determinist position?*

4. *Explain what the libertarian means by claiming that outside forces are influences, not determinants, and that people perform actions for a reason, not just as a result of causes.*

5. *According to the libertarian, how is the theory of determinism inconsistent? In what way does the determinist argue backwards?*

THE RELATIVIST
OBJECTION

 nother source of skepticism about the general validity of ethics comes from the doctrine of relativism, which is an ancient theory that has recently assumed a different form, much like old wine poured into new wineskins. The relativist assumes that all values are simply a function of the particular culture in which people find themselves. We may think our values have an objective foundation but, at base, they merely reflect the social attitudes that surround us. When people say that promises should be kept, they are not really identifying any rightness inherent in promise-keeping but rather expressing their society's attitudes. Likewise, when people declare that exploitation is wrong and being considerate toward people is right, this judgment depends upon the social mores that have been a part of their upbringing. There is nothing intrinsically right about being considerate of the rights and feelings of others and nothing inherently wrong about exploiting others for one's own advantage, the relativist maintains.

DIFFERENT FORMS OF RELATIVISM AND DETERMINISM

▶ **CULTURAL RELATIVISM.** According to *cultural relativism,* different societies form different standards for the satisfaction of their particular needs and there is no universally right way of behaving; the correct way to conduct oneself depends upon one's culture. "Immoral," a prominent sociologist wrote, "never means anything but contrary to the mores of the time and place . . . there is no permanent and universal standard by which right and truth in regard to these matters can be established and different folkways compared and criticised."[1]

▶ **SUBJECTIVISM.** A kindred theory that also denies any objective basis for value judgments is *subjectivism.* Rather than focusing on the unit of society as the basis of values, the subjectivist claims that our moral judgments spring from our personal predilections and aversions. Our morality is a matter of individual taste, and as such it is equally unarguable. As the Romans said, "*De gustibus non est disputandum*": "Taste cannot be disputed or refuted." To the subjectivist, what is right to one person will be wrong to another because individual likes and dislikes vary, and each person is correct in what he or she thinks even if differing views are diametrically opposed. There exists no absolute standard against which a person's preferences can be measured; whatever someone believes is right thereby becomes right. "There is nothing either good or bad," Shakespeare said in *Hamlet,* "but thinking makes it so."[2]

---

1. W. G. Sumner, *Folkways* (Boston: Ginn and Co., 1906), Chap. XI.
2. W. Shakespeare, *Hamlet, Prince of Denmark,* in *William Shakespeare: The Complete Works,* ed. Peter Alexander (New York: Random House, 1952), Act 2, Scene 2, p. 142.

▶ **OBJECTIVISM OR ABSOLUTISM**. Opposed to both of these theories is *objectivism* or *absolutism*, which claims that values have an independent basis apart from either personal or societal beliefs. For example, a person who says, "Rape is wrong," may be identifying something despicable about the act that makes it unworthy of being practiced. He or she is not merely reflecting the disapproval of the culture or venting an idiosyncratic dislike of sexual assault. Rape is wrong no matter what values a society espouses or an individual believes. To the objectivist or absolutist, both people and cultures can be mistaken in the values they hold just as someone can make mistakes in arithmetic or have an incorrect perception of truth; thinking that $8 + 4 = 11$ does not make it so, and the earth is not flat whatever some remote culture might believe.

According to objectivism or absolutism, then, societies can be criticized for holding values that are contrary to objective moral standards. There is an external and independent basis for moral knowledge apart from the attitudes instilled by any given society. This position also thinks subjectivism is misguided in believing that each person creates his or her own moral standards, that what is right for one person may be wrong for another. The objectivist maintains that if something is right for one person in certain circumstances, then it is right for another person in the same circumstances. We do not invent moral values but discover the principles of right and wrong that should govern human conduct. Individuals do not create the proper standards to follow through some act of volition but realize the types of conduct that are morally prohibited or obligatory. And if one speaks about discovering rather than inventing, or realizing rather than creating rules of morality, this makes ethics an objective matter, not something that changes with each individual's attitude.

▶ **CONTEMPORARY TRENDS**. The general fashion today appears to endorse a relativist or subjectivist view (sometimes subsumed under the terms "deconstructionism" and even "multiculturalism," although relativism need not follow from these theories). Perhaps because of a desire to maximize the freedom of the individual and to support tolerance, the contemporary tendency is to declare that whatever a person regards as right is right for that

THE RELATIVIST OBJECTION

person, and that there are no ideal standards of behavior that can be used as a yardstick for measuring the correctness of a person's views. Each individual and each society forms standards that are adequate for themselves, and no one outside the culture or a person's own skin can presume to judge the behavior. By and large, psychologists, sociologists, and anthropologists concur in this view and hold that there are no better or worse values but only those that serve specific purposes and needs. These will be the values selected in social evolution or in an individual's history, and, if they prevail, they are *ipso facto* right. Any allegedly objective evaluation will only reflect the subjective or relative opinions of the evaluator. There is no single model of behavior that will hold true for all people, and to impose on others the values that are compatible with one's own personality is arrogant and oppressive.

THEORETICAL SOURCES OF RELATIVISM

We will examine three theoretical sources of relativism that seem to be dominant as supportive theories today: the findings of sociology and anthropology, the ramifications of Freudian psychology, and the ideas of Marxism as expressed in the *Communist Manifesto*. From each of these vantage points the same conclusion is reached: that values do not have any objective basis but are simply relative to the time and the place from which they spring.

▶ SOCIOLOGY AND ANTHROPOLOGY

William Graham Sumner. To begin with *the evidence of sociology and anthropology*, the book *Folkways*[3] by William Graham Sumner (1840–1910) can be taken as representative. According to Sumner's

---

3. Sumner, *Folkways*.

theory, all ethical ideals concerning the nature of goodness and all conceptions of what is right are derived from the folkways or customary usages that societies have developed to satisfy their needs. Whenever any customs become necessary for the well being of a society, they become part of the mores of that society. These mores do not consist of principles of ethics that are identified as being right but instead are developed in response to the essential requirements of the culture; they are functional and pragmatic means for securing the general welfare of a people. As conditions change and different responses are called for, the mores change correspondingly, and no mores remain fixed over a long period of time (as one might expect if they were objectively based). The mores are not rational or consistent but are shaped by the needs of and the external circumstances surrounding the people who espouse them. Furthermore, the mores can run counter to the group's welfare through the phenomenon known as "cultural lag." A society will gradually change its mores to those most beneficial to it, but a lapse of time may occur between the recognition of the inadequacy of the old mores and the change to a more efficient system.

In this analysis Sumner is not only accounting for the way our ethical values arise, that is, as the necessary mores of a culture, but also dismissing any kind of absolute standards. Because mores change, we can see they are not eternal, and because they change in accordance with needs and circumstances, we can see their true base, viz., the exigencies that exist at a particular time and place. Each culture, therefore, has the norms it needs. A conflict that occurs between cultures cannot be settled by referring to any universal or rational basis of behavior but must be resolved through political means or by force. There is no common standard that cultures can recognize and accept for an adjudication of their differences.

Within a culture, actions are judged to be right when they follow the time-honored customs and wrong when they are opposed to these customs. It is impossible for an individual to get outside the confines of his or her culture and make any kind of independent moral judgment. There simply is not any external standard that can be found, and, even if there were, people are so socialized within a particular tradition that they would not accept a different value system. Whatever a society regards as right becomes the standard for every member of the group, and whatever is considered wrong becomes taboo. To presume to judge one's society is sheer arrogance since no one is capable of removing oneself from the influence of one's culture and there is no outside reference point that can be used as a touchstone for criticism. Even rebels demonstrate the force of social values by the strength of their rebellions; they are trying to overcome enormous resistance, and ultimately become coopted into the system.

Vilfredo Pareto. Vilfredo Pareto (1848–1923) in his book *Mind and Society*[4] echoes this relativistic point of view, and especially emphasizes the subjective character of many of our values. To Pareto, our ethical judgments are not logically based but emerge from the nonlogical parts of our personality. Our judgments are functions of our instincts, sentiments, and emotions, so that whenever we say our actions are right we are only saying we like to behave that way and wish others shared our attitude. To approve of an action is merely to express one's personal preference and the desire that such an action become generally accepted and practiced. The action is in keeping with one's own likes and dislikes and would benefit from group support. The word "right" is used as an honorific term that has persuasive power by virtue of its emotive connotation, and if "right" is claimed to be more than a positively charged term, this claim is either hypocritical, delusional, or mistaken. When people use value-laden words, they usually know they are employing emotive language to persuade others to their own points of view; they are, in fact, rationalizing their desires. "Right," then, means nothing other than "I like to do this and I wish other people felt the same way."

The classic philosophic counterpart of this position, incidentally, was expressed by David Hume (1711–1776).[5] Hume argued that moral judgments are not based on reason since reason is confined to passing judgment on truth and falsity, which applies only to

---

4. V. Pareto, *Mind and Society* (New York: Harcourt Brace and Co., 1935).
5. See D. Hume, *An Enquiry Concerning the Principles of Morals* in *Philosophical Works of David Hume* (Boston: Little Brown and Co., 1854), and C. L. Stevenson, *Ethics and Language* (New Haven: Yale University Press, 1969). A. J. Ayer in *Language, Truth and Logic* (Oxford, England: Oxford University Press, 1936) also contributes to this position in his own way, as does Bertrand Russell.

statements of fact ("The cat is on the mat") and relations of ideas ("Bachelors are unmarried males"). To approve of conduct, on the other hand, means to have positive feelings about it. By and large, if an action tends to bring happiness to significant people in our lives, we treat it with approval. The judgment that behavior is right indicates only that people in our society generally like or favor it, that the behavior meets with most people's approval. But, to Hume, these feelings cannot be argued about, for it would be absurd to try to prove or disprove a feeling. Rational argumentation, then, is inappropriate to morals, and Hume goes so far as to say that, if by flicking a finger, the entire human race could be saved or destroyed, the one choice would not be any more rational than the other—although we might have strong feelings about the matter.

Hume is saying in effect that moral judgments are expressive of an individual's attitude and attempts to evoke a similar attitude in others. We merely vent feelings toward types of actions when we call them right or wrong, shouting "hurrah" for one and "boo" at the other. Argument can legitimately occur over whether certain conduct will produce the goals we like, but there can be no rational arguments over the value of the goals themselves; that is strictly a question of attitude.

Joseph Wood Krutch (1893–1970) summarized the views of Hume and others when he wrote that "all attempts either to enforce a code or persuade others to accept it voluntarily are merely attempts to make others feel as we do, and there is no fact outside our feelings to which our feelings can be referred for justification."

Ruth Benedict. The social anthropologist Ruth Benedict (1897–1948) also argued in the book *Patterns of Culture*[6] that cultural differences account for peoples' way of thinking and behaving, including their ideals and concept of proper conduct. To illustrate her thesis, she described the customs and institutions of three cultures: the Zuni Indians of the American Southwest, the Dobuans who live on Dobu Island off eastern New Guinea, and the Kwakiutl Indians of the northwestern region of the United States. Each is radically dif-

6. R. Benedict, *Patterns of Culture* (London: Routledge and Sons, 1935).

ferent from the other in the values that dominate and permeate the culture.

The Zuni Indians are deeply religious—a sober, hard-working, peaceful people. They are strongly concerned with building a harmonious relationship between human beings, nature, and the gods. Their whole purpose in life is to bring about a balanced and integrated relationship between themselves and their natural environment. The Dobu culture, in contrast, prizes vigilance against evil forces that surround and threaten the individual. If one maintains an attitude of suspicion and defensiveness, and approaches others with equal malignity, then one is living cleverly and rightly. The Kwakiutl culture differs from that of both the Zuni and the Dobu by being highly competitive in nature; a self-aggrandizement that increases personal prestige and pride is of paramount importance. Success over other people is highly valued—not just reaching the heights but being able to look down upon those beneath you. The way that a Kwakiutl is made to feel big is to make others look small. In general, the competitive and aggressive person is considered worthy of admiration and emulation.

Because of the great diversity in standards of conduct between these three cultures, Benedict concluded that there are no absolute moral principles all people can recognize but rather that each culture develops values relative to itself. And what is right in one culture can be foolish or shameful in another. A Dobuan male who acted hatefully would be respected as a strong person by his culture but Zunis would disapprove of him and Kwakiutls might regard his conduct with disdain. If an individual in the Kwakiutl culture should succeed in making himself important, this would be considered unseemly individualism by Zunis and regarded as rather childish by Dobuans. And the Zuni approach to life—the attitude of achieving tranquility, harmony, and peace—would be looked at as absurd by the Dobuan and Kwakiutl cultures.

The implication of this diversity of ethical attitudes and standards seems to be that all values are relative to a person's culture. One cannot find ethical beliefs that are universally held, and one cultural pattern is as legitimate as another. It is not that a pattern of culture *seems* worthwhile to each culture; in point of fact it *is* valuable. For the word "valuable" means nothing other than that which is socially approved.

▶ **FREUDIAN PSYCHOLOGY**. *Freudian psychology* also offers theoretical support to the relativist and, more particularly, the subjectivist critique of universally valid ethical systems.[7] According to Sigmund Freud (1856–1939), the conscious mind constitutes only a small portion of the entire psyche. In the familiar analogy, it resembles the tip of an iceberg whose main bulk lies hidden beneath the surface of the ocean. The greater and more powerful part of the mind is termed the *unconscious*—that dynamic apparatus of the psyche which lies below the level of awareness and is only glimpsed occasionally through slips of the tongue, dissociated acts, or dreams. The unconscious is a seething cauldron of desires that are elemental in nature and basic to every individual.

The Influence of the Unconscious on Human Action. The unconscious is not an undifferentiated, amorphous whole, however, but has three divisions, each of which plays a part in the decisions and actions we take; together these parts are responsible for whatever we do even though we might delude ourselves into believing that we always make conscious, rational choices.

The *id* exercises demands upon each of us that are primarily sexual in nature, totally selfish, primitive, insatiable, and without social or moral restraint. All of our forbidden desires, lusts, and sexual passions come moiling up from the id seeking expression and satisfaction.

The *superego* checks the id and keeps it from wholly controlling our actions. This is the force of social rules and prohibitions that we have internalized and that we call conscience; it is the general voice of society, instilled in us, by and large, by parents and teachers who are the instruments society uses to impose its standards upon us. The superego applies strong controls over each of us, imposing a rigid and puritanical social ethic; its tyranny matches that of the id in strength. The superego opposes the desires of the id, especially the main thrust toward unlimited sexual gratification. A general warfare then takes place within each individual, with the id, on the one hand, demand-

---

7. Freud's theory of ethics is contained in a series of works that have been published under the titles *Collected Papers* (New York: Basic Books, 1959), and *The Standard Edition of the Complete Psychological Works of Sigmund Freud* (London: Hogarth Press, 1966). See especially Volumes 13 and 21 of the latter edition.

ing expression and the superego, on the other, repressing these desires with the weight of social conscience.

Mediating between the demands of the id and the superego is the *ego*, which attempts to reconcile the conflicting forces in a way that will produce the least anxiety for us. The tyranny of desire and the tyranny of conscience can lead to conflict so great that mental disorder will result unless the ego can bring about a satisfactory adjustment between these twin tyrants (which are the mirror images of each other).

Enlisted in the battle is another agent that Freud termed the *censor*. Standing at the gateway to consciousness, the censor only allows us to be aware of those thoughts and emotions that do not violate general moral standards. It filters and selects those appetites that are socially acceptable and excludes from consciousness the large body of desires swirling up from the id. Most wants are too obscene and threatening to be passed by the censor. Nevertheless, they remain operative within each person and their repression can lead to hysteria, depression, and in extreme cases obsessions and neuroses.

The ego in its efforts at conciliation uses various psychological expedients to bring the individual some peace of mind. It uses the device of *rationalization*, for one, which consists in finding plausible but untrue reasons for doing what we desire to do. Rationalization is often employed to make it seem that action which is done from a base motive is motivated by some noble intention. If people think that their awful desires are fine and pure, they can be at peace with themselves; their consciences are satisfied even as the impulses of the id are being expressed. Another ploy used by the ego is called *projection*, whereby we find excuses outside ourselves for the mistakes we make; in that way responsibility is evaded. We pretend we are not to blame for immoral actions, but that the events occurred due to factors beyond our control. Still another device used by the ego is *sublimation*, in which the desires emanating from the id are rechanneled in ways that are socially permissible. If a surgeon uses his scalpel for some beneficial end, then he is not condemned as a criminal even though, from a Freudian point of view, he is actually expressing aggression by unconsciously attacking someone with a knife. Since he does this with a license in an operating room for socially approved reasons, however, he receives a great deal of money and social status, whereas an ordinary person who stabs another on the street is jailed for assault with a deadly weapon.

Freudian Theory and Ethical Skepticism. The relevance of Freud's psychological theory to ethical skepticism is simply that conduct is here interpreted as the product of the battle between the id, the ego, and the superego rather than being the result of reflection on right and wrong. It is these forces that form our concept of ethics and they are completely irrational and amoral. Our conduct is an accommodation and an appeasement of the powers in the unconscious mind. Any attempt at rational or objective judgment regarding values is only a pretext for the unconscious wishes, defenses, and inhibitions, the rationalizations, projections, and sublimations of our psyche. There are no valid reasons behind actions, only a veneer of excuses given by the conscious mind for the dictates of the unconscious. Values, then, are not arrived at through rational reflection on objective standards but are the consequence of the dynamic interactions of the id, the ego, and the superego.

The theory of Freudian psychology lends itself to determinism, relativism, and subjectivism. Our conscious mind must hold the values it does because unconscious forces determine its entire content, that is, these values are relative to the social controls of the superego and the subjective desires surging up from the id. The individual is at the mercy of these forces, a puppet of the unconscious rather than an autonomous entity, consciously deciding which values are worthy of being chosen.

▶ **MARXISM**. Relativism and subjectivism also gain strength from the nineteenth and twentieth century theories of *Marxism*, which has as its cornerstone Karl Marx's *Capital* and the *Communist Manifesto*.[8]

Marxist Economic Theory. Karl Marx (1818–1883) was preeminently a revolutionary who, in the words of his co-worker, Friedrich Engels (1820–1895), strove "to contribute in one way or

8. K. Marx, *Capital* (New York: Modern Library, 1936), and with Friedrich Engels, *The Communist Manifesto* (Chicago: H. Regnery Co., 1954).

another to the overthrow of capitalist society." Or as Marx himself put it: "the philosophers have interpreted the world in various ways; the point, however, is to change it."[9] But in order to effect a change, the laws governing the inner workings of nations had to be scientifically analyzed. This Marx did through a long period of research at the British Museum, and his conclusions were that the structure and history of nations are determined by economic forces.

The "modes of production" constitute the economic foundations of society and produce all social, political, and intellectual forms and institutions. In traditional economic theory the modes or factors of production are usually listed as land, labor, and capital, but Marx analyzed them as materials (resources), labor (purposive activity), and instruments (techniques). In any case, corresponding to these modes of production are "property relations," a concept that refers to the forms of ownership. Property relations are relatively stable through time whereas modes of production change more rapidly, and this differential produces tension and eventual conflict. The modes of production inevitably win the contest and new property relations must be established that are appropriate to them. In this way, new historical realities come into existence, epochs in the progress of society which Marx refers to by such labels as "the asiatic," "the ancient," "the feudal," and the "modern capitalist."

The final struggle, Marx believed, is now occurring in our capitalist era between the property relation of bourgeois ownership and the mode of production in which proletarian labor is intolerably exploited. As the bourgeois power becomes concentrated in the hands of a small number of increasingly wealthy capitalists, and the proletariat become poorer and more numerous, a polarization and antagonism occurs which erupts into violent class conflict. A revolution ensues in which the bourgeois capitalists are necessarily overthrown, and the economic ownership passes into the hands of the proletarian workers themselves. On the political level, after a brief period of proletarian dictatorship, a golden age comes into being—the era of the classless society and the "withering away" of the state.

9. Quotation by Marx from *Theses on Feuerbach*, in *The German Ideology*, ed. C. J. Arthur (New York: International Publishers, 1970), p. 123.

Marxist Dialectic and Ethics. Marx believed that the process of historical change takes place in a "dialectic" or triadic pattern whereby a historic movement is introduced which is then opposed by another movement contrary to it, the finest elements of each eventually being carried forward to form a new and superior historical reality. This new creation contains the best of the previous movements which have become "*aufgehoben*," meaning conserved, overcome, transformed, exalted. The appearance of a historical movement Marx called the *thesis*, he designated the countermovement the *antithesis*, and he called the resolution of their antagonism the *synthesis*. In the continuous unfolding of the dialectic process, the synthesis subsequently becomes a new thesis, which generates its own antithesis, and leads to the formation of a still more encompassing and higher synthesis. The triadic pattern has been repeated innumerable times as history has proceeded, leading to higher and higher stages of development that will culminate in a final, absolute synthesis.

The dialectic process not only forms the pattern for movements in history but also characterizes the development of ideas and even the growth of biological organisms.[10] There is no "either/or" in the dialectic but only a "both/and"—a synthesis of apparently contradictory elements that find their ultimate resolution. No compromise occurs but rather an organic growth takes place with the healthy, vital parts of the thesis and the antithesis combined in a dynamic fusion to produce a greater whole.

In Marx's analysis, all social development and structure depends upon the existing economic base, which determines society's politics, art forms, religious institutions, social classes, and so forth, all of which constitute the superstructure of society with economics as the foundation. What is of importance for our purposes is that Marx regarded ethics also as part of the social superstructure, containing those values consonant with the economic system of the society; with each change in the economic base, the values will change correspondingly. There is a direct correlation and variation

---

10. The dialectic development of biological forms was stressed more by Hegel, who wrote of the bud being negated by the blossom and the two being "resolved" in the growing fruit. Marx obtained the idea of the dialectic from Hegel but, as is frequently pointed out, Hegel conceived of spiritual forces developing in a dialectic pattern, whereas Marx considered the essential forces to be material in nature.

between economic factors and moral factors such that values will follow the existing economic forms. This accounts for the variations in moral codes between nations. By and large, a similarity in ethical views will exist among nations with parallel economic structures, and vast ethical differences will correspond to major economic differences between societies.

An example Marx uses is that of Christian ethics, which conforms, he believed, to the capitalist economy. A great deal has been written about the way in which the Protestant ethic, or more specifically still, Calvinism, harmonizes with the American capitalist system. For the Calvinist ethic stresses that the degree of financial success attained in this life indicates the extent to which one has been favored by God and deserves spiritual rewards in the life to come. One's economic achievement is an index of religiosity and the grace that one has been given by God.[11] But Marx stressed another aspect of Christianity: its concentration on values such as meekness, humility, acceptance, selflessness, and nonviolence, which Marx believed keeps workers in a state of subjection to the capitalist owners. The Christian emphasis on the meek inheriting the earth, its insistence that one must not lay up treasures for moths and dust to corrupt, that God favors the humble over the proud, and that the earth is a vale of tears, a testing ground for the life hereafter, undermines the revolutionary spirit of the oppressed and downtrodden. Instead of revolting against the bourgeoisie, Christians accept their abject state as part of the suffering they must endure as the lot of human beings on earth. For this reason Marx called Christianity "parson power" and the "barking dog of capitalism," thinking that it serves the purposes of the capitalists in maintaining their personally advantageous system.[12]

The point is that ethical values, whether stemming from Christianity in league with capitalism or flowing from some other source, are, according to Marx, relative to the economic system of a society.

---

11. For a classic study of the relationship between Christianity and capitalism see R. H. Tawney, *Religion and the Rise of Capitalism* (London: John Murray, 1926).

12. Marxists would also analyze Hinduism as a case in point, because it stresses that a person's socioeconomic caste in his or her current life is determined by the moral quality of his or her previous incarnation and, therefore, is justified. One cannot change caste in one's lifetime but can only hope to be reincarnated into a higher caste sometime in the future. According to the Marxist view, this suits the rulers perfectly for it sanctions their power, wealth, and privilege.

Right and wrong gain their meaning from the economic structure and are never at variance with it.

A CRITIQUE OF RELATIVISM

In the light of this brief survey, we can see that the relativist or subjectivist doctrine has very strong support from a number of different sources as well as being a fashionable belief in our society. But the question still remains whether this theory gives us the truth about ethics. Popularity does not guarantee the accuracy of an idea, for truth is not established by counting heads or by taking a vote. Neither is it determined by the authority of its advocates (cf. the genetic fallacy, pages 18–19); authority alone is not a good reason for accepting a theory, even if the pronouncement comes from a Freud or a Marx. Relativism and subjectivism must be analyzed in terms of their own merits to see whether they are the most reasonable doctrines to hold. And as was indicated at the beginning of the book, having a criterion of reasonableness in itself argues that all standards are not relative.

▶ **THE SELF-CONTRADICTION OF RELATIVISM**. The main criticism against the relativist and subjectivist is that they either cannot claim their theories are true or, if they do, they then contradict themselves. For they are saying that all of our ideas are reflections of our personal beliefs or of the culture in which we find ourselves. If that is so, then the idea that all of our ideas are subjective or relative must also be a subjective or relative idea. It cannot be held to be true in any objective sense because, according to the theory, there is no objective truth. In other words, subjectivism can only be true for the subjectivist, and relativism can only be true relative to the relativist's culture.

If, on the other hand, the subjectivist or relativist should argue that their theories are true in some objective sense, then they are contradicting themselves in their prior assumption that all ideas are subjective or relative. This idea at least is not true objectively. To put the point somewhat differently, the idea that all ideas are subjective or relative cannot be an exception to the rule that all ideas are subjective or relative without involving a self-contradiction. In order to be consistent, the subjectivist and relativist can only claim that it suits their taste or their society's attitude to think as they do. No argument can be offered for their position without assuming that which is denied, namely, that there are objective grounds for assessing the correctness of ideas. In short, the subjectivist or relativist cannot claim their theories are true in any objective sense of the term.

Thus, the belief of Ruth Benedict (and Pareto and Sumner) that beliefs are relative to one's cultural pattern is only relative to her own cultural pattern. If, according to Freud, all thought derives basically from the unconscious and is not the result of rational understanding, then so does the Freudian theory of psychology. And if all intellectual ideas are, according to Marx, relative to economic circumstances, this must include the Marxist social philosophy. It would be inconsistent for any of these thinkers to maintain that their ideas are actually true.[13]

In terms of logic, the point is that there are certain statements that one cannot sensibly make. A person cannot write that all writers are liars because it would mean he or she is lying when writing this. Or the claim that all generalizations are false would have to include the generalization that all generalizations are false, in which case it is false to say that all generalizations are false, and so on. Or the person who says "I am not speaking" contradicts himself or herself in the very act of stating it. (Camus expressed this logical point when he wrote, "The moment you say that everything is nonsense you express something meaningful.") The subjectivist and relativist are in precisely this position when they claim their theories are objectively true.[14]

---

13. It is sometimes claimed that statements of fact may be true or false but statements of value cannot be judged in those terms. However, this must be proven, for it would seem that the arguments used by these theoreticians would apply to both categories if they apply to either one. That is, their theories would argue that statements of fact and value are both relative.
14. Bertrand Russell attempted to resolve this paradox with his *theory of types*, according to which a class statement cannot be considered a member of its own class. Thus, the proposition "All reasoning is really rationalization" is not itself a member of the class of rationalizations. But many logicians have been dissatisfied with Russell's reasons for exempting class statements from their own categories, and his attempt is not generally regarded as successful.

Plato referred to this self-contradiction in the dialogue called the *Theaetetus*. Protagoras there presents his well-known doctrine that "man is the measure of all things," and means to assert by this that the individual is the yardstick of truth and goodness. Socrates criticizes this subjectivist position at some length, and then concludes "and the best of the joke is that he acknowledges the truth of their opinions who believe his own opinion to be false for he admits that the opinions of all men are true."[15] In other words, if each person creates truth for himself or herself, the individual who opposes that doctrine of personal truth would be correct in believing the doctrine to be false. If each person's opinion is right, then the person who regards subjectivism as nonsense would be correct in thinking so. In essence, Socrates is pointing out that the subjectivist position leads to the paradoxical situation in which contradictory ideas are each held to be true. This is logically absurd because we cannot affirm X and deny X at the same time. It is senseless to say that something both exists and does not exist, is tangible and intangible, is black and white all over. Something can appear to have one set of qualities from one perspective and another from a different point of view, as in the case of a flowing river that appears as a silver ribbon from an airplane, but an object cannot in fact possess contradictory qualities; the river is either stationary or in a state of flux.[16] This rule is called the *law of noncontradiction* and it cannot be abridged without creating chaos among ideas and causing complete anarchy of thought. But this is precisely the position in which subjectivism finds itself because it implies that contradictory ideas are all true if the people affirming them believe them to be true.

In the *Republic* Plato (via Socrates) attacked the subjectivist and relativist in a somewhat different way in a famous passage concerning the nature of justice. A man named Thrasymachus has argued that justice only means "the interests of the stronger,"[17] and Socrates in refuting this view goes on to develop a theory of the ideal

15. Plato, *Theaetetus*, in *The Dialogues of Plato*, trans. B. Jowett (New York: Scribner, Armstrong and Co., 1874), Vol. III, p. 373.
16. In quantum theory, subatomic units of matter sometimes appear as waves and sometimes as particles, and this seemed contradictory when first discovered. Now it is recognized that the paradox arises due to two different ways of viewing matter.
17. Plato, *The Republic*, in *The Dialogues of Plato*, trans. B. Jowett (New York: Scribner, Armstrong and Co., 1874), Vol. II, p. 159ff.

state. Thrasymachus is claiming, in effect, that whatever dominant values are held by the political forces controlling society become the values people accept as authoritative. And these values are always devised by the rulers, not in accordance with any universal principles of right, but in terms of their own welfare. When Thrasymachus says "I declare justice is nothing but the advantage of the stronger," he is declaring that justice does not have any objective status but only exists as an expression of the will of the strongest forces in society. Each new leader or party that gains political power enacts legislation to maintain its own domination and its own interests. Law is not the product of rational reflection or the codification of God's moral will but the arbitrary and self-serving rules imposed on the weaker by the stronger.

In reply to this extreme cynicism, Socrates first makes a distinction. He asks whether Thrasymachus means that justice is what the stronger enforce or what is to the advantage of the stronger. If it is the first, then the stronger might be enforcing that which is not to their advantage; they may, unwittingly, be doing that which is detrimental to themselves. If, however, they are legislating to their own advantage, then they are recognizing that which would be advantageous to themselves and enacting laws in terms of it.

Thrasymachus plays into Socrates' hands by choosing the first as his meaning, and this enables Socrates to expand upon the point that what a person wills may be different from what is advantageous. In other words, what a government may force individuals to accept may be different than what is advantageous—for the leaders or anyone else. There can be a difference between dominant ideas and good ideas. The two can, of course, coincide, but that which is enforced cannot be taken as the definition of that which is advantageous; we cannot equate the political or the legal with the moral. Morality does not depend upon the state's laws but rather the state's laws are judged according to standards of morality. What is right and wrong, then, is not a function of an individual's beliefs, societal norms, or governmental decrees; it has an objective status.

▶ **THE CONFLICT BETWEEN SUBJECTIVISM AND CULTURAL RELATIVISM**. A further defect in the logic of subjectivism or relativism is that the personal values of an individual can be at variance with the values of his or her society, thus setting up a conflict as to which is right. In other words, although subjectivism and relativism are allegedly in the same camp, they might well be in opposition. An African-American, for example, could feel that segregation is demeaning and unconscionable at a time when his or her society regards it as perfectly proper. Furthermore, not only can there be differences between individual and group morals, but various groups can disagree in their values and it would be impossible on relativist grounds to adjudicate the dispute. Republicans and Democrats have very different positions on welfare, homosexuality, and crime, and the Catholic community and the advocates of women's rights have opposite views on voluntary abortion. If values are relative to what a social group believes, which group is the one to select what is right? And since everyone belongs to a number of different groups, people would be divided within themselves, which is obviously an intolerable situation. It is impossible to maintain, as the relativist theory would imply, that an act is right insofar as one is a soldier but wrong as a consumer, right insofar as one is a senior citizen but wrong as an art collector.

▶ **THE DISPARITY WITH EXPERIENCE**. Another criticism that can be leveled against subjectivism and relativism is that they contradict our moral experience. We feel the force of certain obligations and commitments as striking us from without, certain "ought" imperatives that we feel obliged to follow. And it is difficult, if not impossible, to dismiss this experience as relative to our society or as the product of our psyche. To say that when we value human life and feel obliged to preserve it, our response is merely subjective and human life has no real value, runs counter to our most basic feelings.

As mentioned previously, people who adopt an unusual position carry the burden of proof, and must establish their point; otherwise the ideas that are in keeping with common experience are assumed to remain true. In this case, people recognize morals as binding upon them, as basic rules of conduct that transcend particular opinions or mores. Therefore, it is up to the subjectivist or relativist to prove that this is not so. From the theories we have examined and the criticisms of the logic behind them, neither sub-

THE RELATIVIST OBJECTION

jectivists nor cultural relativists have done so; in fact, the argument seems very much the other way. And in the absence of proof for the subjectivity or relativity of values, the common-sense view should prevail: that values are a matter of insight rather than convention, and discovered not created.

► **THE ISSUE OF MORAL PROGRESS.** A fourth criticism of subjectivism and relativism is that neither accounts for moral progress in history nearly so adequately as the assumption of objectivism. Societies have changed throughout the centuries in ways that constitute not just differences but improvements. And these improvements can be explained mainly in terms of a progressive recognition of superior values. If our conceptions of right and wrong were nothing other than a function of our society's ideas, then it would be difficult to account for the evolutionary advances of our civilization. Change can be explained in terms of different historical conditions to which societies respond but progress requires a different explanation. It would seem to be not just a chance happening that societies have become morally better but a matter of people realizing more humane ways of treating one another.

It can, of course, be questioned whether human society has improved. Some people might claim that we are not any kinder today than yesterday, but simply more refined and subtle in our cruelty. Instead of the thumb screw and the rack, we now have economic oppression, toxic chemicals, racial discrimination, and environmental degradation.

Although this point of view may appeal momentarily to our tendencies toward pessimism, it hardly seems tenable. By almost any standard, we are more humane now than in previous times. Civilization does constitute progress from a barbaric state, and the civilization of recent centuries is generally higher in ethical character than that of earlier ages. Rules of war, for example, have been formulated so that when one nation conquers another the women and children are not slaughtered or taken as spoils. Slavery has been virtually abolished whereas prior to the nineteenth century it was commonplace. The conditions of our jails and mental hospitals have improved immeasurably, and our standards of health and housing have become progressively higher. Countless other examples could be cited, but the point does not require very much proof; the evidence is all about us, and the contrary view seems unjustifiably skeptical.

Assuming that the ethical character of society has progressed, it would appear that the improvement is due to people questioning whether the prevailing standards are right, and changing the *status quo* in accordance with their vision of a superior society. We are always able to ask "Is this worthwhile?" or "Will that be better?" when presented with social standards. If society were the measure of those standards, this would not be possible. Americans, for example, have always restlessly explored goals in living and questioned what a better life for themselves might be. And in seeking a worthwhile life Americans are tacitly acknowledging the good as an objective standard against which they can measure the ideals of their own or any society. Values, then, are not assumed to be good or right because society says so, but rather society should say if the values are good or right.

AN OBJECTIVIST POSITION

▶ **OBJECTIVIST VERSUS RELATIVIST VIEWS**. Some people may feel that in order to be scientific they must adopt a relativistic view of ethics, that despite their basic feelings they should be hardheaded in their thinking and follow the contemporary approach to values. But as we have seen, serious doubts exist as to whether the relativist beliefs have been substantiated. The evidence used by Benedict, Sumner, Marx, and others is not in doubt so much as whether it entails the conclusion that values are relative. The logic employed for reaching the conclusion is questionable and may be more soft-headed than tough-minded. According to the standard of reasonableness—whereby a theory must (1) be consistent within itself and with regard to its implications, (2) take the relevant facts into consideration and not contradict those facts, and (3) provide the most probable interpretation of experience—relativism does not fare very well. It is logically inconsistent in various ways and is, in fact, self-contradictory. In addition, it opposes the relevant facts of our moral experience, and fails to offer an explanation of social progress.

Furthermore, our contemporary approach to values is not, in fact, relativistic although we may pay lip service to relativism in earnest academic company. We have not really abandoned objectivism today but have revised our list of the values that we regard as objectively worthwhile. We still feel that some actions are intrinsically right and others intrinsically wrong but the particular acts to which we apply these judgments have changed. We once believed that virginity was a highly important virtue but today we stress the value of personal involvement in our sexual relationships; the sex act does not seem awful to us (as it did to our Victorian ancestors) but depersonalization is thought to be blameworthy in lovemaking or wherever it occurs. Lending money at a high rate of interest (usury) is not now condemned as it was in Biblical times but the exploitation of a person is considered very wrong. Also prominent in our thinking today is the wrongness of rape, terrorism, discrimination, and genocide. Although the list could continue, the point is that we still maintain certain acts are inherently worthwhile and others worthless; only the content of our moral judgments has changed.

This does not mean, however, that because values change the subjectivist and relativist views are vindicated. All it indicates is that although values may be absolute, we are never absolutely certain which values are the right ones. Our belief that a certain action is right may change, but the rightness or wrongness of an action remains constant. Changing beliefs about values, then, does not imply that values are relative but rather that our understanding of correct values is clearer or dimmer at different historical periods.

Since we are never certain that what we believe is in agreement with what is truly right, our commitment to any particular value must always be tentative. Having confidence that there are genuine values gives direction to our search, but it should not make us arrogant about the values we hold. We can never be sure that our insights are correct but it seems reasonable to assume that there are correct moral insights.

Many people fear that objectivists are dogmatic in the values they hold, that they are self-righteous and try to force their values on others, thereby trying to limit their freedom. However, this need not be the case. Although objectivists think there are intrinsic values, they do not assume that they are privileged to know precisely what those values are or that they can instruct others in the truth; as objectivists, they simply presuppose that values are there to be known. They believe we have a finer perception and more accurate sense of right and wrong today than when we were Neanderthals but they never assume that anyone's knowledge is complete. That is, even though they believe there are absolute values, they do not say that we know them absolutely.

▶ **THE SIMILARITY OF THE SCIENTIFIC VIEW AND MORAL OBJECTIVISM.** In this respect, the position of the objectivist is essentially that of the scientist. It has never been an assumption of scientists that they know the whole of reality. But the scientist does assume that there is a reality and that by careful and patient effort we can come to know more about it. Scientists do not think they are inventing scientific ideas or creating truth in the laboratory, but that they are understanding a progressively greater portion of that which is real. When scientists say that the earth orbits the sun, or that atoms are in motion around a nucleus, they do not think these truths are subjective or culturally relative. They are confident that anyone who investigates these phenomena with logical clarity and technical sophistication will reach the same conclusion; the results are reproducible. Since levels of awareness and accuracy of perception differ, they allow for the possibility of disagreement but they feel there is an objective truth that people will come to know and agree upon. Any disagreement, including that implied by different scientific ideas in the past, is taken to be the result of a more or less accurate understanding of a single truth, and scientists hope in time for greater and greater unanimity of understanding.

Objectivists in morals are in basically the same position and have much the same attitude. They too assume that there is a reality and believe that it encompasses moral values. Disagreements about moral truths are thought to be due to more or less accurate degrees of understanding; morality is not considered a personal or social creation. Objectivists hope that, although a universal consensus may never be reached on ethical issues, there will be progressively greater agreement through time. They are no more dogmatic than scientists, for they never maintain that their understanding of moral truth is infallible but, like scientists, believe there is a truth to be known.

MULTICULTURALISM

As a final word on the topic of moral relativism, there is a nationwide movement today in favor of multiculturalism, the inclusion within our national identity of diverse nationalities, religions, races, sexual orientations, and so forth. Rather than thinking of our nation as a melting pot, we are urged to regard it as pluralistic and embracing a wide spectrum of social groups.

Along with this it is sometimes argued that no one culture should be given preference over any other, whether in choosing the canon of good literature or deciding what to include in history courses, and that no culture's practices can be judged as better or worse than that of any other. In other words, it is claimed that the value of all cultures is relative.

Although multiculturalism is a commendable aim, and functions to include people rather than exclude them from the American mainstream, it need not entail moral relativism. The movement is really asking that we have a sympathetic understanding of other cultures and the perspective that different peoples bring to political, social, or cultural issues. We should consider multiple points of view in reaching decisions rather than just the white, Anglo-Saxon, Protestant perspective. That does not mean, however, a moral neutrality in which all values are equal and no behavior is ever condemned.

If a culture practices wife-beating as a part of a manly image, or a particular group considers heavy drinking and intoxication as acceptable forms of entertainment, such practices should not be considered worthwhile just because they are acceptable to certain cultures. We can still differentiate between behavior that is admirable and that which is not, regardless of the culture in which it occurs, including WASP society. Awful conduct does not deserve inclusion even though it is prevalent in a culture. That is, multiculturalism does not mean the suspension of all moral judgments but rather being open to the good that different cultures contribute to American life.[18]

CONCLUSION

In the light of our discussion, therefore, it seems reasonable to assume that there are better and worse ways of living, that people can be morally wrong in their choices of actions, and that it is not a case of actions becoming worthwhile by virtue of having been chosen. Some actions seem to be praiseworthy and others blameworthy; hopefully, we will come to know the difference. And actions should be chosen because they are right, they are not right because they are chosen.

Moral philosophers try to arrive at some broad understanding of moral values and assume they are not merely projecting their attitudes upon others, but are engaged in a serious search for what is, in fact, a right mode of conduct and a good reason for living.

RECAPITULATION

In this chapter we discussed the theories of cultural relativism and subjectivism, which are opposed to absolutism and objectivism as explanations of the basis for values. The relativist and subjectivist positions were elucidated and traced to three modern sources in the finds of sociology and anthropology (using Sumner, Pareto, and Benedict as representatives), the principles of Freudian psychology, and the theory of Marxism. The philosopher David Hume was also mentioned as a supporting figure.

The relativist and subjectivist doctrines were then criticized in various ways. First, they were found to be self-contradictory and logically inconsistent, and parts of Plato's *Theaetetus* and *Republic*

---

18. See Charles Taylor, *Multiculturalism and "The Politics of Recognition"* (Princeton, NJ: Princeton University Press, 1992).

were cited to illustrate the fallacies in such reasoning. The two doctrines were also shown to be at variance with each other in certain situations and not necessarily unified. Relativism and subjectivism were also criticized for running counter to our moral experience, and for failing to account for moral progress in an adequate way.

The chapter concluded with a discussion of contemporary attitudes toward relativism, and by showing that an objectivist is not necessarily a dogmatist.

▼ ▼ ▼

REVIEW QUESTIONS

1. *Discuss the sociological and anthropological foundations of relativism. How do the philosophers C. L. Stevenson and David Hume support this view?*

2. *Explain the relevance of Freudian psychology to the theory of relativism. What does Freud mean by the id, ego, and superego?*

3. *Explain the relevance of Marxism to the theory of relativism. What does Marx mean by the dialectic?*

4. *In his dialogue, the* Theaetetus, *how does Plato show the self-contradictory nature of subjectivism?*

5. *What is meant by the statement that relativism does not account for moral progress in human history nearly so adequately as the assumption of objectivism?*

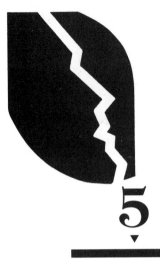

5

HEDONISM

hen people ask themselves what they hope to gain from life, most will reply that they want happiness, that they want to increase the total amount of enjoyment in their lives as a whole. This is the most common theory of what the good life consists of, and is also the definition most frequently proposed by reflective people. It seems a natural way of thinking because from our earliest days we tend to identify the pleasant life with the good life, an enjoyable experience with a worthwhile one. When children taste candy and say, "It's good," what they really mean is that it is enjoyable to taste, thereby making the equation between that which is pleasant and that which is good. We define good in the same way when we refer to an enjoyable experience as a good time.

Furthermore, as philosophers have pointed out, happiness (or pleasure) is an ultimate end rather than a means toward the satisfaction of any other goal. We do many things in order to be happy, but we are not happy in order to attain anything further. It would be an odd question to ask people why they want to be happy, or what they hope to gain from it, because happiness is never the type of state that is a means toward some more ultimate end; rather it is that goal for which a great many things are done. Aristotle pointed out that happiness is totally self-sufficient. Once we have attained happiness, we do not look for anything else. It is whole, complete, and without gaps. If someone lacks something, that person is not wholly happy; if someone is completely happy, he or she lacks nothing. There is a self-sufficiency about happiness that seems to qualify it as being the ultimate good in life.[1]

Other considerations also incline us to accept the idea of pleasure or happiness as the ultimate goal in life. For one thing, both pleasure and pain are regarded as simple feelings, incapable of being reduced to more ultimate psychological terms. In addition, the individual who experiences pleasure considers it as good, while the person who experiences pain regards it as unequivocally bad. Some good may come from suffering but that does not make the suffering intrinsically good; we would just as soon have the good without the suffering. Finally, it seems that all acts considered good have some element of pleasure connected with them. If pleasure is a common denominator, it would appear to be basic.

These are some of the reasons philosophers and laypeople use to justify their commitment to happiness or pleasure as the good. But in a more basic sense, most people take it as a "given," that is, something so self-evident it hardly requires any justification. This affirmation of pleasure or happiness as the goal in life is called *hedonism*, and it is one of the oldest theories in the history of ethics. In its long development various distinctions have evolved regarding the types of hedonism that are logically possible.

1. Aristotle is not technically regarded as a hedonist but his ethic of self-realization does contain some hedonistic elements. He regarded pleasure as the natural accompaniment of virtuous activities, and these activities constitute both our self-realization and our happiness. Pleasure, therefore, is *a* good but not *the* good.

TYPES OF HEDONISM

▶ <u>PSYCHOLOGICAL AND ETHICAL HEDONISM</u>.

Doctrine of Psychological Hedonism. One variety, called *psychological hedonism*, is the doctrine that human nature is so constituted that people necessarily pursue pleasure and avoid pain. Psychological hedonists do not concern themselves with what people ought to do but with what people actually do, not what should be desired but what in fact is desired.

As a description of human behavior it is not, strictly speaking, an ethical theory but a descriptive theory that has implications for ethics. Be that as it may, the psychological hedonist claims that all animals, including human beings, naturally and automatically seek pleasure and avoid pain. This, it is claimed, is a universal law of nature that admits of no exceptions. Pleasure is the prime motivation of all human activities, and people who claim they act for any other reasons are simply rationalizing their basic pursuit of pleasurable experience. To the psychological hedonist, all alleged altruism is seen to be basically a self-interested hedonistic pursuit even if the agent is not aware of that fact. People always behave so as to maximize their pleasure and minimize their pain; it is a necessary and universal law of behavior.

Psychological hedonists claim to see through the pretensions of human conduct. They claim to see that the person who gives a beggar a dollar is motivated not by any anxiety concerning the beggar's state but by the satisfaction that will be derived from this apparently generous act. This interpretation is reinforced by the thought that few philanthropic actions are unknown to other people; most generosity is paraded before an audience for approval, thereby increasing the selfish pleasure of the agent. For example, a college donation usually bears the name of the donor, whether the gift is for buildings, scholarship funds, or an endowed chair. In the case of giving to beggars, the psychological hedonist will further claim that the contributors will also be increasing their own peace of mind. They will think of themselves as superior to those they have helped, and the fact that the beggars are now under some obligation to them adds still further to their pleasure. In general, the gifts of money have increased their pleasure and diminished their pain, and it was because they anticipated this result that they respond as they do to beggars' appeals.

To the psychological hedonist, all actions that claim to be performed in the interest of the public good can be explained in a similar way. Doctors do not enter their profession from humanitarian motives but because of the personal rewards and pleasures they hope to derive from it. Parents who sacrifice to promote the welfare of their child do so because of a sense of pride which they will have in the child's accomplishments. Religious people also do not seek to serve God but hope to gain the admiration of their neighbors, divine protection for themselves in this life, or heaven in the life to come.

A Critique of Psychological Hedonism. We need not spend very long developing this theory since it parallels the position of psychological egoism dealt with in Chapter 1, and the criticisms are very much the same. Experience indicates that many activities are carried on without any desire for pleasure. We often act out of habit or, more importantly, for the attainment of certain goals or values. It is true that pleasure may be the result of these activities but the result cannot automatically be considered the motive. Those people who give a dollar to a beggar may derive pleasure from this generous act but it is doubtful whether they helped the beggar with the intention of increasing their own pleasure. The psychological hedonist may assert that firefighters who risk their lives to rescue a child, or martyrs who die at the stake, or soldiers who volunteer for a dangerous mission are motivated by pleasure; however, the hedonist has no proof of this. The evidence seems rather strong in the opposite direction. A person driving a car, who has a choice between crashing into a tree or hitting a child who darted into the road, would probably choose the tree and thus deliberately risk his or her own life in order to save the child. The driver could not have given any thought to the pleasure to be gained from the altruism.

To look at the matter slightly differently, people seek various goals and when they achieve them they feel a sense of pleasure. But the pleasure is not what they are seeking. The pleasure is an accompaniment or a byproduct of the achievement of their desired goals.

Pleasure might be an emotional tone that accompanies the achievement of our purpose rather than being the thing itself that we desire to achieve. When we want something, we are pleased when we get it, but that is not to say that what we wanted was to be pleased. Pleasure, then, is not the implicit or explicit aim of our actions even though it may be the aim. It is mistaken, therefore, to say that human beings are motivated by pleasure, much less to say that they are never motivated by anything else.

The Theory of Ethical Hedonism. But psychological hedonism interests us much less than *ethical hedonism*, which is often based upon it. This type of hedonism does not maintain that people must pursue pleasure, that it is a law of human behavior or a general description of human conduct, but claims that pleasure *ought* to be that which we seek. Ethical hedonists are not interested in describing what people do but in prescribing what they ought to do. To their minds, pleasure or happiness should be the goal in life.

Ethical hedonism is sometimes based upon psychological hedonism in the sense that pleasure is considered to be natural to human beings and consequently desirable for human beings. What people should do coincides with what they must do, and, in fact, gains its strength from that source. In other words, ethical hedonists will sometimes claim that since people naturally tend to pursue pleasure, they are therefore justified in doing so. But this position not only violates the naturalistic fallacy described in Chapter 2, but can be seen to be basically pointless. For it makes no sense to advise people to do that which they cannot help but do. We never recommend that people should breathe since they necessarily must breathe, and it is equally fruitless to recommend the pursuit of pleasure if pleasure is all that people can pursue. At best, we can only approve of that unavoidable fact.

However, ethical hedonism need not be based on any psychological grounds and is, in fact, on firmer footing as a pure ethical recommendation. Ethical hedonists can say that, regardless of whether people *do* pursue pleasure, they *should* pursue pleasure as the good in life. Even if people are capable of pursuing other goals, pleasure is the preferred one. It is this ethical doctrine that constitutes the dominant form of hedonism and is the one of greatest interest to us.

► INDIVIDUALISTIC AND UNIVERSALISTIC HEDONISM

The Individualistic Position. A distinction that can be made within ethical hedonism is between individualistic and universalistic versions. The person who advocates an *individualistic* position maintains that pleasure for others is regarded as unjustifiable both from a practical and a theoretical standpoint. It is impractical because one never really knows what will satisfy other people; it is difficult enough to determine what will please oneself. Human desires are so strange and various that it is impossible to predict what will satisfy the taste of someone else. If we offer someone a glass of wine, we may find that the person is offended because she is a teetotaler. If we offer a guest a soft bed for the night, we may discover that he is an ascetic and would prefer a bed of nails. And if a man opens a door for a woman, he may find she is a strong feminist who regards the gesture as patronizing behavior.

But even if we could determine what would bring pleasure to other people, the individualistic hedonist sees no reason why we should engage in such conduct. Our sole concern should be to receive pleasure for ourselves. If we forfeit our own pleasure for the sake of someone else, we will have missed life's greatest blessing, and there is no reason for us to make that kind of sacrifice. If each person takes care of himself or herself, society as a whole will be more enriched than if we meddle in each other's affairs, trying to make the other person happy. This aspect of individualistic hedonism is very like the laissez-faire doctrine of the economist Adam Smith, who thought that an "invisible hand" regulates the marketplace so that as individuals seek their private gain in a free-enterprise system the entire economic community prospers.

The Universalistic Position. In sharp contrast and opposition to the individualistic theory is that of *universalistic hedonism.* Rather than advocating that individuals pursue their own pleasure, universalistic hedonists affirm an altruistic doctrine, claiming that we should pursue pleasure or happiness for humankind in general.

All of our actions should be directed toward the maximization of pleasure for society rather than just for ourselves. Our own pleasure is to count as much as that of each person affected by our actions, no more and no less. We should consider ourselves as one and no more than one in the moral equation, neither putting ourselves first nor sacrificing ourselves (except when bringing pleasure to the majority casts us in the minority). Universalistic hedonists believe neither in the selflessness of Christian dedication nor in the selfishness of the individualist's approach. Their concern is with the well being of society, with each person considered as an equal component of the whole. Our attitude toward action should always be "Will this increase the amount of pleasure for humankind?"

Distinguishing between Individualistic and Universalistic Hedonism. Overtly it is very difficult to differentiate between the individualistic and the universalistic hedonist because both will do things for other people. But the motive for individualistic hedonists is to increase their own pleasure through helping others. Their generosity is basically a means toward increasing their personal happiness. The universalistic hedonist, however, helps others for *their* sake rather than for *his* or *her own* sake. Now since motives lie behind actions and are invisible, it is hard to tell when we are in the presence of an individualistic or a universalistic motive. But one way of differentiating between the two is to see whether the individuals would continue bringing pleasure to others even if it conflicted with their own pleasure. Individuals who did persist would be essentially universalistic, not allowing the reduction of their own pleasure to keep them from pursuing wider pleasure for others. Those who stopped at precisely that point where giving pleasure to others conflicted with receiving pleasure for themselves would be individualistic.

An important point to stress is that both the individualistic and the universalistic hedonist are ethical hedonists as well. They both think that pleasure or happiness ought to be sought and differ only in their answer to the question "for whom," the individualist saying "for oneself," the universalist saying "for everyone affected by my action." Individualistic hedonists will very often be psychological hedonists as well, and will frequently claim that people are basically selfish and act mainly for their personal enjoyment. But they need only be ethical hedonists not psychological hedonists to maintain their theory. Universalistic hedonists can also base their ideas on psychological hedonism and say that human nature is so constituted that we always seek pleasure for others, but such a position is much less common. It would more frequently happen that individualistic hedonists would have psychological grounds for their doctrine.

It is useful to keep the various types of hedonism in mind in examining the overall theory. In this way we will be able to make distinctions in analyzing and evaluating the various historical forms that hedonism has assumed.

ANCIENT THEORIES OF HEDONISM

▶ **THE CYRENAICS**. Aristippus (435–356 B.C.) was probably the first hedonist in philosophic history, and he studied under Socrates in Athens before diverging from his teacher's sober rationalism. Subsequently, Aristippus started his own school of thought at a place called Cyrene on the coast of North Africa, and his followers were soon referred to as the *Cyrenaics*.[2]

Cyrenaic Doctrine. Aristippus held that all good is determined by pleasure and, more specifically, that the pleasures which are available to be enjoyed are far superior to any pleasures that we remember or anticipate. The pleasures of the past or the future are pale compared to the enjoyments of the moment, at this knife edge instant of the present. In one of his surviving fragments, Aristippus wrote that the moral good "has nothing to do with the recollection of past enjoyments or with the hope of future ones."

Not only did Aristippus and the Cyrenaics feel that momentary pleasures are best but, as a corollary, they thought we need not pay much attention to the duration of pleasures. The fact that our pleasure might be *brief* does not detract from its worth, and our life aim should be to have as many pleasurable moments as we can cram into the time allotted to us.

Furthermore, they argued, we should strive for maximum *intensity* in our pleasures. The more intense the experience, the more

2. See Diogenes Laertius, *Lives of Eminent Philosophers*, trans. R. D. Hicks (Cambridge, MA: Harvard University Press, 1950), Vol. I, Chapter II, pp. 65–93.

pleasurable it is for the individual. Tranquil, sedentary, passive forms of enjoyment were thought to be tepid and weak compared to the intense experiences available to the pleasure seeker. In addition to feeling that immediate pleasures of a brief and intense kind are best for leading a good life, the Cyrenaics also maintained that the pleasures of the body or *senses* are more desirable than those of the mind. In other words, pleasures such as eating rich and flavorful food, drinking full-bodied wine, making love, enjoying the sea and the sun are to be preferred over the enjoyment of the intellectual understanding, the pleasures of conversation, and the mellowness of aesthetic contemplation. Aristippus did not make any distinctions with regard to better or worse pleasures; he was solely concerned with how intense, physical, immediate, and brief our experiences were. The pleasures of one experience were not superior to those of another—only, perhaps, fuller in the amount of pleasure they yielded and, therefore, preferable.

Critique of Cyrenaic Doctrine. This is essentially a *carpe diem* philosophy, an "eat, drink, and be merry" approach to life. Enjoy what you can today and do not dwell nostalgically on some golden past or pin your hopes on some rosy future you think will be happy; live life to the full, wringing out of the present moment all the joy obtainable. And the more intense and physical your pleasure is, the more satisfying your moments will be. The Persian poet Omar Khayyám, although not a Cyrenaic, expressed this philosophy in *The Rubaiyat* with verses such as the following:

▼ ▼ ▼

. . .

Come, fill the Cup, and in the fire of Spring
Your Winter-garment of Repentance fling:
  The Bird of Time has but a little way
To flutter—and the Bird is on the Wing

. . .

A Book of Verses underneath the Bough
A Jug of Wine, a Loaf of Bread—and Thou

. . .

  Beside me singing in the Wilderness—
Oh, Wilderness were Paradise enow!

. . .

Ah, make the most of what we yet may spend,
Before we too into the Dust descend;
Dust into Dust, and under the Dust to lie,
Sans Wine, sans Song, sans Singer, and—sans End!

▲ ▲ ▲

But certain embarrassing difficulties emerged that constitute a practical criticism of Cyrenaic theory. First, if we simply look for the pleasures of the moment and have no interest in what might occur subsequently, we will often enjoy ourselves now and pay for it very dearly later. For example, if we want to maximize our immediate enjoyment of drinking, to intensify the experience as much as possible, we will find ourselves suffering considerably the next morning. Or if we want to indulge ourselves to the utmost in the pleasures of eating, and gorge ourselves whenever we can, we will find that our body will become ungainly and unhealthy. Then there is the reverse problem of refusing to undergo any momentary discomfort for the sake of future gains, which can be equally self-defeating. There is a story about a Greek boy who was carrying a bag of gold and because it was heavy threw it away. Obviously he should have endured some present discomfort for the sake of the future enjoyment that the money would have brought him. Wisdom dictates that we have to put up with a great deal that is uncomfortable and not particularly to our liking in order to prepare for a future that will be pleasurable for us. For if we refuse to submit to any kind of displeasure now, we will probably come to regret our impulsiveness in later life.

In short, one cannot ignore future consequences in deciding how one should act. Some immediate pleasures ought to be rejected because they are going to lead to considerable pain subsequently, and some immediate pains should be undergone because of the rewards they will bring in the future.

In addition, intensity can also be a state that is not wholly good in terms of what follows from it. It seems that the more one increases the intensity of one's pleasure, the more likely it is that an opposite and equal state of pain will follow. It seems as though the higher the peaks of joyous intensity, the deeper are the troughs of pain, suffering, or despair; the loftier the mountain, the deeper the valley.

For example, if a man decides to intensify his sexual experiences and goes from partner to partner, contemptuous of safe sex practices, he may find that although the experience is more exhilarating, the consequences of his promiscuity can be deadly in the form of AIDS. Or if a woman wants to increase her enjoyment of speeding in a car and drives eighty or ninety miles per hour, the dangers of having an accident are proportionally increased; the faster she drives, the more likely the disaster. The same holds true for the contemporary drug scene, so that if a man progresses from marijuana to heroin or crack cocaine, he will certainly increase the "high," but he runs a commensurate risk of ruining his life and dying an early death. Thus, as one heightens intensity, one seems to multiply the likelihood of pain—whereas if one leads a more tranquil life, the consequences tend to be equally tranquil.

And if intensity is not necessarily valuable, the value of brevity which the Cyrenaics champion is also undermined, for Cyrenaics only accept brevity so that they can maximize intensity. One cannot have a long intense experience but only a brief intense one, so brevity is the price Cyrenaics are willing to pay for having maximum intensity. But if intensity is not necessarily desirable, we need not put up with a brief experience; we would, of course, prefer having our pleasures extended for as long a period as possible.

Finally, the pleasures of the senses can be challenged as not being the most satisfying kind. It can be argued that mental enjoyment is richer, deeper, and ultimately more fulfilling than momentary sensual pleasures. As Walter Lippmann wrote: "It really shouldn't surprise us that the pleasures of the moment are only momentary pleasures." The enjoyment of mental states and activities can be preferred to those of the senses, which are fleeting, shallow, and animalistic.

▶ **EPICUREANISM**. Because of these problems, a series of modifications in theory occurred, which culminated in another variety of hedonism called the *Epicurean school*.[3] The philosopher Epicurus (342–270 B.C.), who founded the movement and gave his name to it, lived in Athens following the death of Aristotle.

3. See W. J. Oates, *The Stoic and the Epicurean Philosophers* (New York: Random House, 1940).

We know that Epicurus studied Plato's system and the ideas of Democritus. We also know that he taught in Asia Minor before he founded his institute of philosophy in Athens, where he conducted classes in a famous walled garden. The garden of Epicurus became as famous as the Academy of Plato or the Lyceum of Aristotle.

Epicurean Theory. Epicurus took as his goal in life an essential serenity or tranquility of the mind and a comfortableness of the body. Anything which disturbed an individual's peaceful state of being had to be avoided. In fact, Epicurus thought it was far more important to avoid pain than to pursue enjoyment. Pleasure, to his mind, is the "absence of pain in the body and of trouble in the soul." The overall aim is to keep ourselves in a state of maximum serenity. The Epicureans criticized the Cyrenaics not only for pursuing exciting pleasures but for concentrating only on immediate pleasures—instead of considering the total amount of happiness attained in one's lifetime. If we are only concerned with the pleasures that can be enjoyed at the moment, we may find that our lives are miserable overall. There should be a long-term balancing of pleasures over pains and this involves a good deal of deliberation, intelligence, foresight, and reasoning. We have to assess pleasures to see which ones would not be contradicted by subsequent pains and which pains are worth enduring for the sake of subsequent pleasures. The rational approach to experience is, therefore, necessary to direct our activities, to temper our passions, and to look for the good in life as a whole.

Because of this emphasis on rational control, the Epicureans began to stress the happiness that the mind can provide over the pleasures that the senses or the body will yield. It is the mind that is most important, both in controlling our activities and receiving intellectual enjoyment. By seeking mental happiness, we avoid intensity and look for tranquility, which is much less hazardous in the long run. We not only avoid the temptations of immediate pleasures, that is, the pleasures near at hand, but we also avoid the temptation of choosing the intense experience over the more tranquil one. With the mind in command, we can choose the overall pleasures that are of a peaceful kind. These pleasures can be of long duration rather than having to be brief, and because they are longer they can prove more richly satisfying; what we seek is a pleasurable consciousness.

As noted, Epicurus regarded pleasure basically as the absence of pain. To him, the good life consists in avoiding pain insofar as possible and not seeking positive pleasures in an active way. If we can maintain ourselves in a condition that is not painful but essentially comfortable, we can say we are in a pleasurable state. If we are not uncomfortable, then we are in a happy frame of mind (or at least in a neutral state, which is desirable because it signifies the absence of physical discomfort or mental disturbance). When we have this peace of mind and body, we have serenity.

The walled garden of Epicurus has always been taken as an appropriate symbol for the philosophy that he advocated because it was a shelter, refuge, or retreat where people could escape from the struggles and vicissitudes of the world and live a life of undisturbed enjoyment. Walls, of course, are ambiguous: They keep things in and keep things out, and it is a matter of emphasis as to which is their primary function. Epicurus' garden wall clearly functioned to keep the sufferings of the world safely outside.

There was something of the monk about Epicurus rather than the saint or martyr, for he did not dedicate himself to others but led a secluded life in the service of an ideal mode of being. His life was ascetic and scrupulously modulated, and he encouraged his followers to practice an equally austere and disciplined existence. Sumptuous food, intemperance, and riotous living were all condemned, and a diet of bread and water was thought sufficient sustenance with a moderate amount of wine on feast days. One's residence was to be modest and economically furnished to satisfy basic needs, and the daily routine was simplified to include only essential activities. Epicurus affirmed the value of friendship—but for the self-gratification it would bring rather than for the sake of the friend, and sharing mealtimes with others was encouraged for the same reason; dining alone was also considered less than human, for as Epicurus said, "To feed without a friend is the life of a lion and a wolf." The body too had to be cultivated, not for sensuous refinements of taste and feeling but to maintain the health of the organism so that sickness would not disrupt a person's tranquility. Exercise and proper rest were essential, but not a regime of athletic training to win honor at the Olympic games. Only enough care of the body was required to keep it from plaguing the person.

The Epicurean way of living, then, favored moderation throughout, the regulation of sexual passion, the control of bodily hungers, and the continual checking of the desire for experiences of the senses. Epicurus strove to move the center of our being from body to mind, from excitement to quiescence, from the active to the passive mode of existence, and from thrilling moments to lasting contentment.

A Critique of Epicurean Theory. It would seem as though the Epicurean type of hedonism is an advance over the Cyrenaic variety, and yet it cannot be judged as unequivocally good. By stressing the avoidance of pain over the increase of pleasure, Epicurus and his disciples adopted an essentially negative attitude toward life. In essence, they were withdrawing from the world, turning inward and choosing to live a comfortable and uninvolved existence, like the attitude characteristic of old age when people simply want to be left in peace and no longer look for excitement and novel experience. The Cyrenaics by contrast were highly spirited, sanguine, and vital. They advocated taking greater risks and seemed more positive in their affirmation of life, saying yes rather than no to experience. And we are not at all sure that intensity should be avoided simply because there can be painful consequences, any more than we are sure that tranquility is a blessing simply because it is unlikely to be followed by negative sensations; the intense joy may be well worth the price.

Similarly, it is not at all certain that we should avoid immediate pleasure that might lead to subsequent pain. To view the world that way means to act without sufficient spontaneity. The Cyrenaic philosophy is, in fact, a young person's philosophy, stressing the pleasures of the body that are immediate, intense, and fleeting, and although this type of approach may not be wise in an Epicurean sense, nevertheless it can yield a better life than the very careful attitudes of wisdom and age. The prudence of Epicureanism tends to chill the blood, a truth that kills.

It is uncertain, then, whether the Epicurean theory was an improvement or a deterioration in hedonist ethics. Both the Cyrenaic and Epicurean theories have their merits, and ideally we might like to combine the two approaches for a valid hedonistic approach to life. This may not always be possible because the factors stressed by each will often be in contradiction. We cannot, for example, have brief enjoyment of long duration, or an intense tranquility. We may vacillate between the alternatives but it is hard to achieve a harmonious blending of the two. And, insofar as we attempt a pleasing mixture, extracting what we regard to be the special merits of each system, we are really choosing an Epicurean balance.

The essentially individualistic character of both the Cyrenaic and the Epicurean types of hedonism has troubled moralists for some time. The Cyrenaics desired physical pleasure of short duration that is immediate and intense, but they wanted it for themselves. The Epicureans sought extended, tranquil, mental happiness in life overall, but they too wanted this for themselves. Neither was altruistic or humanitarian; they did not adopt a universalistic ethic. Epicurus spoke for the Cyrenaics too when he wrote, "No one loves another except for his own interests," and "Injustice is not in itself a bad thing but only in the fear, arising from anxiety on the part of the wrongdoer, that he will not escape punishment." That is, injustice should be avoided because the fear of being caught might make us anxious and disturb our sleep.

UTILITARIANISM: THE SOCIAL THEORY OF HEDONISM

The theory of hedonism did not undergo substantial changes during the Middle Ages or the Renaissance, and appears to have gone into a state of eclipse. Some development of the theory did occur in the seventeenth century at the hands of the English philosophers Thomas Hobbes (1588–1679) and John Locke (1632–1704),[4] but significant work was not done until the nineteenth century when Jeremy Bentham (1748–1832) and, subsequently, John Stuart Mill (1806–1873) gave hedonism a new emphasis. Both men pursued

---

4. Pierre Gassendi (1592–1655) and Francis Hutcheson (1694–1747) also modified hedonism in interesting ways but they are not generally included among the major philosophers.

their theories along universalistic rather than individualistic lines, developing a social hedonism which they termed *utilitarianism.*

The principle of utility, which forms the core of the utilitarian ethic, maintains that we should seek "the greatest amount of happiness for the greatest number of persons." In other words, we should not seek pleasure or happiness for ourselves but for humanity in general, and this happiness should be as great and extensive as possible. We can measure the rightness of our actions and the worth of our goals according to the amount of happiness that has been fostered by our actions. If we have affected more people by our actions, made a greater number of people happy, this is ethically better than making fewer people happy to the same degree. Success in living is thus gauged by the extent to which we have made the lives of others happy.

The utilitarians obviously endorsed a much more altruistic and humanitarian doctrine than that of the Cyrenaics and the Epicureans. The latter were concerned with whether enjoyment should be physical, mental, immediate, extended, and so forth, but it was always enjoyment for the individual that was at issue. The utilitarians, by contrast, were concerned with happiness or pleasure for the community. They considered the individual agent one among those affected by an action, so that the person performing the act does not count for any more than other people—or any less. Therefore, according to utilitarianism, it is not a matter of sacrificing oneself for the good of others or putting oneself first, but of treating one's own happiness as having an equal claim beside that of everyone else.

▶ **JEREMY BENTHAM**. The first hedonist to adopt a utilitarian position was Jeremy Bentham (1748–1832), an English philosopher and social theorist who was interested in political programs aimed at increasing the well being of all classes of society.[5] Bentham was also involved in and impressed by science, which was emerging strongly in his day, and he thought he could conscript science into

5. For a complete presentation of Bentham's views, see his book *An Introduction to the Principles of Morals and Legislation* (London: Athlone Press, 1970). See especially Chapter IV for a description of the calculus. In attempting to make philosophy scientific, Bentham was in company with Descartes, Leibniz, Spencer, Comte, Bradley, Ayer, and Russell.

the service of ethics. He wanted to bring about an increase in the social good through the scientific application of social principles. To Bentham's mind, ethics had been much too vague and imprecise in the past, but the time was ripe to introduce scientific rigor and exactitude into ethical thinking.

Since Bentham was a utilitarian, he was interested in determining the amount of happiness that would be provided by any given action, and he thought this could be quantified and precisely measured. If we are to bring the greatest amount of happiness to the greatest number of persons, we have to know the extent to which various actions provide happiness, and we need to establish which of two actions will provide greater happiness for more people.

The Hedonic Calculus. With this as his intention, Bentham devised what he called the *calculus of pleasures* or the *hedonic calculus*, which was a scheme for scientifically measuring the amount of pleasure and pain that any action would yield. He thought that he could bring pleasure down to certain elements that might be called *hedons*—units of pleasure or pain capable of being added and subtracted. Furthermore, he wanted to isolate each of the factors that were involved in the reception of pleasure and pain, and to rate actions according to the number of hedons provided by all of these factors.

Being aware of the history of hedonism, Bentham knew that the Cyrenaics had identified some important considerations such as intensity, immediacy, and physicality, and that the Epicureans had incorporated several good points in their definition of happiness— tranquility, duration, and the like. It was not a matter of these two earlier forms of hedonism being pitted against each other as mutually exclusive alternatives, Bentham maintained; but both schools of thought could be taken into account and an action given numerical values relative to the degree of pleasure or pain that was attained by either Cyrenaic or Epicurean means. Bentham isolated the factors involved in actions and reduced them to what he termed seven marks, which were, by and large, a combination of Cyrenaic and Epicurean factors.

Intensity, the first mark, was stressed more strongly by the Cyrenaics. All else being equal, we would wish our pleasures to be as intense as possible. *Duration*, the second factor, refers to whether the pleasure is extended or brief. A pleasure of long duration is obviously preferable to one of short duration, and this consideration counted heavily with the Epicureans. By their very nature, intensity and duration are usually opposed, but both seem to be important considerations and many activities have prolongation as their purpose rather than an acute culmination. For example, the purpose of dining is not satiation but extending the pleasures of taste and good company.

Certainty or *uncertainty* is another mark, the meaning of which is self-evident. An experience we are certain to enjoy would be given a higher rating than one we may or may not find enjoyable. In this case, Bentham is recognizing the Cyrenaic concern with enjoyment that is sure rather than enjoyment that is dubious or merely possible. The certainty or uncertainty of a pleasure could be a function of its nearness, and this leads to Bentham's fourth mark, *propinquity* or *remoteness*. This mark states that pleasurable experience that can be enjoyed immediately is superior to that which one hopes to obtain at some future time. The greater the proximity, the better; because as we defer pleasures, hoping to enjoy them at some point in the future, we run the risk of never actually experiencing them at all. Closer pleasures are more certain to be enjoyed, as the Cyrenaics pointed out.

A fifth factor, *fecundity*, refers to the tendency of a pleasure to be "followed by sensations of the *same* kind: That is, pleasures, if it be a pleasure: pains, if it be a pain." If an enjoyable or disagreeable experience leads to similar experiences rather than those of an opposite kind, then it can be rated high in fecundity. Bentham was here recognizing the merit of the Epicurean point that one must be concerned with the future effects of our pleasures and pains rather than seizing or avoiding experience thoughtlessly. By including fecundity, Bentham was also counterbalancing the factor of intensity. For as intensity increases, fecundity tends to decrease; the two vary in inverse proportion, at least with regard to pleasure. That is, the greater the intensity of a pleasure, the more likely it is to be followed by pain and the lower it is in fecundity. The mark of fecundity as well as that of duration, therefore, qualify Bentham's endorsement of intensity.[6]

---

6. Intensity does not vary in exact inverse ratio to fecundity and duration but only in a general way. With regard to duration, for example, an experience of five minutes will not necessarily be lower in intensity than one of two minutes, but an experience that lasts an hour probably will be less intense. The same inexactitude applies to the factor of fecundity.

Still another factor included in Bentham's list is *purity*, which he defined as the chance a pleasure or pain has "of *not* being followed by sensations of the *opposite* kind: that is, pains, if it be a pleasure: pleasures, if it be a pain." This too pays deference to the Epicurean concern with the future consequences of action and the overall pleasure content of our lives.

The final mark is *extent*, meaning the number of persons to whom the pleasure or pain extends. A pleasurable action that affects more people is better than one affecting fewer people, whereas painful action is undesirable and its extent should be minimized. As a utilitarian, Bentham was naturally concerned with pleasure or happiness for the greatest number of people.

Bentham assumed that these seven marks exhaustively account for the principal factors involved in the attainment of the pleasure ideal. He also believed that he had culled the best of hedonistic thinking of the past since he had incorporated into his system the Cyrenaic factors of intensity, certainty, and propinquity, and the Epicurean considerations of duration, fecundity, and purity. In addition, he had added his own utilitarian factor of extent in order to ensure that the happiness of all was included as a value.

Having determined the relevant factors, Bentham employed them in his hedonic calculus. A person would draw up a list of all the pleasures that could be derived from a given action. The specific value of each pleasure would then be determined by applying each of the seven marks, and the sum of hedons would be added together. The same process would be carried out with regard to pains. Then the negatives would be subtracted from the positives to see whether the act was pleasurable overall. If the result proved to be positive, then the act is generally pleasurable and should be carried out, but if a negative result occurred, the act is shown to be largely painful and should not be performed.

Two points about the calculus should be made in passing. First, the individual is the one who decides the number of hedons to award each factor in a given action but the factors involved are an objective matter. Thus, there is a blend of subjectivity and objectivity in the scheme, and two people might well assign very different numbers to the same factor. Second, anyone using the calculus should give a truthful appraisal of the amount of hedons involved in each mark and not "fudge" the numbers so that a preferred result will come about. This would be self-defeating in any case since an honest operation of the calculus will reveal to the person which action is most likely to provide actually greater pleasure.

A Critique of Bentham's Hedonic Calculus. When Bentham's scheme is evaluated, it must be admitted that it possesses a certain elegance in its efficiency and simplicity. Also, the attempt to put ethics on a scientific footing is certainly commendable, although whether the hedonic calculus successfully accomplishes this aim is a moot point.

One criticism that can be leveled against the calculus concerns its utilitarian aspect. As a utilitarian Bentham was strongly concerned with the number of people affected by a pleasurable action, yet the factor of extent is only one of seven marks in Bentham's system, that is, it counts only one-seventh in the sum of hedons. If Bentham had made extent count more than any of the other factors or, perhaps, more than their total value, then a utilitarian result would be more likely. But as the calculus stands, it is not at all certain that the action which touches more people will come out to have the higher number of hedons. Bentham seems to have betrayed utilitarianism in his eagerness to construct a scientific ethic.

In Bentham's defense it should be stated that he believed society as a whole would be made happy by each individual pursuing his or her own happiness. However, this is rather a naive assumption since there is frequent conflict between the happiness of the individual person and that of society generally. A better approach, then, would have been to place a good deal more weight on extent in the calculus rather than assuming that the parts automatically enrich the whole.

A second major problem with Bentham's calculus of pleasures has to do with the specific numerical values that are assigned to each factor. There seems to be considerable imprecision as to the exact number of hedons that should be awarded. If an experience promises to last an hour should it be given a 3, 4, or 2 in duration? Or if an action brings pleasure to five people does that mean it is worth 1, 5, or 3 in extension? With regard to a comparison of two actions, the problem is not so much deciding which action should be given a higher number of hedons but knowing how much higher a number. For example, free fall from a plane is certainly a more intense experience than trout fishing, but is it twice or three times as intense? The overall difficulty comes in trying to obtain an exact measurement of something as amorphous as pleasure, and for the calculus to work, precision is strongly required. With a change of only one or two numbers, the alternative action could be indicated as best in the final arithmetic.

It might seem that a narrower range of numbers would solve the problem, say 1 to 3, so that the variation would not be so great and the decision less arbitrary. But a scheme of this type would not do justice to the extreme differences that could exist between actions with regard to various factors. If one action extended to 10,000 people while another applied only to one person, the difference could only be indicated by awarding the first +1 and the second +3. That hardly indicates the vast superiority of the first action with respect to extent.

On the other hand, if we broaden the range to, say, 1 to 100 in order to show these differences, then we would be at a loss to decide the particular number that would be appropriate to the pleasure quotient involved. For example, would watching a football game in the December cold rate 37 in impurity, or 65, or perhaps 12? In other words, the wider the spread of the numbers, the more inexact the system becomes.

The general problem reduces down to the fact that pleasure is not amenable to quantification. Bentham attempted to apply numerical terms to something that eludes any exact numerical designation. There simply cannot be any exact quantification with regard to states or feelings. As a consequence, Bentham's hedonic calculus breaks down and appears artificial, strained, and unreliable as an instrument for determining the greatest amount of happiness for the greatest number of persons. In a larger sense, there simply cannot be a "moral arithmetic."

Bentham's Theory and Moral Action. One also wonders about the moral aspect of Bentham's theory. That is, by relying upon the maximization of pleasure as the criterion for conduct, one could be led to endorse an immoral act that provides more pleasure over a moral act that yields less. In the hedonic calculus the result of the calculations could be that an immoral action would be indicated as preferable to a moral one because it promised a higher pleasure quotient. This hardly seems defensible, and any theory of ethics that can reach conclusions of this kind is seriously flawed.

Bentham's utilitarianism seems to be equating that which is most pleasurable with that which is most moral, but the two are not logically equivalent. The morally right act does not always produce more pleasure than the act that is morally wrong. An action can be highly pleasurable and highly immoral, as we all know. When we feel called upon to resist temptation, that tension is precisely the reason for our struggle; we want to yield ourselves to a pleasurable experience but feel pangs of conscience because of its immoral nature. Even an action that yields pleasure to a great many people is not necessarily moral as, for example, in the case of a majority that votes to exterminate an unpopular minority (one thinks of Jews in Nazi Germany or Christians in ancient Rome). And the pain of the victims might not be greater than the pleasure of the oppressors. Neither the distribution of pleasure, then, nor the amount is any guarantee of the moral nature of the pleasurable action. Thus, providing the greatest happiness for the greatest number is not a criterion of morality.

With reference to our discussion of good and right, utilitarianism seems to offer a theory of the good which is often at variance with standards of right conduct. This disparity applies not only to Bentham's ethical position but to utilitarianism in general. An action that is highly pleasurable is not always morally right—even if many people find it enjoyable.

In contemporary society we commit this mistake when we use cost-benefit analyses to decide health care issues. A pharmaceutical company might, for example, decide to produce drugs for a common disease rather than for a painful or debilitating one. And on the basis of a cost-benefit analysis we could decide to practice nonvoluntary euthanasia—killing those whose illnesses are incurable and whose medical costs are high in order to use the dollars for the treatment of general and curable illnesses that are widespread in the society. When we engage in this type of utilitarian calculation, we ignore our moral obligation to alleviate suffering and to preserve life.

Bentham's Theory, Psychological Hedonism, and the Naturalistic Fallacy. Two additional problems with Bentham's theory should be pointed out. For one thing, he based his ethical hedonism on psychological hedonism, and the difficulties with this structure have already been shown. "Nature has placed mankind under the governance of two sovereign masters," Bentham wrote, "pain and pleasure. It is for them alone to point out what we ought to do, as well as to determine what we shall do." Bentham was also accepting here the account of human nature given by psychological hedonism as well as psychological egoism, and this explanation of conduct is highly questionable.

Bentham tended to base his belief that pleasure ought to be pursued on the fact that we must pursue it, thereby not only committing the naturalistic fallacy but making the recommendation of pleasure utterly pointless; according to Bentham's statement, we have no choice. If we inevitably pursue pleasure, then Bentham could (at best) approve of that fact but he cannot logically argue for the adoption of a pleasure ethic as he appears to do; commending is not the same as recommending. In addition, even if people do pursue their own pleasure, that does not furnish any grounds for the utilitarian ideal of seeking the happiness of others.

The Quantity versus the Quality of Pleasure. A final criticism of Bentham's hedonism is that he only takes into account the *amount* of pleasure that an action promises to yield and is unconcerned with the *kind* of pleasure involved. By implication, Bentham would compare activities such as hearing a classical concert and wallowing in mud only with regard to the quantity of pleasure produced by each activity; if the latter were more pleasurable, it would be the preferred activity. Bentham even went so far as to state that "quantity of pleasure being equal, pushpin (pick-up-sticks) is as good as poetry." But surely pleasures should be differentiated in terms of higher and lower kinds and not judged solely in terms of amount. Qualitative distinctions between pleasures seem at least as significant as quantitative considerations—and are probably more important altogether.

Because of Bentham's failure to consider quality as well as quantity in his assessment of pleasures, and his treatment of animal pleasures as equal to those of human beings, his philosophy was referred to as "pig philosophy" (by Thomas Carlyle). The pleasures of a pig and a person were not considered to be any different in value provided they were the same in degree. Bentham's concern was with more or less pleasure not with better or worse, and this implies that he would approve of the mode of life of a happy pig as much for human beings as for pigs.

When we see animals grazing, we sometimes experience a sense of envy and think it would be marvelous to lead the life of a sheep or cow, with food readily available and nothing to do but roam about, sleep, stare, and reproduce the species. But even though an uncomplicated existence of elemental pleasures might be momentarily appealing, we really would not want to trade places with any animal. If we had the choice, we would elect being human even if it involved more pain. We believe human life to be better qualitatively in the kind of happiness that it brings, and we are not impressed by the fact that a pig, a sheep, or a cow might lead a life of greater pleasure.

We are also unimpressed by the number of people who enjoy a particular activity, because if that activity is inferior it is not preferable no matter how many people enjoy it. We are not inclined to change our art galleries into beer halls, our colleges into sports arenas, and our libraries into television lounges even though by doing so we would provide pleasure to a greater number of people. Deep experience for a few can be worth more than trivial pleasures for the majority.[7]

▶ **JOHN STUART MILL.** Because Bentham's utilitarianism consisted only of quantitative considerations, a reform was needed and this was introduced by his compatriot and successor John Stuart Mill. According to Mill, hedonism had to take into account the qualitative aspect of pleasure if it was to become a doctrine dignified enough to be the goal of life. In his book *Utilitarianism*, Mill wrote, "It is quite compatible with the principle of utility to recognize the fact, that some kinds of pleasure are more desirable and more valuable than others. It would be absurd that while, in estimating all other things, quality is considered as well as quantity, the estimation

---

7. A problem also exists with what constitutes "the greatest number." Mill defined it as "the whole sentient creation," but that could include animal life as well as future generations of people, in which case people alive today could be asked to sacrifice their happiness for the sake of the larger group of animals and future human beings.

of pleasures should be supposed to depend on quantity alone."[8] Mill was here acknowledging the need for a modification and refinement of utilitarianism in terms of the quality factor.

The Quality of Pleasure. But how are we to determine which of two pleasurable actions is qualitatively superior? What makes one pleasure higher and another lower? Mill's answer is that the better pleasure is the one chosen by the majority of people. He wrote, "Of two pleasures, if there be one to which all or almost all who have experience of both give a decided preference, irrespective of any feeling of moral obligation to prefer it, that is the more desirable pleasure." The choices of experienced people, then, can be safely taken as the index of higher quality since no knowledgeable person would ever elect a worse pleasure over a better one. As Mill noted: ". . . no intelligent being would consent to be a fool; no instructed person would be an ignoramus, no person of feeling and conscience would be selfish and base, even though they should be persuaded that the fool, the dunce, or the rascal is better satisfied with his lot than they are with theirs." Mill went on to say, "It is better to be a human being dissatisfied than a pig satisfied; better to be a Socrates dissatisfied than a fool satisfied." The superior pleasures are also the ones that engage the higher faculties of human beings.

A Critique of Mill's Theory. Certainly utilitarianism needed the addition of qualitative considerations as a corrective since the principle of the greatest happiness for the greatest number can produce a vulgar philosophy. Also, Mill's criterion for establishing higher and lower pleasures appears persuasive. Upon analysis, however, certain flaws appear that throw Mill's utilitarianism and, indeed, the whole of hedonism into question.

First, it is simply mistaken to believe that people who have experienced two pleasures will necessarily choose the higher one—however widely one wants to define "higher." The millions of people who watch dramatically poor soap operas on television are by and large acquainted with good plays but they prefer to watch these programs instead. And in choosing soap operas they do not claim

---

8. John Stuart Mill, *Utilitarianism,* in *Collected Works of John Stuart Mill* (London: Routledge and Kegan Paul, 1969), Vol. X, p. 211.

these programs are a higher pleasure; they simply want the lower one. The same holds true with regard to attending boxing events as compared to visiting an art gallery. Blood sports attract far more people than cultural events but that hardly shows them to be more elevated activities. Even within the same field, the higher type of pleasure is less popular than the lower type, and not because people have never been exposed to excellence. Better literature sells fewer copies, classical music is played less often, and artistic films have a shorter run at the cinemas than commercial types. In short, mass taste is usually the opposite of good taste, which means that, contrary to Mill's contention, the choice of the majority cannot be taken as an indication of higher-quality pleasures.

Second, Mill's concern with qualitative experience inadvertently led him to deny the primary importance of pleasure itself. When Mill stated that it is better to be a dissatisfied person than a satisfied pig, or a Socrates dissatisfied rather a fool satisfied, he was saying that a certain quality of life is more valuable than a pleasurable life. A consistent hedonist would never approve of *dissatisfaction* (unless it led to greater pleasure in the long run) but Mill accepted this over animalistic or foolish pleasures. In this way, he was subordinating the hedonistic goal of pleasure to a better type of existence associated with the higher life of human beings.

The general point is that when Mill (or anyone else) attempts to refine hedonism by introducing qualitative distinctions, he places himself outside of hedonism altogether. That is to say, the criterion used to differentiate between higher and lower pleasures becomes the basic ethical standard, displacing pleasure as the criterion for the good life. Without realizing it, Mill ultimately took as his standard the life of a more fully developed human being or, perhaps, the choices of finer people as indicative of that higher life. But, at this point, hedonism has been left behind. By introducing qualitative considerations one goes beyond hedonism, yet the quality of existence must be taken into account in any theory of the good.

As a minor criticism of Mill, we should also mention that, as in the case of Bentham, he based his ethical views on descriptive information. Mill wrote, ". . . the sole evidence it is possible to produce that anything is desirable, is that people do desire it. . . . No reason can be given why the general happiness is desirable except that each person, so far as he believes it to be attainable, desires his own happiness. This however being a fact, we have not only all the proof which the case admits of, but all which it is possible to require, that happiness is a good."[9] The fallacy in this type of thinking, of deriving values from facts, is clearly evident. Furthermore, what people desire may not be desirable, that is, worthy of being desired.

AN EVALUATION OF HEDONISM IN GENERAL

Our discussion of Mill's ethical theory, particularly the criticisms regarding qualitative factors, leads us to an evaluation of hedonism in general. To many moral philosophers, experiencing maximum pleasure does not seem sufficiently dignified or substantial to serve as the pivot of human existence. We feel the need to uplift this doctrine from its animal associations but, as we have seen, any refinements point beyond hedonism and suggest other theories of the good life. Pleasure or happiness may be a common and natural goal to seek but, upon analysis, we find it lacking; we look for a life purpose that can make us proud of ourselves rather than one that would cause us to blush.

Also, as was pointed out in the discussion of Bentham, there is no necessary connection between moral conduct and conduct that will secure maximum happiness either for oneself or the majority. An extremely pleasurable action can also be highly immoral. It would be very odd, therefore, to endorse a theory of ethics that sanctioned all actions yielding pleasure regardless of the immorality of those actions.[10]

In an effort to counteract such criticisms, Mill argued that

9. Ibid, p. 234.
10. Mill did mention two "sanctions" that he believed would keep people from pursuing their own happiness at the expense of others. There are the external sanctions of law, public opinion, and religious belief, and the internal sanction which is "the feeling of unity with our fellow creatures"; the latter supposedly makes it impossible for us to be happy unless we make others happy also. But not only are these points rather weak but they would allow immoral pleasures provided they were shared.

utilitarian principles in no way contradict morality but rather function as the basis for moral precepts. Murder, for example, can be judged as wrong on utilitarian grounds because it militates against the social welfare and runs counter to the greatest happiness for the greatest number; therefore it would be immoral, in general. This has been called *rule-utilitarianism* as distinguished from *act-utilitarianism*, for instead of evaluating actions it evaluates the rules by which actions are judged. According to Mill, this forges a necessary link between the greatest happiness principle and moral rules. An act-utilitarian might condemn a murder if that act failed to maximize happiness, but he could not offer any objections if the general happiness was increased by the action. A rule-utilitarian, on the other hand, could disapprove of murder and similar crimes because they would be injurious to the happiness of society; such actions, therefore, could not be justified as rules of behavior. In this way Mill believed he could escape the charge that utilitarianism would condone immoral actions that produced an increase in human happiness. According to rule-utilitarianism, that could never occur because the meaning of "immoral" is "deleterious to happiness when practiced as a rule," and "moral" refers to whatever is conducive to the happiness of the majority. Mill referred to justice, for example, as "a name for certain moral requirements which, regarded collectively, stand higher in the scale of social utility, and are therefore of more paramount obligation."

However, the basic objection still remains, namely, that actions should be judged right or wrong in themselves, independent of the pleasurable consequences for the majority, and our endorsement of moral rules does not depend on the happiness they promote necessarily but on their intrinsic rightness. Even if most people were to derive happiness from child molesting, we would not call it morally justified as a rule of conduct. Utilitarian ethics, therefore, does not provide us with a proper standard of behavior even in its rule-utilitarian form, and could well approve of immoral actions.

Finally, individualistic hedonism has been plagued from its inception by an inherent problem known as "the hedonistic paradox."[11] The paradox, quite simply, is that pleasure or happiness is not an object that can be obtained by direct pursuit but comes about

11. Mention was made of the hedonistic paradox in Chapter 2 in discussing the good.

as a side effect or unintended consequence of the pursuit of other goals. People who strive to serve others, for example, may well find that they are happy in their dedication, but people who deliberately try to be happy usually discover that happiness eludes them. Happiness or pleasure seems to be a state that is attained indirectly, and any conscious pursuit is self-defeating. Pleasure is a byproduct of the fulfillment of our striving and is destroyed when it becomes our goal. (Sexual neurosis, in fact, often stems from a failure to act in terms of this truth.) Therefore, the search for happiness is, paradoxically, usually an unhappy one, and hedonists are faced with the further paradox that by advocating happiness they are decreasing the likelihood of people's achieving it.

Mill made this concession in his *Autobiography* (to the embarrassment of hedonism): "Those only are happy who have their minds fixed on some object other than their own happiness. . . . Ask yourself whether you are happy, and you cease to be so. . . . Treat not happiness, but some end external to it, as the purpose of your life . . . and if otherwise fortunately circumstanced you will inhale happiness with the air you breathe."[12] This observation appears to be true but it also gives the game away; Mill was here recommending some other purpose in life besides the pursuit of pleasure.

As we have seen, hedonism contains some serious defects whether formulated by the Cyrenaics, the Epicureans, or the utilitarians, and these defects serve as a counterfoil to the common-sense notion that happiness is the reason for living. But the advantages and drawbacks of hedonism must now be judged by the reader. At this point, after a critical exposition of hedonism in its various forms, the individual must decide whether the weaknesses render the theory untenable or whether hedonism is still sufficiently strong to be chosen as the good in life. For, in the last analysis, there is a natural appeal to hedonism that was expressed by Joseph Butler (1692–1752) in his frequently quoted comment that "when we sit down in a cool hour we cannot justify any pursuit 'til we are convinced that it will be for our happiness, or at least not contrary to it."

---

12. John Stuart Mill, *Autobiography*, in *The Harvard Classics* (New York: P. F. Collier and Son, 1909), Vol. XXV, p. 94.

RECAPITULATION

In this chapter we have examined the theory of hedonism, beginning with the various justifications given for its adoption. We then distinguished between psychological and ethical hedonism, and individualistic and universalistic hedonism, with an analysis of each type. The historical and theoretical development of hedonism was then presented using Aristippus and the Cyrenaics as the first representatives. Following an explanation and evaluation of the Cyrenaic view, the Epicurean philosophy was critically examined. This led to a consideration of utilitarianism as developed by Jeremy Bentham and John Stuart Mill. Bentham's hedonic calculus was discussed, then Mill's corrective to Bentham's approach. Finally, the problems with both versions of utilitarianism were shown, and criticisms were offered of hedonism as a whole.

▼ ▼ ▼

REVIEW QUESTIONS

1. *Differentiate between psychological and ethical hedonism, and between individualistic and universalistic hedonism.*

2. *Compare and contrast Cyrenaic and Epicurean hedonism. On what grounds do you judge one or the other as a stronger theory?*

3. *Discuss Jeremy Bentham's hedonic calculus, describing its operation and assessing its validity.*

4. *Explain the grounds on which John Stuart Mill asserts that one action can be qualitatively superior to another. Why would you agree or disagree with Mill?*

5. *Discuss "the hedonistic paradox" and the way in which it undermines the hedonistic theory. Does it apply equally well to utilitarianism?*

6

SELF-REALIZATION

elf-realization is an ancient doctrine, first articulated by Greek philosophers several centuries before Christ, as well as being a contemporary theory as to the purpose of human existence. Perhaps it is not surprising that the ancient Greeks, emerging from a more unreflective to a more reflective state, should develop the same ideals as modern thinkers who negate the past and create their values from the individual.

It was Aristotle among the Greeks who developed the theory of self-realization most fully, although the virtue "know thyself" and the value of achieving excellence as a human being were part of the general culture. Another prominent name in the history of the movement is G. W. F. Hegel (1770–1831), a major nineteenth century philosopher, but his theory is highly specialized and integral to an elaborate system of thought. Other representatives include

T. H. Green (1836–1882) and F. H. Bradley (1846–1924) in Great Britain,[1] and the American philosophers W. E. Hocking (1873–1966) and Josiah Royce (1855–1916).[2] Interestingly enough, some of the strongest advocates of self-realization in this century are psychologists rather than philosophers—humanistic psychologists such as Abraham Maslow (1908–1970), Carl Rogers (1902–1987), and Erich Fromm (1900–1987).[3]

THE AIMS OF
SELF-REALIZATION

As a theory of the good life, self-realization maintains that the fulfillment of our capacities is the ideal goal. We should strive to develop our potentialities and actualize our talents, or, in other words, to develop our selfhood to the utmost. The self to be realized is not the self of any given moment or any particular time in our lives but our ideal self—the self that would exist if all of our abilities and interests were fully developed. The self-realizationist is looking for the closest approach possible to what we conceive of as our perfect self or ideal being. Sometimes the self-realizationist will concentrate upon human nature and say that we should be as human as we can be, that is, strive for the ideal of becoming a complete human being. At other times, the emphasis is placed upon our individual personalities, on developing our own unique self. But whether our human nature is emphasized or our individual person is emphasized, the self-realizationist takes complete development as the goal.

As with all ideals, of course, the state of total realization of

---

1. T. H. Green, *Prolegomena to Ethics* (Oxford, England: Clarendon Press, 1883); and F. H. Bradley, *Ethical Studies* (Oxford, England: Clarendon Press, 1927).
2. W. E. Hocking, *The Self, Its Body and Freedom* (New Haven: Yale University Press, 1928), and *Human Nature and Its Remaking* (New Haven: Yale University Press, 1918); and J. Royce, *The World and the Individual* (New York: Macmillan Publishing Co., 1904).
3. See A. Maslow, *Motivation and Personality* (New York: Harper, 1970); C. Rogers, *On Becoming a Person* (Boston: Houghton Mifflin, 1961); E. Fromm, *Man for Himself* (New York: Rinehart, 1947).

---

ourselves can never be achieved, for we can always imagine becoming more than we ever are. We are never complete, never full grown, for there is always more that we could do or know or be. Unlike a frog or a squirrel that develops to a maximum point where it resembles every other frog or squirrel, human beings can always conceive of other states that they have not yet achieved. We are always short of our goal, forever lacking, so that a gap continually exists between what we are and what we want to be. Perhaps a hedonist will one day be able to say to herself or himself, "At last I am happy," but the self-realizationist knows that her or his ideal will never be realized. We throw the ball ahead of ourselves and chase after it in a recurrent and continual dance. But in that process of continually challenging ourselves to reach more distant goals, our selves are expanded and enriched. By striving to realize their selves as fully as possible, the self-realizationists feel they are alive and growing and have what they regard as a worthwhile existence. Their ideal gives shape to their conduct and provides an overall orientation to their lives.

In order to develop ourselves in the best way possible, it is necessary to decide which of our tendencies are dominant, for they are the ones that should take precedence and govern the realization of the rest. Some of our capacities, interests, and abilities are rather minor and should not be given much emphasis. Others of our capacities, talents, and the like are the principal ones that deserve our primary attention and cultivation. It would be impossible to develop all of our talents equally; there simply is not enough time and, inevitably, even if we tried to do so conflicts would occur. Furthermore, it is not desirable to achieve breadth at the expense of depth or to award equal place to the major and minor parts of ourselves. Unless our main interests are given priority we will not realize our basic self.

For this reason the self-realizationist wants us to develop as fully as possible but always under the guidance of our dominant interests. And this provides a principle of selection when we are debating which action we ought to choose. We should engage in those actions that will realize more of our essential selves rather than selecting those that are relatively minor and inconsequential. We should develop ourselves as widely as possible but always with the qualification in mind that the realization of our essential self is more important than the variety, diversity, or range of our development.

The American philosopher George Santayana (1863–1952), in discussing Goethe's *Faust*, explained this point as follows:

> It is characteristic of the absolute romantic spirit that when it has finished with something it must invent a new interest. It beats the bush for fresh game; it is always on the verge of being utterly bored. . . . [However] man is constituted by his limitations, by his station contrasted with all other stations, and his purposes chosen from amongst all other purposes. . . . His understanding may render him universal; his life never can. . . . To be at all you must be something in particular.[4]

Our contemporary attitude stands opposed to Santayana's wisdom. We want to do everything and be everything, to expose ourselves to all possibilities. We resist making commitments to jobs or people or to determine ways of being. We refuse to decide upon the type of person we want to become and imagine ourselves capable of any number of different roles. We want to leave all options open and not close any doors, thinking of ourselves as flexible, diversified, open-minded.

But if we try to be everything in general, we will be nothing in particular. If we regard every type of life as consistent with ourselves, then we are generalized beings rather than individuals with unique identities. We must decide what we are and what we are not; otherwise, we are a set of random numbers and have no selves at all. This is Santayana's point and the attitude of most advocates of the self-realization ethic. In order to become someone, we must focus upon our dominant interests and abilities; then self-realization can occur.[5]

Utilizing this type of approach, the self-realizationist can make qualitative distinctions between experiences that the hedonist is debarred from making. Higher kinds of activities to the self-

---

4. G. Santayana, *Three Philosophical Poets* (Cambridge, MA: Harvard University Press, 1910), Chapter IV, passim.
5. In the play *Peer Gynt* by Henrik Ibsen the same idea is expressed through the figure of the Button Molder, who melts down all souls who, instead of being true to their essential selves, have sought diverse experience.

realizationist are those that will develop the more essential parts of one's being. The qualitatively inferior activities are those that will realize only a minor part of one's being. If we are looking for the maximum development of our personalities under the control of dominant tendencies, then we can say that certain activities are higher and other activities are lower, some behavior qualitatively superior and other behavior inferior in terms of our overall goal of self-realization. In that regard, self-realization has the advantage over hedonism. We might want to quibble with the definition of better and worse but at least it is consistent with the self-realization theory to make a differentiation of this kind.

SELF-REALIZATION AND HEDONISM

In relation to hedonism, self-realizationists are not saying they want to realize themselves in order to be happy. It is not that full realization is thought to lead to happiness and is therefore desirable as a means. Self-realization is not instrumental to happiness, but is something *preferred* to happiness as the goal or ultimate end of all activity; like a mountain peak, it leads nowhere. Rather than pursuing lives aimed at happiness, self-realizationists want to have lives that will realize their capacities—which can be a very different thing. If, in the course of realizing themselves, self-realizationists find happiness, that would certainly be welcome but it would be regarded as an accidental consequence—not the final aim. Very often the realization of one's self will conflict with the achievement of happiness because the self-realizationist will perform actions that do not bring pleasure but lead to some type of personal development; the growth is preferred over enjoyable experience. For example, a millionaire's son could choose to strike out on his own rather than depending upon the family fortune. He may know that the money he is due to inherit will give him an enjoyable life but he may also understand that his chances at developing his talents and abilities would be commensurately reduced. The pleasures that the wealth would provide him would militate against his becoming a worthwhile person, seducing him away from the labor involved in actualizing his potentialities. Knowing the weaknesses of his own character and preferring a life of self-actualization to one of pleasurable experience, he could decide not to run the risk of remaining in the "land of the lotos-eaters."[6] *Becoming* might be thought more important than *having*, even if one would "have" a considerable fortune and one would not, in the last analysis, "become" an outstanding person. (The person who chooses to be a second-rate flutist rather than a first-rate insurance salesman, incidentally, has a similar motive in mind, viz., to fulfill the essential self.)

In our hypothetical case, the potential heir is not afraid he will be unhappy but that he will be happy, and, being happy, he will be stunted in his growth as a person. He is concerned that he might be tempted to take the line of least resistance rather than choosing the path of greatest advantage.

In brief, then, self-realization is not necessarily a means to happiness, but an end in itself that a person might very well prefer to the goal of happiness. It would make no sense, therefore, to ask people why they wanted to develop themselves, implying that it must be for the sake of a further end. Self-realization is itself a final goal of action and, in this sense, stands on a par with happiness, competing with hedonism as a theory of the good life.

HUMANNESS AND SELFHOOD

One of the first questions faced by the self-realizationist is that of deciding what the self is that is supposed to be realized. It is all well and good to say that we should realize ourselves, but what exactly is that self, in actual or ideal terms? This is a more

6. See A. Tennyson, *Poetical Works* (Boston: Ticknor and Fields, 1864), Vol. I, pp. 90–96.

difficult question than one might think, for in attempting to answer it we become involved in issues concerning the nature of humanness. How are human beings to be defined? What differentiates man and woman from other organisms and objects in the world, and what specific definition can be formulated of humankind? We also become involved in identity issues concerning the particular factors that constitute an individual. How is a person to be defined such that one individual is distinct from others and unique as a particular human being? These issues of humanness and selfhood are by no means identical but they are related and, of course, important to the self-realization theory.

▶ **HUMANNESS**. With regard to humanness, an extensive list could be compiled of the definitions that have been proposed throughout intellectual history (and some philosophers assert that human nature is a myth altogether). Human beings have been variously called the social or political animals, the intelligent or rational animals (*Homo sapiens*), the language-users or tool-users (*Homo faber*), the beings who possess consciousness, the beings who have self-consciousness, the aesthetic or religious beings, and so forth. However, if we are to define human beings in ways that differentiate them from other creatures or machines (which seems to be the type of definition usually proposed), all of these definitions are questionable. Humans are not the only social or political organisms since a variety of animals from ants and bees to deer and beavers arrange themselves in organized groups with hierarchical orders and distinct divisions of labor. Intelligence and reasoning, including problem solving, are certainly not unique to human beings. Although we may be the most intelligent of creatures, that does not make us unique in kind but only indicates that we stand at the top of the intelligence spectrum that runs throughout the animal kingdom. In a very real sense, computers too may be said to think.

The use of language and tools is also shared by animals—for example, by chimpanzees who crack nuts with rocks and have learned an extensive vocabulary of sign language, including the use of abstract terms; they converse in a very sophisticated way with their trainers, as do dolphins, who have an elaborate communications system of their own. As for consciousness, this is certainly not an exclusive possession of human beings, and self-consciousness, long thought to be a distinctively human characteristic, has recently been found in the higher apes; gorillas, chimpanzees, and orangutans.[7] The same holds true for the creation and appreciation of art, for chimpanzees paint and their paintings have won prizes in juried competitions.[8]

The same criticisms apply to other definitions of human beings, for it is not at all certain that humans are the only creatures that become bored, kill their own kind, want to know (that is, are inquisitive), eat when they are not hungry, perform homosexual acts, have imagination or a sense of humor, or love to play. We certainly cannot say "to err is human" or "man is mortal" since these are not distinctive to humans (and may not always continue to be true). And to call a human being an "*animal bipes implume*" ("two-legged animal without feathers") seems beside the point. What then is human nature?

▸ **THE SELF**. A parallel problem exists with regard to the meaning of selfhood or individuality. If the emphasis is placed on the development of the self, we must know what a self consists of, what constitutes a person's identity. We are not concerned with the peripheral or transitory qualities that may serve to identify a person at a particular time but with whatever is constant and essential to selfhood, that without which a person would no longer be the same self.

7. An account of the recent and remarkable research in primatology can be found in D. Premack, *Intelligence in Ape and Man* (New York: Erlbaum Assoc., 1976); and A. J. Premack, *Why Chimps Can Read* (New York: Harper and Row, 1976). It was formerly believed that apes could not use language because they did not speak, but now it is known that they possess the capability for language but lack the necessary vocal apparatus for speech. Some gorillas and chimpanzees have been taught sign language and have progressed to a relatively high level. The methodology of some experiments has been questioned, but the results cannot be entirely dismissed.

8. Perhaps we are unique in conceiving of religious reality, but one intriguing suggestion regarding our belief is that we long for God as herd animals seeking the lost pack leaders; essentially we are wolves baying at the moon when we offer up prayers.

The Self and the Physical Body. One initial response when faced with a question of this kind is either to reject it as absurd, a concern of only fools or philosophers, or else to identify ourselves with our physical form. We are tempted to respond that we know ourselves and other people through bodily appearance, and this means of identification is a person's identity. Dennis is the person with brown hair and pale skin, who dresses in rough clothing, talks a lot, and has an ambling walk. But if Dennis dyed his hair blonde, got a deep tan, began to dress up more, talked less, and walked more briskly, he would still be Dennis nonetheless. We would say that Dennis had changed but we would not mean that he had actually become another person; he would remain Dennis with a different appearance. If that is so, then physical appearance cannot be the constituent of selfhood. That is to say, if Dennis is still himself with a changed appearance, then physical appearance cannot be that which makes him Dennis.

A somewhat more difficult case would be if Dennis had a change-of-sex operation and subsequently renamed himself Debbie. We might be tempted to say that he was now another person but it would be more accurate to conclude that the same person had assumed a different gender and a new name. He would now be a she but not someone else. Even with a physical change of such a radical character, the same self would exist. This indicates that the essence of the self does not lie even in sexual characteristics much less in physical qualities such as hair color or complexion.

Reflections of this kind suggest that the identity of the self may not consist of a person's physical aspects at all. If a person happens to lose an eye or a leg in some terrible accident, that person's self is not diminished; he or she still remains that person but without the eye or the leg. Similarly, people who have heart transplants or receive artificial joints are not that much less themselves, and they do not become someone or something else.

One objection that may be made to the above remarks is that people can change when a bodily trauma occurs. The actor whose face is disfigured in a fire, the athlete who is crippled in a war, the pianist whose fingers are gnarled by arthritis surely can become very different people as a result of those physical events. But in these cases the people are different not because of the physical changes but because of their inner reaction to these changes. They have become embittered or introspective or despondent and this is what may make us say they have become different people. If these individuals had not undergone any psychological transformation, then, regardless of the physical alterations, they would remain the same selves.

The Self and the Mind. Selfhood, then, would appear to lie in that which is internal rather than that which is external, a matter of mind not body, the spiritual not the material dimension. It would seem that a severe constriction of a person's emotions or feelings, a loss of memory or thinking ability could constitute a changed self in a way that the loss of a limb could not. That is, a major mental change as contrasted with a major physical change could more easily be viewed as a change in identity.

However, certain difficulties also accrue to this interpretation of self. For example, if there could be such a thing as the isolation of a person's mind, suspended in a tank and connected by tubes and wires to a variety of life-support equipment, it would be difficult to say that the person was there. Just the presence of mind does not seem sufficient to declare that a person is present. A disembodied mind cannot be identified as a self.

For this reason the Christian idea of the soul as the self has been difficult for people to accept. The self seems more than just the spiritual part, and the soul that is alleged to survive the body when "we give up the ghost" may be an important element of the self but it is not synonymous with it. Even within theological circles a debate has continued for centuries over whether resurrection should be interpreted as including the body as well as the soul. Many laypeople and theologians alike feel that an afterlife without the body would be seriously lacking; the full self would not be present.

If, then, mind alone is insufficient to constitute a self, and body is inessential to the self, how are we to define selfhood? We are left as perplexed as Oscar Wilde when he wrote,

> Soul and body, body and soul—how mysterious they were! There was animalism in the soul, and the body had its moments of spirituality. The senses could refine, and the intellect could degrade. Who could say where the fleshy impulse

> ceased, or the physical impulse began? How shallow are the arbitrary definitions of ordinary psychologists! And yet how difficult to decide between the claims of the various schools! Was the soul a shadow seated in the house of sin? Or was the body really in the soul, as Giordano Bruno thought? The separation of spirit from matter was a mystery, and the union of spirit and matter was a mystery also.[9]

The Self and Time. A further problem that increases the difficulties of identifying the self with either mind or body (and that generally affects the entire issue of selfhood) has to do with the continuity of the self through time. That which defines a person should remain constant throughout his or her life. Whether we are referring to an aspect of mind or body as making up an individual, that element must be the same from birth to death; otherwise the person is not the same. The problem comes in identifying the common denominator, the thread of continuity, in determining what it is that makes a person the same continuous self.

An analogy with an automobile may clarify the problem. If a car owner should replace the engine of a car, and then the upholstery, the electrical wiring, the tires, the body, and so on, until nothing of the original car remained, we could not call it the same car. Similarly, if we had an axe and we changed the head, and then the handle, it would not be the same axe. With regard to people, if someone changed in all respects from one time to another, logically and by analogy, we could not regard the person as the same. And it seems as though that is, in fact, the case with all human beings; nothing of either a mental or a physical nature, which would make a person the same self, remains constant throughout a lifetime.

Our bodies grow, mature, and decay, changing radically in size and character from birth to death. Our skin expands and grows slack; our hair thickens, then becomes sparse and changes color; our muscles gain in strength, then atrophy; our senses become more acute, then degenerate in old age. Even our skin cells are replaced every seven years, the RNA in our nerve cells changes, and although our organs perform the same function throughout our lives, they change in composition.

---

9. O. Wilde, *The Picture of Dorian Gray* (London: Oxford University Press, 1974).

Perpetual flux and mutability also characterize our mental makeup, for every element from thoughts to disposition appears to change. Our ideas are different at six years of age and at sixty, our attitudes can change from an optimistic orientation toward life to profound pessimism (cynics, in fact, tend to be former idealists), our memory and will can change from strong to weak or vice versa, our disposition can be substantially altered as a result of our experiences, and so forth.

It should be added that even though a person always remains the son or daughter of the same biological parents, this only serves as a means of identification in the way that a birth certificate does; it hardly defines a person. Furthermore, what would then differentiate a man from his brother, a woman from her sister, or, for that matter, identical twins where the DNA for both is identical?[10]

What, then, constitutes the identity of the self through time? If a person changes in all respects (which seems to be the case), he or she would not be the same person but rather a series of different selves at different times. And, as a corollary, people would not be responsible for what their previous selves did, and no future selves would be bound by a promise.

A CRITICAL APPRAISAL

The self-realizationist has a difficult time defining the nature of the self, as do all philosophers, because of the problems that have been described. And these difficulties stand as a stumbling block to the affirmation of self-realization as an ethical theory. Quite obviously, if we are to pursue the development of our selves, each of us should know what the self is that we are striving to develop.

10. At the time of writing, frogs have been successfully cloned and biologists may be close to producing a human clone from a male cell (and without a mother). Clones are identical to their parents and the problem of differentiation is greater than that of identical twins.

For a subtle contemporary discussion of personal identity see the works of Derek Parfit.

But passing over the difficulty of precise definition for the moment, self-realizationists do present a rough conception of humanness and selfhood which, they believe, adequately serves their purposes. They view people in terms of interests and needs, the desire for material goods, relationships, friendship and love, the wish to acquire knowledge, to pursue ideals, and to experience beauty, the biological drives for food, for sex, and for shelter. These factors may not uniquely define people, differentiating them from chimpanzees and robots, but they are a definite part of being human whatever else they may be part of, and our development should include them. The self-realizationist would want our development to occur in terms of these elements.

▶ **THE GOODNESS OF HUMAN NATURE**. However, if human beings are described in this way, further difficulties are encountered that penetrate to the heart of the self-realization theory. For to drive toward the development of our human nature can only be good if human nature is, in fact, good; and this assumption is highly questionable. Judging by human history, the impulse to murder, rob, and rape seems very much a part of the human being, but it is hardly a worthwhile trait. Sadomasochism—the desire for exploitation, domination, and degradation of others or ourselves—is likewise characteristic of people but should be suppressed rather than cultivated. We seem able and willing to destroy as well as create, to be lazy as well as vital, to harm as well as help, but surely we would not want to become as destructive, lazy, or harmful as possible. The list of undesirable potentialities could be extended much further, but the point is that not everything human is commendable; a portion, at least, is shameful. And if that is so, we cannot take as our ideal the unrestricted development of our human capabilities.

Self-realizationists may reply to this criticism by stating that they would not want people to realize the undesirable parts of human nature but only the attractive aspects. They would say, in rebuttal, that the self to be realized is the good self, the pure gold within the coarse ore. But that brings us back to square one. Self-realization, as an ethical proposal, defined good as the development of our human capabilities, but if that is not always desirable then the development of our capabilities cannot be the definition of the good. Perhaps it would be clearer to say that in making the judgment that some actualization of humanness is bad we are referring to a more basic standard of what is good than self-realization. The theory of self-realization thereby shows itself to be superficial and inadequate.

To bypass this criticism, self-realizationists may reply that they have consistently advocated the development of the *dominant* tendencies of human beings, and, in the main, human nature is good. Therefore, there is no ethical tension within their system. However, self-realization has consistently championed the development of as much of our nature as possible, with our dominant tendencies having priority and a controlling function. Therefore, even if our main tendencies are considered to be positive, the minor tendencies should also be developed, according to the theory, and that would necessarily include some negative aspects.

Furthermore, the assumption that human beings are good at heart is far from being an established fact. A continual debate has been in progress for several hundred years over this very point. For example, Jean Jacques Rousseau (1712–1778) believed that people are basically and naturally good but society and modern civilization corrupt their pure nature.[11] On the other hand, his predecessor Thomas Hobbes (1588–1679) claimed that a protective selfishness lies at the core of each person's being, so that prior to the establishment of governmental protection each individual lived a life that was "poor, nasty, brutish, and short."[12] The contemporary argument is conducted between psychologists and anthropologists, and in newer subfields of child development. Some social scientists are convinced that there are no genetically transmitted, innate tendencies that constitute human nature, that each person, to use John Locke's phrase, is a *tabula rasa*, a "blank tablet." Others claim that people are basically loving, compassionate, and generous, and will remain so unless their development is blocked or distorted. Still others maintain that our basic drives are toward self-preservation, acquisitiveness, and power over others—which is in keeping with the Freudian characterization of the unconscious lying at the root of

11. J. J. Rousseau, *The Social Contract and Discourses* (London: J. M. Dent, 1913).
12. T. Hobbes, *Leviathan* (London: J. M. Dent, 1914).

conduct and with the Christian notion that man has inherited the original sin of Adam.

The issue is vast and far from decided, so that at this point in time we cannot be sure that humanness necessarily means goodness. We cannot, therefore, advocate the realization of our essential humanness and feel assured that we are thereby promoting what is good. That which is human is not necessarily humane, and a substantial portion of human potential may not be worth bringing into being.

▶ **THE GOODNESS OF THE INDIVIDUAL**. But what of the individual self? The self-realizationist could be advocating not the development of our human nature but of our individual natures. Here the emphasis is placed on people realizing their particular talents, interests, and abilities. In popular and modern language, the self-realizationist is recommending that we should find out "who we are" and concentrate on becoming the person we discover ourselves to be. The more we actualize our latent self, the better our existence will be as a whole.

In elaborating and affirming this position Erich Fromm wrote,

> *Existence and the unfolding of the specific powers of an organism are one and the same.* All organisms have an inherent tendency to actualize their specific potentialities. *The aim of man's life*, therefore, is to be understood as *the unfolding of his powers according to the laws of his nature.*
>
> Man, however, does not exist "in general." While sharing the core of human qualities with all members of his species, he is always an individual, a unique entity, different from everybody else. He differs by his particular blending of character, temperament, talents, disposition, just as he differs at his fingertips. He can affirm his human potentialities only by realizing his individuality. The duty to be alive is the same as the duty to become oneself, to develop into the individual one potentially is.[13]

13. Fromm, *Man for Himself,* pp. 19–20.

But this version of self-realization, as persuasive as it may appear, hardly fares any better than the ideal of becoming complete as a human being. For one's individual potential can lie in useless or harmful activities. A torturer might well be developing his personal abilities—in fact, calling into play his major tendencies. He may be extremely talented at inflicting pain and derive very basic satisfaction from it, but his life could hardly be called commendable. Perhaps he has found his calling, his niche in the world, and is realizing the principal potentialities of his nature; nevertheless torturing people cannot be judged to be a worthwhile existence—even though a self is being realized. In the same way, the drunkard may be satisfying his or her main interest in life and developing it to the utmost, but living in a continual alcoholic stupor seems a wasted existence. More significantly, we do not praise Jack the Ripper or Al Capone, Hitler or Attila the Hun even if they were expressing their true selves in their actions. We would rather that they had suppressed the dominant tendencies of their selves (for brutality) and favored their minor tendencies (for benevolence). We would prefer that they had actualized less of what they were and became more of what they were not. Contrary to Fromm, their duty lay more in not becoming themselves.

This implies, of course, that the realization of one's self is not necessarily desirable; it very much depends upon the nature of the person. And if it is not always good to realize one's self, then the good cannot be defined as self-realization.

As mentioned previously in regard to the development of our human nature, self-realizationists cannot say that we should develop only the good tendencies in ourselves since they have defined "good" as complete self-realization. We need some external criterion for differentiating between our good and bad parts, and this takes us outside of self-realization for our ultimate standard of conduct. If, for example, our good tendencies were defined as those that bring happiness to others, then a utilitarian ethic would become our goal and guide in living, replacing the ideal of self-realization.

As a parallel criticism to the "humanness" version of self-realization, not all of our individual traits are worth developing, yet the theory of self-realization favors the maximum realization of our selves. That would include the worse as well as the better parts so long as they did not conflict with our dominant tendencies. Such a view is morally intolerable since miserliness, cruelty, insensitivity, and so forth would all have to claim to be developed if they were part of the person.

Similarly, just as our essential human nature is not necessarily good, our essential self may not be good. The claim that awful actions do not express a person's *real* self is dubious at best. It assumes that the basic part of any person cannot be bad, which is an unproven assumption if it is not patently false altogether. There may be some good in everyone, as the Quakers believe, but that is not to say that everyone is basically good inside.[14]

To become yourself, then, does not necessarily mean becoming something commendable, either in terms of one's own life or the well being of other people. This reference, to the welfare of others, introduces a final criticism of both forms of the self-realization ethic.

 CONCERN FOR OTHERS. Whether in the form of a theory that recommends the development of our selfhood or of our humanness (or both), self-realization offers no restraints whatsoever to an egotistical and selfish life. There is nothing in the self-realization position that encourages us to consider others as we pursue our own self-actualization. Sometimes it is suggested that we cannot realize our own selves without helping others to realize their selves, but this necessity is never made clear. It seems more likely that we need not pay much attention to the development of humanity at large in order to expand personally. We may need others to develop our social dimension but we do not have to be particularly concerned with their development in order to further our own; we only need be concerned with the nourishment others can provide.

This means that self-realization, as a theory of the good, can be at variance with what is right. It cannot condemn immoral actions

---

14. It has been claimed that we should develop every *real* aspect of ourselves, and that negative traits are not real in themselves but are the lack of something positive. This view can be traced to the Medieval notion of evil as the absence of good, which is too complex and extraneous to discuss here.

that lead to the fulfillment of a person's primary needs and interests. In many situations, it could be the case that by realizing our self we would not be behaving in the right way. And if self-realization by its very nature has to approve such conduct, then it contains a gross moral defect.

This essential selfishness has often been noted and stands as a major obstacle to the acceptance of self-realization as the ultimate goal in life. Any ethical theory that condones the pursuit of one's own advantage at the expense of other people is difficult to justify.

▶ **SELF-REALIZATION COMBINED WITH OTHER THE-ORIES**. As we see, then, self-realization can be criticized in several fundamental ways, and if we are to accept it as the purpose of our existence, these criticisms must be met. The full realization of one's being appears to be a finer goal than the hedonistic ideal of attaining maximum pleasure, but it is by no means unequivocally good. Perhaps a combination of self-realization and another theory would be best in order to eliminate the weaknesses, but that must be left to each individual to explore. For example, perhaps our goal should be the realization of those aspects of ourselves that yield happiness to ourselves or to others. But what if our development lies in one direction and personal or societal happiness in another? . . .

ARISTOTELIANISM

A particular type of self-realization ethic that should be explored to complete our survey is that of Aristotle (384–322 B.C.), who advocated a doctrine that is still influential today.

Although Aristotle's ethic is self-realizationist in nature, it nevertheless contains certain components of the hedonist theory that were previously examined. Aristotle is, in fact, sometimes classified as a hedonist (as well as a rationalist and a teleologist), but this is misleading because he only regarded pleasure as the accompaniment of activities aimed at self-realization.

Aristotle studied at Plato's Academy before founding his own school, called the Lyceum—an institute of philosophy that vied for prestige with the Academy in the ancient world. The name survives today in the French "*lycée*" which is modeled on the Greek example; all teachers, however, are still referred to as "academics." The main expression of Aristotle's ethical views occurs in a book entitled the *Nicomachean Ethics* (which was named after his son, Nicomachus) and this work stands as one of perhaps four outstanding treatises in the history of ethics.[15]

▶ **ARISTOTLE'S NOTION OF THE GOOD**. At the beginning of the *Nicomachean Ethics,* Aristotle made the famous statement that ". . . the good is that at which all things aim." Then in a typically systematic way, he defined what he meant by the central terms "aim" and "good."

The aim Aristotle referred to signifies the ultimate end of all activity, something that is not a means toward anything further but that for which everything else is done. To illustrate his meaning, he took the case of bridle making, saying this activity is not an end in itself but a means toward the end of fine horsemanship. But horsemanship is not a final goal either; it is, in turn, a means toward victory in war (horses being used primarily for military purposes at the time). Aristotle was showing by these examples the distinction between means and ends, and saying that the aim he was referring to is the final aim, which is never an instrument for reaching a more ultimate goal.[16]

Aristotle defined good as "*eudaimonia*," which has been translated as "well being," "vital well being," or simply "happiness." "Vital well being" is perhaps closest to the Greek, for it implies a dynamic state of personal satisfaction as well as health, good looks, material comforts, achievements, etc., which seems to be what

---

15. The other three are Plato's *Republic,* Immanuel Kant's *Foundations of the Metaphysics of Morals,* and John Stuart Mill's *Utilitarianism.*

16. Aristotle, *The Nicomachean Ethics,* trans. F. H. Peters (London: Kegan Paul, Trench, Trubner, 1901), Book II, 6. The problem of means and ends is an interesting one in philosophy. If, for example, we were to climb a mountain, would we regard scaling a cliff as a means toward climbing the mountain or the end of climbing the mountain itself? Is climbing a mountain a different activity than mountain climbing?

Aristotle had in mind. In any case, Aristotle took *eudaimonia* to be the *summum bonum*, the "highest good" which human beings can attain.

▶ THE CONCEPT OF FUNCTION. In order to achieve *eudaimonia*, we have to understand what it is to be human—which is the question we posed earlier. Aristotle believed that the ethical ideal must be integral to the being of man. If we know what it is to be human, then we know the domain within which the good can be attained.

Aristotle addressed the question in a unique way by asking what can be the "function" of a human being. A knife's function is to cut; a bird's wing, to enable the bird to fly; a house, to provide shelter. Since everything has a function, what, then, is a human being's function?

Initially, Aristotle examined the possibility that nourishment and growth may be man's function but he dismissed this conjecture by pointing out that this is basically a vegetative level of existence, fit for plants but not for people. The good cannot lie there, he concluded.

Aristotle then considered the suggestion that the fact of having feelings or emotions, of being able to sense the exterior world, is distinctively human; perhaps the good for man may be found in this function. But he immediately rejected this possibility by reminding us that animals also have sensations and feelings and live appetitive lives. There is nothing preeminently human in that.

But if plants are the organisms that feed and grow, and animals are the organisms that feel and sense, what function has man in the scheme of things? Aristotle's answer was that reason alone distinguishes human beings, and the good for man must in some way involve our reasoning faculty. Humans are the rational beings ("a thing that thinks," as René Descartes (1596–1650) later phrased it), and man's purpose in living must be connected with the proper use of this central and primary ability.

▶ THE EXERCISE OF REASON. The next question, of course, is "How should we exercise our rational function so as to attain the good?" The best life for human beings may involve the use of reason, but how, exactly, ought our powers of reason to be employed so as to achieve *eudaimonia?*

Aristotle replied in a somewhat circuitous way by saying that we should aim at achieving excellence for ourselves as rational beings. *Arete* or excellent functioning in our area of supremacy (which is reasoning) will yield a good life. Just as the excellence of flutists consists in the artistry with which they play the flute, and the excellence of sculptors lies in their skill at sculpting, human excellence must be judged by the degree to which we excel at being rational in the conduct of our lives. Since reason is central to man *arete* in the functioning of reason will bring about the ultimate good for man which is well being or *eudaimonia.*

More specifically, reason should be exercised in two ways: to control the extreme tendencies of our passions and make wise choices, and to engage in reflective contemplation. The former use of reason occupies a more prominent place in Aristotle's system, so we will examine that first and at greater length.

The Golden Mean. For Aristotle as for Plato, it is the unruliness of the passions that causes a great deal of trouble for individual human beings and for the human race in general. We have to control, not develop, the sensuous and impulsive parts of ourselves, the emotive and animal aspects of our being, through the exercise of reason. Our rationality should be taken as our guide in striking the proper balance in actions between the extremes that the passions tend to promote.

Specifically, Aristotle maintained that we must strive to attain the *mean between extremes* by allowing reason to adjudicate between the conflicting claims of the passions and choose that area of moderation between excesses and deficiencies. What is needed is for reason to select, deliberately and objectively, mean states and activities, and not allow the individual to be misled by his feelings into extreme behavior and consequently into an unharmonious life. "*Meden agan,*" Aristotle declared: "nothing in excess." And it is reason that will keep us from excessive states or actions.

The emotions can cause people to miss the mark by swaying them to sin either to the right or to the left—either by bringing about an excess or a deficiency of the quality that is required. Moderation is best, Aristotle believed, for just as it can be said of a good work "that nothing could be taken from it or added to it," implying that excellence is destroyed by excess or deficiency, but secured by observing the mean, so in action we must aim at the mean under the guidance of reason. Aristotle elaborated upon the point by saying, "For instance, it is possible to feel fear, confidence, desire, anger, pity, and generally to be affected pleasantly and painfully, either too much or too little, in either case wrongly; but to be thus affected at the right times, and on the right occasions, and towards the right persons, and with the right object, and in the right fashion, is the mean course and the best course . . . excess is wrong and deficiency also is blamed, but the mean amount is praised and is right. . . ."[17] We should strive to achieve what is called the *"aurea mediocritas"* or the "golden mean" (although Aristotle never used the word "golden").

Aristotle realized that these generalizations do not help us in a practical sense in the conduct of our lives, and since he wanted to give us a type of handbook of morality, he then specified particular states and actions that would be covered by his doctrine of the golden mean. With regard to feelings of fear and confidence, the mean is courage, the excess an extreme foolhardiness, and the deficiency cowardice. With respect to pleasures and pains, the mean is temperance, the excess profligacy (dissipation), and the deficiency, Aristotle said, has not been given a name because it is hardly ever found (sic!). In money matters involving large sums, moderation is magnificence, while excess and deficiency are vulgarity and meanness, respectively. With regard to honor and disgrace, the mean is pride, the excess vanity, and the deficiency humility.

Aristotle supplied us with an extensive list including, for example, the virtue of wit as a mean between buffoonery and boorishness, and friendliness as the moderate path between obsequiousness and quarrelsomeness. In all cases, following the middle of the road constitutes the virtuous and ideal behavior. Aristotle did not say that we should try to strike a precise midpoint between extremes, but rather that we find a middle range along the continuum from excess to deficiency.

Aristotle also stated that certain virtues may not fall toward

17. Ibid.

the center of the range. In other words, if 10 is an excess and 2 a deficiency, the mean may not be 6; it might be closer to 8 or 5. In order to determine where correct behavior lies, Aristotle advised us to avoid that extreme which is more opposed to the mean. (By and large, this usually works out to avoiding the deficiency more than the excess.) If we are looking to achieve courage, for example, that would be closer to foolhardiness than to cowardice, so we would probably want to act more rashly than cowardly. In the same way, being without a sense of humor is farthest away from wit, so in trying to achieve wittiness, we would move closer to the side of clownishness. Or being a miser is much further from generosity than being a spendthrift, so we would avoid miserliness more.

Aristotle also instructed us to notice the errors to which we are ourselves most prone and to resist those the most. In other words, if our inclination is to be vain, we have to fight that tendency in order to strike the mean of pride. We must lean away from our personal vices after first analyzing ourselves to discover our particular weaknesses.

Last, Aristotle warned us to be on guard against what is pleasant and against pleasure. An action may be pleasurable but not especially right in terms of not being the mean virtue between extremes; pleasure can, in fact, induce us to adopt nonvirtuous actions. By saying this, Aristotle clearly differentiated his ethical theory from that of hedonism.

To forestall criticism, Aristotle also wrote,

> . . . it is not all actions nor all passions that admit of moderation; there are some whose very names imply badness, as malevolence, shamelessness, envy, and, among acts, adultery, theft, murder. These and all other like things are blamed as being bad in themselves, and not merely in their excess or deficiency. It is impossible therefore to go right in them; they are always wrong: rightness and wrongness in such things [e.g., in adultery] does not depend upon whether it is the right person and occasion and manner, but the mere doing of any one of them is wrong. It would be equally absurd to look for moderation or excess or deficiency in unjust cowardly or profligate conduct; for then there would be moderation in excess or deficiency, and excess in excess, and deficiency in defi-

> ciency. The fact is that just as there can be no excess or
> deficiency in temperance or courage because the mean or
> moderate amount is, in a sense, an extreme, so in these kinds
> of conduct also there can be no moderation or excess or
> deficiency, but the acts are wrong however they be done. For,
> to put it generally, there cannot be moderation in excess or
> deficiency, nor excess or deficiency in moderation.[18]

This would also imply that we cannot practice the doctrine of the mean too much and that being moderate about moderation would be an extreme.

In summation, Aristotle argued that if we use our primary function of reasoning in an excellent way, we will choose the mean between extremes and thereby bring about our vital well being. It is unlikely we will feel a sense of well being if we behave in a foolhardy way, or as buffoons or spendthrifts. It is equally unlikely we will attain a sense of well being if we are cowardly, humorless, or miserly. But if we reach a condition in which we are courageous, witty, generous, and the like, we will have arrived at the ideal state of being. When we develop ourselves thus under the control of our dominant trait of rationality, we can achieve the highest good of *eudaimonia*.

Reflection. We said previously that reason has two uses, according to Aristotle, and the second is to engage in reflection. Reason is sometimes considered as an end in itself rather than a means for threading one's way between excess and deficiency. Reason, for Aristotle, is the highest activity of which human beings are capable, the fullest development of a human being. Here we are not concerned with accomplishing any kind of practical goal through our contemplation but with contemplation as something worthwhile in and of itself. Aristotle referred to it sometimes as "*theoria*," pure intellect or theoretical understanding. At one point he called it consummated knowledge of the most exalted objects. In other words, if we reflect upon eternal, timeless objects, if we meditate upon basic questions and are involved in deliberative activity, this will be good in itself. In a sense, even here reason is being used as

18. Ibid.

a means for the development of the person and to achieve well being, but since reason is central to the person its exercise is, at the same time, personal development. Reason is both means and end.

This portion of Aristotle's theory, as well as his list of virtues, has been criticized as being too elitist and smacking of privilege. Contemplation may be fine for people who have a good deal of money and leisure time but that hardly characterizes the mass of humankind. Nevertheless, in a larger sense contemplation is not just a rich person's luxury since people in any walk of life can engage in it just as they now may practice transcendental meditation or yoga. So this particular criticism does not seem to be well taken.

In any case, we are more concerned with the use of reason for achieving moderation in our behavior, and certainly this notion has great appeal. It is part of conventional wisdom that we should not be extravagant or miserly but spend our money in the right degree, that we should not be too silly or too serious but instead have a good sense of humor. We speak of people loving not wisely but too well and not keeping their emotions in proper proportion, being blinded by passion or, at the other extreme, being incapable of loving themselves or other people. All of this has a certain common-sense appeal.

Aristotle's position is certainly not the modern type of self-realization theory that appeals to us, but he can be classified in that category because of his concern with the nature of being human and the application of our essential function to the achievement of overall well being. He was concerned with homeostasis and the equilibrium of the person, an overall harmony in our feelings and activities. If we go to extremes, our balance will be destroyed and our development distorted. To live in such a way that we achieve just the right amount, at the proper time and place, guided by our dominant element of reason—that is successful living.

▶ EVALUATING ARISTOTLE'S ETHICS

A Critique of Function. In criticizing Aristotle, we should first notice his concept of function. He inquired into man's function because the good is connected with it, and in this inquiry he presupposed that since everything has a function, human beings do

SELF-REALIZATION

also. But this assumption is questionable. Artifacts such as knives or hammers, mills or houses have been designed to serve a function but that is not to say that natural objects such as plants, animals, or people have a function in the same way. Natural objects do have various characteristics and capabilities but these are not necessarily their function in existing. A date palm may grow dates but growing dates is not necessarily its function in the sense of its purpose for being.

Aristotle embraced what is called *teleologism*,[19] the belief that everything has an end or purpose, a potentiality seeking actuality. (Christianity later adopted this notion in the thought of St. Thomas Aquinas by conceiving of God as the being responsible for the purpose behind all life.) But there may not be an end for which everything is intended or an inherent purpose that all things must fulfill. Rain may water the land (or erode it), lightning may scorch the earth, cows may give milk, plants may give oxygen, but that is not to say these activities are their function. They are merely capabilities or primary characteristics and not necessarily purposes. There may not be a purpose to anything aside from the artifacts man creates specifically to serve some purposes.

Human beings in particular may not have a function aside from a self-created one. Perhaps we have no intrinsic function or calling or purpose that can be discovered through introspection and subsequently actualized. The entire approach of seeing objects, animals, or people in terms of function may be wrongheaded.

The possible error of this perspective is illustrated by the argument often used to suppress women in their career aspirations. "A woman's function is to be a wife and mother," it is said. "Unless you are a wife and mother, you are hardly a woman because you have failed to fulfill your purpose." But this kind of reasoning seems fallacious. Although women have the capabilities of marrying and having children, they are not necessarily women's functions. Women

---

19. Teleologism has already been discussed as an ethical theory which states that actions are to be judged in terms of their consequences not their nature or the intention of the agent. Aristotle's teleological theory is a metaphysical one which holds that the universe as a whole and every object in it is arranged according to ends and purposes. Events are therefore explained not by their prior or "efficient" causes but by their purpose or final causes. The metaphysical theory of "mechanism" maintains the former, teleologism the latter.

can choose whether or not they wish to realize this potential, depending upon what they want to gain out of life. They may not be suppressing their functions by deciding to remain single and/or not to have children.

Thinking in terms of functions can be very misleading and damaging, and Aristotle's notion that everything has a function is highly suspect.

Another criticism of Aristotle in connection with this concept is that, when Aristotle tried to determine the human function, he meant by this our unique function as distinguished from that of animals, and he concluded that the human function is reason. But as was said earlier, humans do not necessarily differ from animals in their ability to reason; animals also reason, albeit at a lower level. Reason is not something unique to human beings. We also realize today that if human beings are unique (which is questionable) they could be unique in other respects besides reason—in aesthetic or religious awareness, for example. Why not choose one of those as man's unique function?

Third, why look for uniqueness at all in order to find out what human beings are? It could be that a major aspect of being human is something shared with other animals: In the present day we are rediscovering that pure animal energy is good; that running or swimming, eating natural foods, or drinking fresh water is a marvelous experience. We would not want to do away with those activities just because we share them with animals; we think that these things are worthwhile for people too. Aristotle seemed to cut people off from their animal roots; but it could be that we should concentrate on certain things we share with other animals and not just on whatever we can find that differentiates human beings from them.

A Critique of Moderation. Apart from the problems surrounding the concept of function, a second criticism of Aristotle has to do with his championing of moderation. Reason achieves *arete*, Aristotle stated, when it serves as a reliable guide to the mean. But is the mean always best? Surely we would be justified in going to extremes in some cases, and perhaps temperance should not be our guiding principle if we want to lead a rich life overall. A painter, for example, might be justified in going to extremes in his or her passion for art as van Gogh and Gaugin did, and Christianity is based on complete dedication to God and an extreme self-denial and altruistic love for humankind. Should the artist, the devotee, the political reformer, the explorer, and the gifted scientist live in moderation or to the limits of their abilities?

We also feel that we ought not to be moderate in our pursuits of justice, goodness, truth, or virtue itself. As was mentioned, Aristotle defended his principle of moderation by saying that these virtues are good in themselves and can be taken to extremes; moderation in them would be a vice. But this implies that moderation is not always best, which is inconsistent with Aristotle's position. And how do we know in advance which feelings and actions are virtuous and should not be done in moderation when virtuous behavior is defined as that which is moderate? Correct conduct is supposed to emerge from Aristotle's scheme, but how do we know beforehand which cases fall outside of the scheme? It would seem as though Aristotle had already established to his own satisfaction the states and actions that are right, and then took these pre-established virtues and fit them into his general system. But neither he nor anyone else can determine ethical behavior by asking whether an action is a mean or an extreme. In short, Aristotle's system does not tell us how to conduct ourselves and thereby fails in its intention. [It should be noted that Aristotle addressed this point through the concept of *phronesis* (practical wisdom) in Book VI of the *Nichomachean Ethics*, but it is arguable whether he resolved the problem.]

Aristotle's Ethics and Commonplace Morality. This leads to a third problem in Aristotle's ethics, which every philosophic analysis has disclosed. Far from presenting us with an original theory of ethics, Aristotle merely took the conventional Greek virtues and found a system of thought to contain them—a system that is itself the product of conventional wisdom. Aristotle stated that we should be temperate, courageous, truthful, gentle, modest, and so forth, enumerating a string of cliches and truisms that cannot be disputed but are also embarrassingly banal. And the system within which we find these prosaic virtues, the system of choosing everything in moderation and nothing in excess, reflected an equally pedestrian mentality of the orthodox segment of Greek society. They are the values emphasized by conservatives and conformists, the middle class and middle-aged, the people opposed to risk and afraid of emotion. Aristotle thus became a spokesman for a customary and commonplace morality that is reassuring but not inspiring.

▶ __CONCLUSION__. In view of the problems connected with Aristotle's version of self-realization, it may not be the way to successful living. But the reader must now make this determination for himself or herself in the light of the positive and negative features of Aristotle's system. As in the case of hedonism, the final judgment must rest with the individual as to whether self-realization in general or Aristotelianism in particular can be adopted as one's fundamental reason for being.

RECAPITULATION

__W__e began the chapter by describing the position of self-realization in its broadest meaning. The role of dominant tendencies in the development of self was explained, and the theory of self-realization was differentiated from that of hedonism. The problem of defining humanness or selfhood was then pursued at some length, the latter in terms of mind and body and continuity through time. Self-realization was subsequently criticized both in its form as human development and its form as self-development.

Aristotle's theory was then examined, including his notions of aim, good, function, and excellence. The doctrine of the mean was described in relation to reason, with qualifications concerning its application and illustrations of its functioning. Criticisms were then offered of several features of Aristotle's system to conclude the chapter.

▼ ▼ ▼

REVIEW QUESTIONS

__1.__ *Explain what the self-realizationist means by asserting that our dominant tendencies should take precedence in our development, and that if we try to be everything in general, we will be nothing in particular.*

__2.__ *Describe the two tracks that self-realization can take: developing humanness or selfhood. Why is it difficult to define human nature and the self?*

3. *What is meant by the criticism that self-realization offers no restraints to an egotistical or selfish life? Why would you agree or disagree?*

4. *Explain Aristotle's doctrine of "the golden mean" with examples of how various virtues are derived within his system.*

5. *Present an exposition and critical analysis of Aristotle's concept of function. Why would you affirm or reject the notion that all objects have a function?*

7

NATURALISM

the word "natural" is one of the vaguer and more ambiguous words in our language, if we mean by vagueness seeing dimly and by ambiguity seeing double (or multiply). The term has caused particular trouble to students of ethics examining naturalism and to those who want to follow a "natural" way of life, because living naturally or being natural is hard to translate into concrete conduct. What does it actually mean to oppose an unnatural or artificial existence and to endorse the ideal of living in a natural way? Our first task, then, in elucidating this theory of ethics is to differentiate the various senses of naturalism and the several ways of living that are intended.

By a naturalistic ethic one can mean:

(a) being natural, or living physically close to nature and satisfying our basic needs in simple, elemental ways—the type of naturalism of Henry David Thoreau (1817–1862), of some of the nineteenth century romantic poets, and of the "back to nature" movement of the 1960s;

(b) following the divine spirit within nature and being guided by its inherent character, laws, and ways—the view of American transcendentalism and ancient Roman Stoicism; and

(c) cooperating with the natural development of life as it has progressed and unfolded throughout biological history, doing nothing to counteract its dynamic movement and tendencies, its thrust toward greater being.

Evolutionism is characterized by the last approach and, to a certain extent, so is Hegelianism. We will examine each of these interpretations in turn as being the principal forms of naturalism; other alleged types will be subsumed under these categories as subspecies.[1] The first two will be covered in this chapter. Evolutionism will be dealt with in Chapter 8, for it is sufficiently distinct from other forms of naturalism to warrant separate treatment.

BEING NATURAL

In the 1960s a movement principally concerned with the values surrounding a natural life spread across the country, fostered mainly by young people. The advocates of this mode of living preferred the natural environment of the country over the artificiality of urban life, the tenderness of making love in place of the violence of making war; they sought the rhythm of the days and seasons as their measure of time, the simplicity and space and silence of the land to make them gentle, balanced, sensitive, and

---

1. We do not discuss the special types of naturalism of John Dewey (1859–1952) and George Santayana. Neither do we cover the ethical naturalism in terms of following one's own nature, doing what is natural to oneself, or being true to one's real self, which is actually closer to a self-realization ethic. A philosophic naturalism of a technical kind, which is also excluded, is the claim that all moral judgments are about some natural quality in actions rather than being based on some nonnatural (or spiritual) quality. See the *Concise Encyclopedia of Western Philosophy and Philosophers*, ed. J. O. Urmson (London: Hutchinson and Co., 1960), pp. 275–76.

tranquil. They wanted to eat organic foods without pesticides or preservatives, to drink pure water and breathe unpolluted air, to maintain good health through balanced nutrition and physical activity with minimum reliance on machines. They also wanted to express themselves through folk crafts and popular music rather than being spectators of high art, and to wear comfortable working clothes instead of dressing up in the latest expensive fashions; following Thoreau, they said that security does not consist in what you have but what you can do without. There was an emphasis on joy instead of status, feeling rather than intellect, communion in place of verbal communication, and direct experience rather than ideas contained in books. They also believed in magic and, perhaps, the insights obtained through hallucinogenic drugs rather than the methods of science and discursive reasoning. Culture, learning, sophistication, achievement, urbanity were all considered suspect as artificial overlays on the natural life while plainness, simplicity, openness, rusticity were prized as elemental and good.

In the 1990s some of these ideas have been absorbed into our thinking. The concern about the environment, pollution, and conserving natural resources derive from this movement, as does the interest in being healthy and physically fit, eating natural foods—especially fruits and vegetables—dressing informally and in natural fabrics, protecting endangered species, banning animal experimentation, and so forth.

▶ **A HISTORY OF THE "BE NATURAL" MOVEMENT.** The roots of naturalism can be traced far back in intellectual history, perhaps to the Cynics in ancient Greece. But the "be natural" movement was precipitated by specific ills of modern life, including industrial pollution, unhealthy packaged foods, and overcrowded, noisy, impersonal cities.

Thoreau. In the nineteenth century Thoreau expressed the idea of retreating to nature for the sake of achieving clarity and simplicity in living. "I went to the woods because I wished to live deliberately," he wrote in *Walden*, "to front only the essential facts of life, and see if I could not learn what it had to teach, and not, when I came to die, discover that I had not lived. I did not wish to practice resignation, unless it was quite necessary. I wanted to live deep and suck out all the marrow of life, to live so sturdily and Spartan-like as to put to rout all that was not life, to cut a broad swath and shave close, to drive life into a corner, and reduce it to its lowest terms. . . .''[2]

Thoreau was retreating from a world that entices people to obtain more and more in the way of inessential goods, to live in debilitating comfort, and to spend an unnecessary portion of their lifetime earning money to support a wasteful, superfluous, artificial existence. He believed that life in the towns diverts people from the satisfaction of their primary needs and encourages them to rounds of frivolity and superficiality. It separates them from the beauties of nature and the dignity of labor—especially labor which bears the stamp of their personality. Instead of being self-reliant, people grow weak and dependent, self-indulgent, and pusillanimous. Above all, towns render people oblivious to what is essential in life whereas the demands of rural living make them aware of the basic terms of human existence.

The Romantic Poets. The nineteenth century Romantic poets also found in nature the "truths" and models that they sought, and evoked an ideal of passive receptivity to the lessons that nature could impart. In "The Tables Turned," for example, Wordsworth urged readers to "let Nature be your teacher":

▾ ▾ ▾
Books! 'tis a dull and endless strife:
Come, hear the woodland linnet,
How sweet his music! on my life,
There's more of wisdom in it.

. . .

One impulse from a vernal wood
May teach you more of a man,
Of moral evil and of good,
Than all the sages can.

. . .

---

2. H. D. Thoreau, *Walden* (London: Walter Scott, 1886), pp. 88–89.

Enough of Science and of Art;
Close up those barren leaves;
Come forth, and bring with you a heart
That watches and receives.

▲ ▲ ▲

Nature, not books, has the wisdom that will nourish us, and the truth it contains can only be absorbed through a "wise passiveness" not a deliberate and earnest effort. Communion with nature was thought to be an experience that happened to the sensitized person rather than something that could be made to happen by an act of will. It is almost as though we have to become one with nature in a pantheistic sense to absorb its message. "Are not the mountains, waves, and skies, a part/Of me and of my soul, as I of them?" Byron asked in "Childe Harold."

We must also become like children or perhaps even infants, Wordsworth declared in "Intimations of Immortality"; they are nature's priests who come into existence "trailing clouds of glory":

▼ ▼ ▼
. . . trailing clouds of glory do we come
  From God who is our home:
Heaven lies about us in our infancy!
Shades of the prison-house begin to close
  Upon the growing Boy,
But He beholds the light, and whence it flows,
  He sees it in his joy;
The Youth, who daily farther from the east
  Must travel, still is Nature's Priest,
  And by the vision splendid
  Is on his way attended;
At length the Man perceives it die away,
And fade into the light of common day.

. . .

Thou, whose exterior semblance doth belie
  Thy Soul's immensity;
Thou best Philosopher

. . .

Mighty Prophet! Seer blest!
On whom those truths do rest,
Which we are toiling all our lives to find,

. . .

Thou little Child, yet glorious in the might
Of heaven-born freedom on they being's height,

. . .

▲ ▲ ▲

According to this perspective, the innocent and natural child is wiser than any adult and closest to God. The sophisticated person must learn from the simpler souls, children, animals, from the wilderness, the sea, the seasons, the diurnal pattern of nature. "Except as ye turn and become as little children ye shall in no wise enter into the kingdom of heaven" the gospel of *Matthew*, Chapter 18, verse 3, tells us. And *Luke* Chapter 12, verse 27, enjoins: "Consider the lilies of the field, how they grow; they toil not, neither do they spin;" lilies are the models of beauty and purity in living, a part of nature as we were until we severed ourselves from our origins. Now the prodigal must return to the mothering arms of nature which is, as Wordsworth declared in "Tintern Abbey":

▼ ▼ ▼

. . .

The anchor of my purest thoughts, the nurse,
The guide, the guardian of my heart, and soul
Of all my moral being.

. . .

▲ ▲ ▲

Or as he wrote elsewhere in the same poem, in extolling his boyhood emotions,

▼ ▼ ▼

. . . For nature then
(The coarser pleasures of my boyish days,
And their glad animal movements all gone by)
To me was all in all.—I cannot paint

What then I was. The sounding cataract
Haunted me like a passion: the tall rock,
The mountain, and the deep and gloomy wood,
Their colours and their forms, were then to me
An appetite; a feeling and a love,
That had no need of a remoter charm,
By thought supplied, nor any interest
Unborrowed from the eye. . . .

▲ ▲ ▲

Keats too celebrated nature, conceiving it as our fundamental solace, an infinite balm against despondency through the beauty of its being.[3] In his celebrated "Endymion" he wrote,

▼ ▼ ▼

A thing of beauty is a joy for ever:
Its loveliness increases; it will never
Pass into nothingness; but still will keep
A bower quiet for us, and a sleep
Full of sweet dreams, and health, and quiet breathing.
Therefore, on every morrow, are we wreathing
A flowery band to bind us to the earth,
Spite of despondence, of the inhuman dearth
Of noble natures. . . .
Some shape of beauty moves away the pall
From our dark spirits. Such the sun, the moon,
Tree old, and young, sprouting a shady boon
For simple sheep; and such are daffodils
With the green world they live in; and clear rills
That for themselves a cooling covert make
'Gainst the hot season . . .
. . . whether there be shine, or gloom o'ercast,
They always must be with us, or we die.

▲ ▲ ▲

3. In addition to Wordsworth (who may be the best example of a Romanticist intoxicated with nature) and Byron and Keats, one could also list Shelley and Coleridge as having a strong naturalism at the heart of their poetic works.

▸ **A CRITICAL APPRAISAL**. Many poems extolling nature are lyrical and lovely, but can commitment to a natural life survive the harsh light of logic? If we are to be natural in these various ways, admiring and emulating nature, will that provide us with a good life? Is the natural the ideal, and is nature a model teacher? In a realistic rather than a romantic sense, does country living yield the best type of existence?

Country Living. Being in the country certainly has some advantages over city life but it lacks a great deal as well. In practical terms, good theater and films are difficult to find in rural areas as are museums, art galleries, and concert halls. If we enjoy performances of modern dance or ballet, or seeing fine architecture in buildings or cathedrals, we will probably be at a loss in a farm community, and if we want a variety of food or the pleasure of dining in excellent restaurants, we are much more likely to satisfy our tastes in the city. Urban areas also offer a wide range of entertainment from sports events to night clubs, and provide a more extensive selection of products and services including clothing, cars, books, furniture, appliances, repair work, and so forth. One also finds people to converse with who are generally better educated and more sophisticated than country people. The main cultural achievements of civilization are concentrated in cities, as well as the latest technological advances that provide increased comfort and convenience in living. Dental and medical care are also superior in cities, which have more highly trained doctors and better equipped hospitals, and social services are more extensively developed as are systems of public transportation. The educational level of people in urban areas tends to be above that of rural people, and city newspapers, libraries, and broadcasting stations (both radio and television) are generally better than their rural counterparts.

Furthermore, a country existence may be more peaceful and serene but it also can be dull, monotonous, and lonely, deadening people rather than enlivening them. It can reduce us to an animal level where we only satisfy our biological needs and do not live the higher and more complex existence of a human being. The means for satisfying a variety of our human interests are less readily available, and with limited access to educational, social, and cultural institutions our personal development can be severely constricted.

And is it, in fact, an advantage to minimize our material goods or to eliminate the labor-saving devices that modern science has developed? Surely it would be more impoverishing than enriching to do without refrigerators, stoves, washing machines, cars, running water, indoor plumbing, central heating, or electric lights. Too much time would be spent on sheer survival, on providing the basic necessities for maintaining ourselves in a reasonably comfortable way. And not only would the burden fall on the woman (if she were the one keeping the home) but on the man as well if he tried to operate a farm without machinery or to produce goods without mechanization. At least some technological devices free us from exhausting, repetitive, routine labor, and some material objects such as musical instruments, attractive interior furnishings, paintings, and cooking utensils enhance our lives and give us the means for self-expression. Having a spacious, well-decorated house can do more for our spirit than living in a cave or shack, even if the latter is a more natural dwelling.

Country living, then, with a minimal use of technological equipment and material goods is not necessarily better than living in the city in a tastefully decorated home with a variety of labor-saving devices at our disposal.

The Natural State. In addition, the "be natural" theory does not tell us how elemental or primitive we should be in order to lead a truly natural life. Should we, for example, do without metal for our tools, without written language or the wheel? Should we go without clothing even in winter, as animals do, and never wear shoes? Should we bathe very seldom, pay little attention to sanitation or manners, or never consult doctors, undergo surgery, or use any medication other than herbs? Must we abandon the use of silverware, napkins, and plates, or even tables, chairs, and beds, in keeping with the ways of early peoples? Should we only gather fruits, nuts, and berries rather than raising cattle or crops? If we eat meat, must it be raw? Is it enough to use a hand plow to work the land rather than a tractor or should we use a stick in order to farm the natural way? And when we travel should we simply forgo trains, airplanes, and cars, using horses instead, or do we have to walk to be truly natural? Are boats and bridges natural or must we swim across rivers? Just how far back must we go in evolutionary history in order to reach the natural state—to an eighteenth century peasant, ancient Egyptian, Neanderthal man, an ape, an amphibian, an amoeba, a particle of inanimate matter? The dictum "be natural" simply does not tell us which stage of development is the truly natural one.

We could begin with the first human being, *Homo erectus* (although that stage of human life does not seem ideal). But the moment we admit that certain changes in our natural state still constitute a natural life then we do not know where to stop; we cannot then say how extensively human beings can change the environment and still be living naturally. We certainly cannot claim that whatever human beings devise is natural by virtue of the fact that it is a natural product of people's minds, because then every development in science, medicine, engineering, and so forth would be natural. In this case, there would be no distinction between living naturally and living unnaturally; whatever people did would, *ipso facto,* be natural.

Therefore, in addition to the criticism of the "be natural" ethic that urban living in all of its implications has numerous advantages over a rural existence, we can also find fault with that ethic for failing to provide a criterion for a natural as opposed to an unnatural or nonnatural life.

Nature as a Model for Conduct. A third criticism has to do with the emphasis that is placed on nature as a model for human conduct. We are told we should emulate nature, live as the animals do, and draw our inspiration from their example. But in addition to possessing pastoral beauty, nature also contains savagery; it is "red in tooth and claw," as Tennyson said. We would not want to imitate nature insofar as that includes animals preying on each other, maiming and devouring one another for food, or perpetrating acts of mindless cruelty. And to duplicate natural catastrophes would hardly be desirable. Hurricanes, earthquakes, forest fires, tidal waves, avalanches, floods, volcanic eruptions, and so forth are undoubtedly part of nature but they are not events that we would wish to duplicate in human life. Civilization is in many ways a fortress in the wilderness, and we fight to keep out the more brutal aspects of the natural environment. To a greater or lesser degree, we feel we should oppose nature as the enemy.

John Stuart Mill wrote,

> In sober truth, nearly all the things which men are hanged or imprisoned for doing to one another, are nature's every day performances. Killing, the most criminal act recognized by human laws, Nature does once to every human being that lives; and in a large proportion of cases, after protracted tortures. . . . Nature impales men, breaks them as if on the wheel, casts them to be devoured by wild beasts, burns them to death, crushes them with stones like the first Christian martyr, starves them with hunger, freezes them with cold, poisons them by the quick or slow venom of her exhalations, and has hundreds of other hideous deaths in reserve. . . . All this, Nature does with the most supercilious disregard both of mercy and justice, emptying her shafts upon the best and noblest indifferently with the meanest and worst. . . . She mows down those on whose existence hangs the well-being of a whole people, perhaps the prospects of the human race for generations to come, with as little compunction as those whose death is a relief to themselves, or a blessing to those under their noxious influence. Such are Nature's dealings with life. . . . Next to taking life (equal to it according to a high authority) is taking the means by which we live; and Nature does this too on the largest scale and with the most callous indifference. A single hurricane destroys the hopes of a season; a flight of locusts, or an inundation, desolates a district; a trifling chemical change in an edible root, starves a million people. The waves of the sea, like banditti seize and appropriate the wealth of the rich and the little all of the poor with the same accompaniments of stripping, wounding, and killing as their human antitypes. Everything in short, which the worst men commit either against life, or property is perpetrated on a larger scale by natural agents.[4]

Nature, then, is by no means exemplary in all of its manifestations. Animals are often vicious to each other and suffer under the vicissitudes of their natural environment just as human beings do. When we say, "Don't behave like an animal," we mean that we

4. J. S. Mill, *Nature, The Utility of Religion, and Theism* (London: Longmans, Green, 1874), p. 28–29.

NATURALISM

should not be selfish, violent, or base. For the beasts are often beastly, the brutes can be brutal, and we are all subject to disasters of the sort described by Mill. Suffering and death are certainly part of nature; nevertheless we would not want to call them good.

Nature and the Good. This brings us to a final point to which we will return repeatedly in discussing the various types of naturalism: The natural is not necessarily good. Some aspects of nature and a natural existence are worth following but others are not, just as that which is unnatural contains both good and bad. For example, eating natural foods seems far better than consuming prepared meals with large doses of chemical preservatives, but we would not want to cure a ruptured appendix with herbal remedies; here we want the civilized skills of modern medicine. Or we might want to build into our lives some of the harmony and tranquility found in nature but it is doubtful that we want to follow the example of nature by deliberately introducing pain, disease, and starvation.

In short, to call a practice "natural" is not always to commend it, and if something can be natural but not good then good cannot be defined as the natural. In addition, this point implies that, when a natural event is called good, the judgment is not made because the event is natural but for some other reason. A natural event could be judged good because it enhances happiness, provides rich experience, preserves life, and so forth, just as an unnatural event would be judged by those standards. But the event is not good simply because it is natural; as we have seen, that fact alone does not necessarily make it worthy of praise or imitation.

This criticism stands as a stumbling block to all forms of naturalism that attempt to equate the good with the natural. For our present purposes it certainly constitutes a viable criticism of the "be natural" ethic. Rather than blindly following a natural life, it seems far more sensible to select from among natural and unnatural options those features that are most worthwhile.[5]

5. A comparable criticism can be made of aesthetic naturalism, which may not be surprising when one considers that ethics and aesthetics are both concerned with values and are classified as species of axiology or value theory. The point is that a work of art is not good because it is a naturalistic representation of the world, flows naturally from us in a sincere way, or faithfully mirrors some natural object. Not all naturalistic works are, *ipso facto*, good art, and not all good art is naturalistic.

FOLLOWING THE INNER SPIRIT OF NATURE

A second naturalistic ethic stresses following nature in the sense of harmonizing with its essential purposes and spirit, its inherent character and structure. According to this viewpoint, there is a universal force moving through nature to which we should ally ourselves, finding our reason for being in discerning and fulfilling its will. Without conceiving of a God behind natural phenomena, this type of naturalism sees nature as a transcendental force in itself, moving through all things and imbuing them with destiny. Nature here becomes God, not a personal being but an abstract spiritual power with an overall purpose and design. Unconsciously, without direction from a cosmic mind beyond itself, nature tends toward certain ends and contains an internal structure that is orderly and dynamic. Without being directed nature contains a direction, and the natural world is shot throughout with discernible order. All events occur as a consequence of the operation of its grand scheme, and everything happens in a beneficial way, for the scheme is ultimately and supremely moral. If human beings live in tune with the system of nature, understanding its inherent tendencies and conforming to its ways, they will achieve a satisfying existence for themselves, individually and collectively. If, on the other hand, they oppose the plan of nature, they will live in a state of disequilibrium, divided from both the natural order and their own natural being.

The "be natural" movement seems to stress conformity to nature in a more external and romantic sense, whereas this theory looks to the active power within natural phenomena and stresses becoming one with nature in a more fundamental way. Here the purposive thrust of nature is emphasized in contrast to its external manifestations, which are only indicative of an underlying reality. Our duty is consequently seen in deeper perspective; it consists in following the inner principles of the natural order, not the behavior but the disposition of nature, its vital, spiritual essence.

We can take as representatives of this type of naturalism the nineteenth-century American movement of transcendentalism and the ancient Roman philosophy of Stoicism. Both have a somewhat

NATURALISM

dated flavor, but at the same time they have been absorbed into our psyche and form part of our contemporary outlook.

Of the two, Stoicism has probably affected us more deeply. We say, as part of our unconscious Stoic philosophy, "There's nothing you can do, so you might as well make the best of it," or "No sense in worrying; it doesn't do any good." In repeating these maxims, we usually fail to realize our debt to the Hellenistic-Roman period. Whether or not Stoicism exerts a greater influence on our thinking today than transcendentalism, we will deal with it more extensively as the clearer illustration of this version of naturalism. Transcendentalism, like the Eastern Taoism of the *Tao Te Ching*, offers a naturalistic ethic which is too diffuse and multifarious for our purposes; we will treat it first, but only briefly.

▶ **TRANSCENDENTALISM**. The American transcendental movement embraced a Neoplatonism usually identified with Plotinus (A.D. 205–270) as a founder. From Neoplatonism it derived the idea of nature as the expression of "mind," and natural laws as embodying moral principles. A supreme but impersonal force was thought inherent in the natural world and, as Ralph Waldo Emerson (1803–1882) phrased it, "at the center of nature lies the moral law, radiating to the circumference." In order to understand the inner workings of the universe, an intuitive perception is needed to carry us beyond the appearances of natural phenomena. Systematic reasoning or scientific discoveries can only present arguments and teach us facts; a direct vision of reality is required. The truth disclosed to those who discount empiricism and dismiss the outer world as "a dream and a shade" is that nature is divine, and insofar as human beings are a part of nature they too carry a spiritual spark and transcendental worth. "Every natural fact is a symbol of some spiritual fact," Emerson wrote. ". . . The whole nature is a metaphor of the human mind." And he claimed, "Within man is the soul of the whole." Therefore, by looking either outward or inward, by understanding ourselves or nature, the fundamental reality is revealed to the aware and patient seeker.[6]

6. For excellent expositions of the philosophy of transcendentalism see G. Hicks, *The Great Tradition* (New York: The Macmillan Co., 1933); L. Mumford, *The Golden Day* (New York: Harcourt, Brace and Co., 1929); and W. G. Muelder, L. Sears, and

In addition to opening our minds to nature's spirit within and without, we also have a duty to correct injustices against humankind in civil society. Crimes against human beings are sins against nature because the two are one, and we can have confidence in the judgments we make about societal practices because our consciences are rooted in the natural moral law. We are, therefore, obliged to adopt a humanistic stance; for the nineteenth-century transcendentalists this took the form of an active protest against slavery. Most of the major figures of the movement defied the Fugitive Slave Law and several were imprisoned for subversion. But whatever the particular issues of the age, the transcendentalists advocated a life of moral commitment that attempted to redress the offenses committed against humanity. It was conceived as something on the order of a holy mission to resist the desecration of the human spirit—a spirit that was the epitome of nature and the divine.

Because of its insistence on a supernatural reality within the physical world of nature, transcendentalism is sometimes considered to be in opposition to naturalism, and a good case can be made for that position, particularly if naturalism is closely identified with the materialism of, say, Lucretius (97?–54 B.C.) in *De Rerum Natura*. But insofar as the transcendental movement regarded nature as having an inner soul, it was a type of spiritualized naturalism; the belief in the reality of the unseen was a faith in nature's divine essence. "Everything in Nature contains all the powers of Nature. Everything is made of one hidden stuff," Emerson declared. Spirit is immanent in nature, residing in every part, not a separate force behind it.

It is difficult to judge whether transcendentalism was correct in its assessment of reality, particularly since it disqualified the rational and scientific approaches to truth. Is there a cosmic spirit permeating the natural world, and a mind or soul in each human being reflecting nature, a "ghost in the machine," or do only biological and physical laws operate in the universe? Perhaps the tran-

A. V. Schlabach, *The Development of American Philosophy* (Boston: Houghton Mifflin Co., 1960). To consult the primary sources see Ralph Waldo Emerson, *The Complete Works of Ralph Waldo Emerson* (Boston: Houghton Mifflin Co., 1903–1904), especially *Nature: Addresses and Lectures*, Vol. I; Walt Whitman, *The Complete Works of Walt Whitman* (New York: G. P. Putnam's Sons, 1902), especially *Democratic Vistas*, Vol. II; and the works of Theodore Parker and William Ellery Channing, respectively.

scendentalists felt the force of conscience so strongly that it seemed an obligation from outside themselves (which may also explain Socrates' *daimon* or moral voice), and perhaps their entrancement with nature was so great that they imagined an animistic spirit within natural phenomena. This is the metaphysical question that has come down to us from the transcendentalists, and our acceptance of their ethical theory depends upon our answer to it.

▶ <u>STOICISM</u>. To examine naturalism in the form of Stoicism, we must go back to ancient Rome. Stoicism was a philosophy most closely identified with Seneca (c. 5 B.C.–A.D. 65), Epictetus (c. A.D. 55–c. 135), and Marcus Aurelius (A.D. 121–180), but its intellectual framework lay in the Greek thought of Zeno of Citium (c. 334–262 B.C.) and Chrysippus (c. 280–207 B.C.). The term derived from the painted *stoa* (or colonnade) where Zeno taught in Athens.

Stoic Theory. The Stoic philosophy was a blend of Greek rationality, Roman practicality, and an abiding theological belief in *logos*, which is an active, divine, and rational force informing every aspect of the universe. The external manifestations of nature were considered to be expressions of *logos*, and the spiritual force within directed all natural events in an orderly and purposive way. As in transcendentalism, there was in Stoicism the idea of a divine power coursing through nature, but the power was considered to be rational and, therefore, comprehensible through the human intellect. And God and nature were so closely identified that the universe was sometimes spoken of as a living whole; the physical world was considered the body of God, its inherent *logos* God's very spirit.

According to the Stoics, nothing occurs in vain or by chance in this universe suffused with divine reason, and the good for human beings therefore lies in conforming to its benevolent purposes. We must live "in harmony with nature,"[7] acting "with good reason in the selection of what is natural,"[8] and "hold fast to the things that

---

7. Epictetus, *The Works of Epictetus*, trans. E. Carter (Boston: Little Brown, 1865), Chapter I, p. 6.
8. Diogenes Laertius, *Lives of Eminent Philosophers*, trans. R. D. Hicks (Cambridge, MA: Harvard University Press, 1950), Chapter VII, p. 88.

---

are by nature fit to be chosen; for indeed we are born for this."[9] By definition, nothing that is natural can be evil in any ultimate sense, and it is childish of people to fear or criticize natural occurrences. It is equally foolish to seek our life purpose anywhere except in universal nature and the answering call of our human nature. "Do not look around thee to discover other men's ruling principles, but look straight to this, to what nature leads thee . . . following thy own nature and the common nature."[10] As in much Eastern philosophy, the inner and the outer are one; internal and external nature are fundamentally the same, and both embody the workings of reason.[11]

When the rational governance of the universe is understood, a necessary pattern of events is revealed, for nothing happens fortuitously or by chance. A rigid predestination operates throughout the natural world, an infinite chain of causes and effects to which human beings too are linked in their physical life. The fatalistic universe always works for the good of the whole but no material event is free from its ineluctable progress, including the events that constitute the outer experience of human beings. The happenings of human life are wholly beyond our control despite the fact that some actions may appear to be the result of our will. All events occur as they must and we have no choice in the matter. As in the case of material objects, everything that befalls us is part of the necessary design, a thread in the tapestry of destiny.

However, human beings are not only physical entities any more than the universe is purely material. We have an inner spirit that is capable of responding to the inevitable occurrences in our lives. Events may be predestined but our attitude toward those events is not; here we possess free will and are our own masters. Our reaction to fate lies within our own power.

Although we are free in our response to nature's inevitable decrees, if we are wise we will respond in a positive and rational way. We

9. Epictetus, *Works*, Chapter II, p. 10.
10. Marcus Aurelius Antoninus, *The Meditations of the Emperor Marcus Aurelius Antoninus*, trans. George Long (New York: A. L. Burt, 1864), Chapter VII, p. 55, and Chapter V, p. 2.
11. Several of the Eastern religions contain basic ideas which parallel those of Stoicism, including the Hindu and Buddhist belief that we must free ourselves from desire; the Confucian ideal of "*li*" or equanimity, poise, and decorum; and the Taoist notion of passivity, quietism, and receptivity to the harmonious flow of the universe. The *Tao Te Ching*, for example, says, "There is no greater calamity than not to be contented."

can rail against our fate, which is particularly tempting when trage-
dies occur, but that would be pointless and, in a sense, blasphemous.
We cannot do anything about the diseases or disasters that afflict us,
neither to prevent nor to avoid them, and since destiny is ultimately
good it ought not to be opposed in any case. Just as the Christian or
Jew says that, despite the suffering we experience, we must have faith
that God is good, the Stoic believes that everything happens for the
best in a world governed by the divine logos of nature.

The only rational and moral response, then, is to condone
actively whatever occurs. Not only should we accept our lot in life
and remain poised and tranquil even in the face of catastrophe, but
we should positively endorse whatever circumstances fate has ordained for us. Although our emotional reaction to disasters might
be anxiety or frustration, curses or rebellion, we should exercise
rational control over our feelings; we must behave with equanimity
and maintain an attitude of calm approval. "Ask not that events
should happen as you will," Epictetus advised, "but let your will be
that events should happen as they do, and you should have peace."
Any other attitude is foolish and contrary to our duty to follow
nature's will.

Intelligent persons distinguish between that which is within
their control, principally their mental attitude, and that which is
not, namely, external events. They realize that their well being depends on knowing the difference between the two, accepting what
they cannot change and intelligently managing that which is within
their control. Nothing can be done about a drought or a plague but
we can cultivate the right attitude toward these disasters and achieve
inner peace of mind. As Epictetus stated, we should "make the best
of what is in our power, and take the rest as it occurs," separating
"what is *ours*, and what is not *ours*—what is right, and what is wrong.
I must die, and must I die groaning too? I must be fettered; must I
be lamenting too? I must be exiled; and what hinders me, then, but
that I may go smiling, and cheerful, and serene? 'Betray a secret.' I
will not betray it, for this is in my own power. 'Then I will fetter you.'
What do you say, man? Fetter me? You will fetter my leg, but not
Zeus himself can get the better of my free will."[12]

12. Epictetus, *Works*, Chapter I, p. 6. Cf. the following statement by the Roman Stoic
and Platonist Boethius (c. 480–c. 524), from his famous book *The Consolation of
Philosophy*. Boethius was wrongly imprisoned by Theodoric the Great after a life of

Our essential self, then, possesses free will, which means that we are capable of gaining power over our lives in a very basic sense. But in order to do this, we must agree to be ruled by our rationality. Only reason can give us freedom because it enables us to recognize those circumstances which we cannot change and to rise above them, not allowing any physical happening to affect the felt quality of our existence.

Conformity to nature, therefore, has a deeper meaning than it appeared to have at the outset. To the Stoic it signified following the rational part of our being that corresponds to the rational spirit within nature. It also meant using this rationality to realize that all operations of nature are beneficial to the universe at large and therefore should be approved. We cannot control our fate but we can and should actively assent to it, and by this assent we will lead tranquil and satisfying lives. In our inner and inaccessible being we will remain unharmed by any catastrophe and pass through life in a serene manner, confident that the divine spirit moving through the natural order will inevitably bring about the ultimate good. In this way we will attain the ideal state of *apatheia,* the complete absence of feeling or emotional involvement.

Stoicism Critically Evaluated. The Stoic approach to successful living is extremely appealing at times of insecurity when people live in unsafe conditions and the political and social order is in ferment—which was the case during the later period of the Roman Empire. In such times, the tendency is to turn inward for our well being rather than relying upon anything external, to concentrate on the satisfactions that are within our power to achieve and not the external goods of life that are beyond our reach and, therefore, uncertain. We are impressed by the fact that our health or safety

outstanding public service. He wrote the following words in prison one year before he was executed: "He who has calmly reconciled his life to fate, and set proud death beneath his feet, can look fortune in the face, unbending both to good and bad. . . . Why then stand wretched and aghast when fierce tyrants rage in impotence? Fear naught, and hope naught: thus shall you have a weak man's rage disarmed. But whoso fears with trembling, or desires aught from them, he stands not firmly rooted, but dependent: he has thrown away his shield; he can be rooted up, and he links for himself the very chain whereby he may be dragged." [Boethius, *The Consolation of Philosophy*, trans. W. V. Cooper (New York: Modern Library, 1943), p. 8.]

cannot be guaranteed any more than we can count on gaining wealth or fame; and if we pin our hopes on these things, we may well be disappointed. But we can take the proper attitude toward anything that occurs, and even find contentment in pain or poverty.

This polished sphere of Stoic philosophy can be attractive today also when economic conditions are so unstable in the West. People often feel that they have little power over their wealth or their positions, that larger economic forces determine their fate. Working hard will not ensure employment, a record of success will not ward off economic ruin, and, in general, achievement will not guarantee any personal rewards. The system is no longer expected to keep its promise of providing to those who do their part. Rather, people feel that their efforts are largely inconsequential in affecting their economic future; what happens is outside their control.

However, adherence to Stoic attitudes can be problematic. There are four main criticisms, to which we now turn.

(1) By adopting the Stoic approach, either in ancient Rome or contemporary America, we may be turning away from the world too much, denying ourselves its benefits in order to minimize its pains and the possibility of disappointment. We might be inclined to take too few chances and therefore gain less than we could. In brief, our concern with avoiding discomfort can severely limit our satisfactions, making our lives more cramped and stultified than they need be.

This point has often been made against the Stoic mentality, which seems overly concerned with personal control and ensuring peace of mind to the detriment of fullness of living. In this Stoicism echoes a recurrent theme in Eastern philosophy and religion (especially Buddhism) that attachments to this world render us subject to pain at their loss. According to this view, if we love or desire nothing, then we are invulnerable. But surely certain satisfactions are worth the risk of attendant pain.

Furthermore, if we adopt the Stoic viewpoint, we may become convinced that we have less control over our affairs than we actually do, resigning ourselves to our fate when we should be masters of it. We might be inclined to make the best of our situation or make a virtue of alleged necessities when an expenditure of effort could improve our circumstances. In short, by following Stoicism we tend to underestimate the degree of control we have over external events, and, lacking confidence in our own powers, give up before we have adequately tested our ability to change our lives.

A first criticism of Stoicism, then, is that it needlessly constricts our lives by advising us to forgo certain anticipated satisfactions for fear of disappointment (much as Epicureanism does), and to accept various circumstances that we well might be able to alter. It seems far better to try to gain all we can out of life even though we run the risk of pain or frustration. Being safe is no substitute for being fully alive. Our efforts may be fruitless but that is hardly a good reason to avoid trying for a richer life. *"Abstine et sustine,"* "abstain and endure," is a sad motto for living.

(2) This leads to a second criticism, which has to do with the Stoic belief in fate ruling all external events. Obviously, there is no point in trying to improve our situation if we have no control over it. However, few people today believe in the doctrine of a predetermined fate; it has lost the widespread acceptance it had in the ancient world (see pages 64–66). Even contemporary Christianity holds a strongly limited view of providence, which allows for free will and our consequent responsibility to God for the lives we lead.

Although predeterminism has been discarded more than disproven, the grounds offered by the Stoics for its acceptance appear to be extremely weak. The Stoic argument is that all past events are frozen in time and cannot be altered by any act of will; as the English poet John Dryden wrote, "Not heaven itself upon the past has power." Certain future events are also unalterable, such as the succession of night and day and the inevitability of our deaths. From these considerations the Stoic concluded that, since the past and part of the future are fixed and determined, we can assume that *all* temporal events occur in accordance with the plan of destiny. The entire universe, past, present, and future, is one bloc, a predetermined whole.

Great acumen is not needed to detect the fallacies in this reasoning. From the fact that one class of phenomena, that is, past events, are unchanging, we cannot infer that another class of phenomena, namely, future events, are unchangeable. Equally illogical is the claim that because some future occurrences are inevitable, therefore the future is as fixed as the past. This is technically referred to as the *fallacy of composition*, for it claims that what is true of the part is true of the whole. Not only is the logic faulty, but one cannot claim that there are future necessities or inevitabilities—even with regard to common-sense notions such as day following night and human mortality. The earth could cease its rotation at some point in time, and if we should control the aging process, then it will not be true that people must die. No future event is certain to occur; only the conclusion to a logical train of reasoning may be called certain.[13]

(3) In addition to the weaknesses in the arguments for predeterminism, another objection against Stoicism pertains to the fact that a doctrine of predestination makes all effort pointless. This has become such a standard objection that it has acquired a name: the *lazy argument*. According to this criticism there would be no point in doing anything at all if every event were predestined. We could simply lie about, confident that to do so was fated. Furthermore, no one would be accountable for anything that occurred since events must happen as they do. No person would be guilty of having done anything wrong but would be regarded as an innocent instrument in the hands of destiny. Blame or praise would be inappropriate just as punishment or reward would be. (Of course, if a person was imprisoned for a crime, that imprisonment could always be treated as having been predestined, but it could not be regarded as punishment for wrongdoing or an attempt to reform the criminal.)

There is some question as to the extent to which our will has an effect on our actions according to the Stoic system. It would seem odd to believe that when a person decides to throw a rock, and the rock then flies from the person's hand, the internal decision had nothing to do with the external event of the rock hurtling through

---

13. Another Stoic argument for predeterminism (to which we can only refer) is that statements about events are either true or false; they do not become true or false relative to future happenings. We may know in the future whether a statement is true or false but the statement is not made true or false by subsequent events. The proposition "There will be a world war" does not become true when war breaks out but is verified as being true at that time. Therefore, the Stoic would argue, a true proposition about the future states an unavoidable event, a false proposition, an impossibility.

This problem, of whether there can be true propositions about the future has been extensively debated among logicians. Aristotle, for example, took the position that truth refers to reality, which encompasses only the past and the present. The future is not real and therefore no proposition about the future can be true now; it can only become true as the future passes into the present.

the air. The Stoic is rather vague on this point, sometimes extending the power of will only as far as speech (as when Epictetus said he would not betray a secret) and sometimes implying a greater degree of power over our actions. By and large Stoicism separated volition and action in a radical way, and this produced certain paradoxes which have plagued the movement from its inception. And if the Stoic did not see the will as causing events to occur, then all effort would be fruitless and the "lazy argument" would be valid. Why try, after all, if nothing we do makes any difference, and why hold people responsible for anything that happens?

Another way of presenting the objection is to say that if we do believe a connection exists between will and action, and if we do think people are largely responsible for their conduct, then we are rejecting the validity of Stoic predeterminism. One way of criticizing an ethical theory is to show that its consequences violate certain basic beliefs and contradict our moral experience. Stoicism does this, and its philosophical standpoint becomes highly questionable.

(4) A final criticism has to do with the impoverishment of our emotional life that comes about when we only allow ourselves to respond to events in practical and beneficial ways. For example, if we were concerned about someone we love who is undergoing surgery, the Stoic would advise us to rationally suppress our emotional concern because it serves no useful purpose; it does not help the situation and it works against our peace of mind. But in this case, we are feeling concern not because we think it will do any good but as a result of our love for the person; our concern is not meant to be a cause of anything but is an effect of our caring. And to refuse to feel this emotion would mean a stifling or suppression of our love—a love which is expressed by concern.

If the Stoic recommendation were carried out, it would make genuine love impossible, for the emotions associated with love are not always "useful." A great deal of our emotional life, in fact, would be disallowed because it "does not do any good" in the way of producing changes in our circumstances; it would be considered "wasted emotion." But surely we want to have the full range of emotional experience, including those emotions that serve no practical purpose. And the very process of controlling our emotions to the extent advocated by the Stoic is destructive in itself. To allow ourselves only to feel certain emotions severely reduces our openness, sensitivity, spontaneity, and involvement, and transforms the richness of feeling which human beings are capable of enjoying to a carefully regulated set of prudential and advantageous responses. It would seem very odd for a person to say, "I will feel a certain emotion if it is helpful; otherwise I will not feel it." Reason might be used to tell us whether we have any real cause for worry or rejoicing, but it should not function to limit our emotions to those that are practical. Blaise Pascal (1623–1662) once remarked "There are two equally dangerous extremes, to shut reason out, and to let nothing else in." The Stoic obviously commits the latter mistake.

This attitude is characteristic of the authoritarian person who is highly controlled, rational, and deliberate. The authoritarian (as contrasted with the democratic) personality has such a rigid structure of responses that any genuine reactions are deeply buried beneath an extensive defense system. To be affected by genuine emotion means to risk a crack in the foundation of the personality, threatening it with collapse; therefore, a strict, strong, implacable, enameled surface is presented to the world. But such strength is basically weakness, for it is grounded in an anxiety about exposing oneself; the person is most afraid of being unguarded, that is, of being himself and vulnerable. The real person lies cowering behind an elaborate network of fortifications.

Oddly enough, this self-protective attitude that is assumed to provide freedom from injury becomes the opposite of authentic freedom, for one locks oneself away from others and oneself, becoming separate and self-alienated. The fortress is actually a prison, with little nourishment being delivered from outside the walls; the person feeds off the self like a snake swallowing its own tail; he or she cannot be injured very readily but also cannot communicate with others or be touched by them. In gaining the invulnerability of a citadel (in the form of an obsessively ordered routine, or psychological calluses that make the individual unable to feel, or machine-like performance, or membership in a hierarchical organization), the authoritarian personality loses his or her reality as a person. Petrified by fear, the individual becomes part of the castle rock itself, unassailable and less than human.

It should also be added that genuine independence does not come through total self-dependence but by being secure enough within ourselves to risk depending on people and happenings external to us. Because of their insecurity, those who espouse the Stoic attitude are afraid to rely upon anyone or anything except themselves, thereby showing that they are not in command of their lives at all.

All four of these criticisms make the Stoic doctrine questionable as a theory of ethics. Following nature as Stoicism would have us do tends to constrict our conduct, to make moral effort futile, and generally to impoverish our emotional life. And as we have seen, the belief in predeterminism, which lies at the heart of Stoicism, can be questioned as a metaphysical description of the way in which the universe actually functions.

RECAPITULATION

In this chapter, we have examined the major types of naturalistic ethics, beginning with the naturalism of Thoreau, the nineteenth century romantic poets, and above all, the "be natural" movement. This theory was criticized in various ways and certain questions were raised about the value of country living, how "natural" is to be defined, and how much of a model for wise living nature actually is.

A second variety of naturalism was then discussed, namely, the view that the order of nature embodies a divine essence. American transcendentalism was treated as representative of this approach and, more importantly for our purposes, ancient Stoicism. The defects of both positions were analyzed, particularly Stoicism, in terms of its doctrine of predeterminism and its implications for morality and the emotions.[14]

---

14. For an exhaustive discussion of the self and naturalism see C. Taylor, *Sources of the Self: The Making of the Modern Identity* (Cambridge, MA: Harvard University Press, 1989).

1. Describe and criticize the "natural life" as an ideal for the good life.

2. Explain the philosophy of transcendentalism and show how it is a form of naturalism despite its spiritual dimension.

3. How is free will possible within a Stoic system? In what ways does the Stoic live in harmony with nature?

4. Discuss the grounds on which Stoicism maintains that all external events are fated. Why would you agree or disagree?

5. Explain and evaluate "the lazy argument" as a criticism of the Stoic ethic.

8

EVOLUTIONISM

 third type of nature theory is far removed from the "be natural" ethic and the spiritual-centered naturalism of transcendentalism and Stoicism. This is the evolutionary theory of ethics advocated principally by Charles Darwin (1809–1882), Herbert Spencer (1820–1903), and, somewhat less importantly, by T. H. Huxley (1825–1895). Evolutionism differs from the first type of naturalism principally in looking to the inner process of nature's development, not just the external phenomena; but in finding the processes to be basically natural rather than supernatural, it differs markedly from the transcendentalist or Stoic assumptions as well.

Evolutionism created a furor at its inception when Darwin published *The Origin of Species* in 1859, because it opposed several of the articles of orthodox religious belief. The Bible stated that "God made the beast of the earth after its kind, and the cattle after their

kind, and every thing that creepeth upon the ground after its kind"
(*Genesis*, Chapter 1, verse 25). In other words, there were fixed
species created at a certain point in time, all of which are in existence now (having been preserved by Noah). Darwin opposed this
tableau with the theory that a sequence of progressively more sophisticated species developed over a period of millions of years.
Using evidence from fossil records and the bones of animals (com-
parative paleontology), Darwin concluded that one species emerged
from another, and that the origin of all species consisted of specks
of protoplasmic jelly in the scum of tides. Microorganisms developed
from these bits of protoplasm by the action of the sun's rays, and all
organic life subsequently evolved from them. Darwin maintained that
the process of evolution was really a movement from greater homogeneity to greater heterogeneity among organisms, and from lesser to
greater integration of functions. The less integrated and homoge-
neous species evolved to more integrated, heterogeneous forms, with
various reversals along the way. During glacial periods, for example,
there was a devolution to more elementary forms but, in general, a
gradual upward movement had occurred; that is, a genuine evolution
had taken place and not mere change.

The second radical aspect of the theory of evolution was the
claim that this process had not only been ongoing through time but
that an explanatory principle could account for it; this was the principle of *natural selection*. Those species that had the proper adaptations to their environments produced offspring so that they were
perpetuated, whereas those species that did not possess the requisite
adaptations perished in the struggle for survival and their lines were
extinguished. A continual warfare occurred in nature for the means
of life, which took the form of battles for territory, sexual domi-
nance, and food, and to the victors went the spoils of continued
existence. The strongest species were able to dominate an area, and
drive out or exterminate other species in the competition for the
available land and food supply. In the same way, within a given
species those particular members that were strongest were able to
drive off competitors and to mate, thus carrying forward a successful
strain for the species. The weaker members did not reproduce their
own kind, and their poorer characteristics were eliminated through
the natural-selection process. Thus, only the fittest members of the
fittest species were able to survive.

Darwin's theory of evolution is now treated as commonplace biology and a natural law rather than a scientific theory. Few, if any, biologists doubt its basic premises, although certain biologists such as J. B. de Lamarck (1744–1829) and T. D. Lysenko (1898–1977) proposed an unusual interpretation of the way in which evolution operates, arguing that species can acquire new characteristics through interactions with their environment and genetically transmit these changes to their offspring; the orthodox Darwinian interpretation is that those species already possessing certain genetically determined variations are "selected for" by competition. But the scandal that Darwinism caused in the nineteenth century was due mainly to the challenge it offered to the religious position. Not only did the theory of evolution assert an origin of species but it accounted for the characteristics of species and all order in the world, not as God's work necessarily but as the result of natural selection.

DARWINISM AND RELIGION

▶ **THE ARGUMENT FROM DESIGN**. Prior to Darwin's writings, theologians had frequently employed the *teleological argument* in their apologetics in attempting to prove the existence of God. This argument, first stated by St. Thomas Aquinas in *Summa Theologica*, pointed to the regularity and orderliness of the natural world, its apparent design and harmonious arrangement. And the conclusion they reached was that design necessarily implies a designer, order entails belief in an orderer, a plan means a planner must exist. If the universe presents itself as a vast architectural scheme, there has to be a cosmic architect, and if nature is a work of art, with brush strokes visible in every landscape, then God exists as the divine artist.

More specifically, the teleological argument, or the argument from design, trades upon such facts as the rotation of the earth around the sun, which occurs in an arc to bring about the changing seasons and at a perfect distance from the sun's heat to sustain life;

the ability of human beings to eat plants and animals and the avail-ability of edible plants and animals for people to eat; the marvelous functioning of the human body, its intricately balanced and inter-meshing systems and organs, its delicate chemistry. Or, within the animal kingdom, the argument from design points to the ideal dis-tribution of attributes needed by the various species: the hard shell of the turtle, without which it would be practically defenseless, the ability of the chameleon to escape detection by changing into the color of its background, the giraffe's long neck, which enables it to eat the leaves at the tops of trees, and so forth.

None of these remarkable phenomena could be adequately explained, it was claimed, without the assumption of a conscious and intelligent designer of creation, that is to say, a god. William Paley (1743–1805) buttressed this argument from design with his famous watchmaker analogy, arguing that if we found a watch upon the ground in perfect working order, with the gears properly posi-tioned so as to interlock, the teeth, pointer, and balance all of the right shape and size to regulate the motion, the wheels made of brass to keep them from rusting, a spring of flexible steel, and glass over the face where a transparent material is required, we would be forced to conclude "that the watch must have had a maker . . . who formed it for the purpose which we find it actually to answer." By analogy, when we encounter the intricate mechanism of the world we must infer that it too had a maker; the parts could not have fallen together by chance in just the right combination to produce a per-fectly functioning system. "There cannot be a design without a de-signer," Paley wrote, "contrivance without a contriver; order without choice; arrangement without anything capable of arranging." That is, unless we assume "the presence of intelligence and mind" the world in its orderliness is inexplicable.[1]

▶ **DARWIN'S ALTERNATIVE EXPLANATION**. Darwin, however, offered an alternative explanation to account for the ideal arrangement of the physical world. He argued that if turtles had not possessed hard shells, chameleons their ability to alter their skin

---

1. W. Paley, *Natural Theology* (London: J. Faulder, 1809), pp. 3 and 11. See also Chapters VIII to X, and XIX to XXII.

pigmentation, or giraffes their extended necks, they would probably not have continued in existence as a species. These were the adaptations that were needed by them for survival; therefore, it is not remarkable that these and other surviving species possess these adaptations. It is no more astonishing that animals have their necessary attributes than that all Olympic winners are good athletes; if they were not good athletes, they would not be Olympic winners. In the same way Darwin explained the perfect position of the earth relative to the sun, the edibleness of plants and animals, and the efficient functioning of the human body: If these factors had been different, then human life or indeed any life might not have existed (as it does not exist on less favorably positioned planets). Therefore, it is reasonable to expect the elements needed for life to be present; otherwise there would not be any life.

In short, Darwin proposed a scientific theory of evolution to account for the orderliness of the universe, using the concepts of natural selection and survival of the fittest, and in this way undercut the teleological argument for God's existence. A naturalistic theory was presented in place of a supernaturalistic one, and it explained the biological facts more adequately. For example, it is difficult to account for extinct species such as dinosaurs using the Biblical account of creation, but they can be understood in terms of the Darwinian assumption that these species lacked the adaptations necessary for survival.

Theologians found it difficult to argue against Darwin's theory, although some tried to retain a portion of the teleological argument by claiming that God lay behind evolution, and that he used the process of evolution as his device in forming the universe. The billions of years of biological history, reckoned in the scale of human time, was sometimes viewed as corresponding to the six days of creation described in *Genesis*, a day in the life of God being that much longer. But even this modest interpretation met with considerable resistance because of a rule of thought called *Occam's razor*, also known as the *law of parsimony*. Named for its originator, William of Occam (1300–1349), this rule states that an explanation should not be compounded beyond what is required. As applied to this case, since the theory of evolution alone can explain the orderliness and arrangement of the physical world, we need not have recourse to a further explanation in the form of a divine being behind evolution.

Debate about this point persists to the present day, but, by and large, Darwin's work seriously undermined the teleological argument so that theologians became reluctant to use it as a basic proof of God's existence. It should be emphasized that the theory of evolution did not disprove the existence of God but, at best, only showed the teleological argument for God's existence to be faulty. God may exist, but the argument from design was pointed up as a dubious way of trying to prove it. Nevertheless, since this argument had been a mainstay of theology, its loss or diminished status was felt as a powerful blow to religious belief. Furthermore, Darwin's writings were regarded as supporting a naturalistic alternative to the religious *Weltanschauung* or world view; in that sense, Darwinism presented a more general threat to religion. It regarded the universe as essentially indifferent to the teeming life on earth.

DARWINISM AND ETHICS

▶ **SOCIAL DARWINISM**. Some of the ethical implications drawn from the theory of evolution were also disturbing, particularly the more literal interpretations such as social Darwinism (also discussed in Chapter 1, pages 13–15.) According to these readings, the evolutionary development of the natural world was thought to provide a clear model for human behavior. The principles of conduct that should govern human interactions were seen as having been manifest in the law of survival of the fittest, and the overall purpose of life as having been revealed by nature's thrust toward perpetuating existence in more advanced forms. Anything that promotes the survival of more complex and better integrated forms of life was declared good, and whatever impedes evolutionary development was declared bad. In this view, if we allow the law of the jungle to operate and the fittest alone to survive, then our conduct is right, for the main direction of evolution is thereby abetted, but if we interfere with the course of evolution by helping the unfit to survive, then our conduct is ethically wrong. In evolutionary terms, following the ways of nature was taken to mean emulating in human life the operation of nature's laws so that continual progress would be achieved.

Using this doctrine, the "robber barons" or industrial entrepreneurs of the late nineteenth century attempted to justify various types of exploitation, including low wages and long hours, arguing that their financial success revealed their fitness to succeed; it showed they were brighter, stronger, and more capable than other people, and therefore deserved their wealth and social position. By the same token, those who failed to succeed thereby showed their unfitness for success, and their low status was justified on evolutionary grounds. (Poverty was, in fact, considered shameful because it indicated that the poor did not have "what it takes.") The entrepreneurs and their apologists argued that it was not unjust that certain people succeeded, that they had used unscrupulous means and therefore did not deserve their success, because the fact that they had succeeded legitimized their success. They had thereby shown themselves to be superior individuals in an evolutionary sense, that is, the highest members of their species who could then transmit their outstanding qualities to their offspring; in this way the human race was strengthened and improved.

Following the same reasoning, social welfare programs were sometimes condemned as offering artificial help to the feebler members of the species, thereby enabling the unfit to survive. It was considered contrary to nature to have minimum wage laws, social security programs, retirement benefits, health-care plans, and so forth; even unionization was considered immoral because it permitted the weak to band together against the strong. All of these were thought to run counter to natural evolution, for they allowed lazy or defective people, the misfits, the infirm, and the aged to be carried on the backs of the competent and the industrious. With this approach of supporting the weak and allowing their weaknesses to be perpetuated for generations, the entire species would deteriorate and the evolutionary process, as realized through natural selection, would be thwarted.

We have experienced the same thinking in the 1980s under Reaganomics, when a militant capitalism was championed. Economists such as Milton Friedman argued that business has no social responsibility, and people should practice the work ethic rather than expect handouts. The climate of the times was opposed to "entitlements" such as welfare, student loans, and Medicare, and self-help was lauded, not government-assistance programs. The underlying assumption was that those who succeeded deserved their success and owed nothing to those who happened to fail in the free-market competition.

► FALLACIES IN SOCIAL DARWINISM

Social Circumstances versus Inherent Qualities. This rather superficial reading of Darwin is, of course, fraught with flaws. One point that the nineteenth century entrepreneurs and the twentieth century capitalists neglected is that people do not necessarily succeed or fail because of their inherent qualities. A great deal depends on circumstances such as the opportunities that are available, luck and timing, contracts, financial backing, and so forth. For example, a person who inherits ownership of a railroad needed to transport an essential product such as wheat or oil is in a good position to make a great deal of money, and if that individual subsequently becomes a millionaire it will be mainly due to these favorable circumstances rather than superior intelligence, industry, or competence. Antitrust legislation was enacted, in fact, because of the realization that owners of monopolies have an unfair advantage over others. Financially successful persons, then, do not necessarily deserve their wealth by virtue of having superior natural abilities, and the poor are not necessarily poor as a result of their biological deficiencies; many impoverished people are simply unfortunate victims of social forces. There does not seem to be any natural hierarchy in society which correlates directly with people's inherent qualities.

Of course, some Marxists would say that even if there were such a hierarchy it would be an unfair one because people would have been rewarded for abilities they happened to inherit. Gifted people, they argue, have a greater responsibility to give to society because of their exceptional attributes rather than having a greater claim on society's goods. Hence the Marxist dictum, "From each according to his abilities," to which is added "and to each according to his needs."

In any case, no automatic correlation between success and inherent qualities exists. Those at the top of the economic and social scale do not necessarily have superior natural attributes of the kind that can be genetically transmitted. The genes of the wealthy do not enrich the human race more than the genes of the poor. The economically successful people are not necessarily the most outstanding biological specimens; in fact, they may not be the fittest at all but only the most fortunate.

The Fittest versus the Best. The concept of the fittest has been subject to various criticisms including the fact that it is circular, for an organism is called "fit" because it survives, and it survives because it is fit. But a more substantive criticism has to do with the implicit assumption that the fittest means the best. That is, it is not at all certain that the victors in the struggle for survival can be equated with the finest of a species, particularly the human species. People who are deceitful and ruthless, self-centered, and manipulative, for example, may have the qualities that fit them for success, but that is not the profile of the most admirable type of person. The fact that such a person succeeds does not mean that he or she deserves that success in the sense of having excellent attributes. The worst people may, in fact, "win" and the best may "lose," but ethically speaking that is no index of what they "deserve" in terms of their character traits. The fact that some people achieve worldly success where others fail does not show that the former are the fittest in the sense of being the best of the human race, nor are their characteristics necessarily the ones we would want perpetuated, either biologically or through the social environment.

Obviously, we would not prefer the human race to consist of people who cannot survive, for that would lead to the extinction of humanity, but neither would we want the race to be composed of individuals who have the characteristics needed for survival but are deficient in moral character. In the latter case, the human race would continue to exist, but in a shameful condition; and it is questionable whether a race of morally unfit people is worth preserving. Rather than either of these extremes, it would seem preferable to promote as an ideal individuals of good character who have sufficient survival ability to maintain themselves in existence. In other words, we should value moral character above mere survival skills while not denying the importance of succeeding in the struggle for existence.

Civilization versus the State of Nature. Civilization has as one of its primary purposes the fostering of a high level of cultural development rather than the simple preservation of existence. Instead of the harsh principle of survival of the fittest that pertains in nature, civilization aims at a refinement of conduct, taste, and thought that transcends sheer survival. And rather than importing the brutal law of the jungle into civilization, it seems preferable to push back the jungle with the standards of civilization, to build a garden in the wilderness rather than allowing the wilderness into the garden.

In keeping with this aim, we would not want to duplicate the brutal competitiveness characteristic of many animals in a state of nature but rather build into our civilized world some moral improvements over nature such as care for the elderly and medical treatment for the sick and injured. In this way the infirm and disabled will be shown compassion and will not be abandoned as unfit for survival. Instead of following nature in its awful aspects, we can improve upon nature and live like human beings, closer to angels than beasts.

SPENCER'S EVOLUTIONARY ETHIC

Some of these points were recognized by the more astute proponents of evolutionism, including Herbert Spencer; we will examine his theory as an example of these more sophisticated systems of ethics based on evolution.

▶ LONGEVITY VERSUS RICHNESS OF EXISTENCE.

Like other evolutionists, Spencer was certainly concerned with the longevity of the human race and the maintenance of individual lives, for he wrote that "other things equal, conduct is right or wrong according as its special acts . . . do or do not further the general end of self-preservation."[2] Spencer clearly recognized that survival is a necessary condition without which all other values become impossible. He also agreed with the overall position of evolutionary ethics "that the conduct to which we apply the name good is the relatively more evolved conduct; and that bad is the name we apply to conduct which is relatively less evolved."[3] But he placed special and unique emphasis on what he called breadth or fullness of life, which is the supreme value and the goal of evolution. The richer our lives the better.

The meaning of richness can be understood by examples Spencer drew from biology. The oyster, for instance, may live longer than the cuttlefish, but the oyster's life consists only of streaming water through itself and absorbing nutrients, while the cuttlefish has more numerous and varied activities; in that respect, the cuttlefish experiences a higher mode of existence. The earthworm too, living in a secure and protected environment in the soil, might have a longer life than an insect exposed above ground. But the insect, Spencer wrote, "during its existence as larvae and pupae may experience a greater quantity of the changes which constitute life."

With regard to human beings, he made the same point: Civilized people may have shorter life spans than savages, but they have a greater aggregate of thoughts, feelings, and actions. Spencer thought that greater breadth of life tends to increase longevity also for he wrote that "each further evolution of conduct widens the aggregate of actions while conducing to elongation of it." In other words, more evolved means broader and richer, but along with this usually comes greater longevity. Length of life seems to follow richness of life in an automatic way, so that with the improvements of civilization modern people live longer than did primitive people. However, even if this were not true, Spencer favored breadth of life as the actual and ideal goal of evolution.

▶ **COOPERATION VERSUS INDIVIDUALISM.** Breadth of life, to Spencer, did not just mean whatever is more complex and varied but a *moral* existence also, which takes into account the har-

---

2. H. Spencer, *The Data of Ethics* (New York: A. L. Burt, 1897), p. 26.
3. H. Spencer, *The Principles of Ethics* (New York: D. Appleton and Co., 1895), Vol. I, p. 15.

monious development of the race. He saw evolution as tending toward a fullness of life that includes concern for the welfare of others. According to Spencer, the line of evolution does not lead to a selfish individualism but to cooperation and community, which are essential to the survival and satisfaction of human beings, individually and as a species.

Although conflict now occurs between the individual and the group over their separate interests, Spencer believed that, in the long run, the two will be recognized as not being at variance. At some advanced stage of evolution, when an understanding is achieved of the interrelatedness between society and the individual, this conflict will disappear and human beings will live in peace. Altruism will completely replace egoism as the human race evolves to the moral stage of development. "Conduct gains ethical sanction," Spencer wrote, "in proportion as the activities becoming less and less militant and more and more industrial, are such as do not necessitate mutual injury or hindrance, but consist with, and are furthered by, cooperation and mutual aid."

In taking this position, Spencer was actually following the lead of Darwin, who wrote, "The term, general good, may be defined as the rearing of the greatest number of individuals in full vigour and health, with all their faculties perfect, under the conditions to which they are subjected."[4] Spencer then went on to say that rearing and preserving healthy, vigorous individuals could only be brought about by mutual justice and consideration among people. Since human beings possess a capacity for sympathy and are able to retain past experiences, social justice is thereby able to flourish.

Spencer elaborated and developed this idea of social justice and cooperation as an intrinsic part of evolutionary development by arguing that mutual helpfulness rather than competition tends to promote breadth of life for the group and, consequently, for the individual. When a community cooperates, each individual benefits from the goodness of the whole, and the species is advanced by the efforts of each of its members "to further the complete living of others." Murder, for example, is not justified because it works against the good of the species but, at the same time, refraining from murdering does not involve any self-sacrifice because everyone

4. C. Darwin, *The Descent of Man* (New York: D. Appleton and Co., 1876), p. 612.

profits from having a nonthreatening environment. Benevolent conduct therefore furthers evolution and is good; selfishness runs counter to the evolutionary flow and is no way sanctioned by the law of survival of the fittest.

> ► **SPENCER'S THEORY AND HEDONISM**. Spencer also noted that those activities conducive to survival and richness of living are also the ones that bring pleasure, and those that are destructive bring displeasure and suffering. Thus, by seeking pleasure, human beings as well as other species act in ways that promote their continued existence. For example, eating brings pleasure through the experience of taste, and consuming food, of course, is necessary for survival. Rest provides the pleasure of refreshment from fatigue, and shelter offers the pleasures of warmth and comfort; both rest and shelter are vital to human existence. Spencer also mentions the pleasures that accompany being married, rearing children, and accumulating property, all of which are necessary to the survival of the species. Pleasure and survival are, therefore, perfectly adjusted to each other, which is a fortunate occurrence for as Spencer wrote, "those races of beings only can have survived in which, on the average, agreeable or desired feelings went along with activities conducive to the maintenance of life, while disagreeable and habitually avoided feelings went along with activities directly or indirectly destructive of life." If hunger, fatigue, and cold have been pleasurable feelings, the human race would never have continued.

By combining these elements Spencer constructed an ethic that is basically evolutionist but with hedonistic aspects. Pleasure is the index that our conduct is in conformity with evolutionary development, and evolved conduct is always "immediately pleasurable" and "conducive to future happiness." Spencer did not favor the pursuit of pleasure *per se* but advocated actions conducive to higher evolutionary development, which, it so happens, are accompanied by pleasure. In any case, Spencer declared, we never pursue pleasure but only objects that further evolution. If we are hungry, we want food not the pleasure of eating, and if we are cold, we seek heat not the pleasure of warmth. These activities are basically conducive to evolutionist goals and are not essentially hedonistic; pleasure is always a byproduct not an end in itself, whether we realize it or not.

There is an interesting parallel between Spencer's refinement of the evolutionist ethic in terms of breadth of life and John Stuart Mill's addition to hedonism of qualitative considerations. Mill declared that of two pleasures, equal in amount, one could be judged higher because of its quality (for example, poetry over pushpin), while Spencer maintained that of two lives, perhaps equal in length, one can be judged superior to the other by virtue of its breadth, fullness, or richness (for example, the life of a civilized person versus that of a primitive person). In their separate ways, each thinker tried to raise the level of the ethical theory to which he adhered and to render it sufficiently dignified to serve as an ideal for human life. Both chose quality over quantity as the more important factor in the good life.

▶ **AN EVALUATION OF SPENCER'S EVOLUTIONISM.** Spencer, then, can be commended for including a qualitative factor in his evolutionist ethic and a pleasure component, for pleasure in life is surely important. He also seems praiseworthy for integrating into the survival-of-the-fittest doctrine the concepts of cooperation and community, both of which are more helpful to the survival of individuals and the species than ruthless competition. For these reasons, and because it offered a scientifically based ethic, Spencer's theory was highly celebrated in the late nineteenth century. Today, however, Spencer is rarely read, for although his theory is appealing, it is also seriously flawed.

Progress Through Evolution May Not Be Inevitable. For one thing, Spencer assumed that evolution will necessarily progress through all future biological history, and it will do so by continually producing increased complexity and integration of functions, that an inexorable process of change from "incoherent homogeneity" to "coherent heterogeneity" will necessarily occur. His optimism echoed that of Darwin, who concluded the *Origin of Species* by saying "we may look with some confidence to a secure future of great length. And as natural selection works solely by and for the good of each being, all corporeal and mental endowments will tend to progress toward perfection."

However, since the nineteenth century when these confident

words were penned, we have experienced two world wars of unimagined destructiveness, and we possess the capability through nuclear weapons of extinguishing life on earth. Furthermore, because of human greed and irresponsibility, we have polluted our natural environment to the point where we may have done irreparable damage to the ecological balance of nature—a symbiotic harmony necessary to maintain ourselves and other species in being. In the wake of these events, we can no longer believe that evolutionary progress is inevitable or that natural selection works toward perfection. Because human beings can intervene so significantly to alter natural processes, we cannot be sure that the pattern of improvement will remain the same.

In addition, the theory of evolution is not compatible with the principle of entropy, or the second law of thermodynamics in physics, which holds that matter and energy are continually being transmuted into unusable forms, and this degradation tends toward a state of inert uniformity for the entire universe. This presents a countermovement to evolutionary development.

In short, evolution will not necessarily produce greater complexity and integration, breadth of life, harmony, and pleasure, and this presents an uncomfortable dilemma for Spencer's evolutionary ethics. For if it is claimed that we should follow evolution wherever it leads, we may well find ourselves endorsing a less coherent and diversified world, or one in which selfishness, violence, and ugliness are the principal elements. If, on the other hand, we are meant to affirm the values of complexity, integration, fullness, richness, cooperation, pleasure, and so forth, then we may no longer be endorsing evolution as our model.

Spencer seemed to adopt the latter position, which means he embraced a nonevolutionist and nonnaturalist position, which in turn implies the need to justify his ideals in ways other than by invoking evolution or nature. In other words, he appeared to claim that breadth of life is best, whether or not it is evolved or natural, which means that he would have to base that value on some grounds besides evolutionary naturalism. But in either case, Spencer's theory seems untenable. For either he endorsed an evolutionism that could be morally monstrous, or he violated his basic evolutionist ethic by affirming moral ideals that could run counter to the thrust of evolution.

In a sense, Spencer and Mill fell into the same trap. In trying to refine their respective theories, they placed themselves outside of those theories altogether, which could mean each theory has a fundamental defect that cannot be eliminated without abandoning the ethic altogether.

Evolution May Not Depend on Cooperation. Besides this major deficiency, Spencer's evolutionism has been criticized with regard to its emphasis on the importance of cooperation and mutual helpfulness. Neither necessarily characterizes evolution, and according to other interpretations nature is "the tyrannically inconsiderate and relentless enforcement of the claims of power" (Nietzsche) or "ruthless self-assertion," a "thrusting aside, or treading down" of all competitors, a "gladiatorial" existence (T. H. Huxley). Some creatures such as bees or beavers may live in cooperative communities but tigers and cobras lead lives of brutal competition; it is an open question as to which is more representative of the natural evolutionary process.[5]

Pleasure May Not Be Conducive to Evolutionary Progress. Spencer's belief that pleasurable activities are conducive to evolutionary advancement may also be challenged. Sometimes pleasure can accompany activities that do not have survival value or produce an enrichment of life, as in the case of gluttonous persons who enjoy eating to the point where their movements are restricted by obesity and their health is seriously endangered. People can enjoy food so much that, in psychological terms, they are attacking themselves with knives and forks.

Complexity Is Not Always Best. Still further, the integrative complexity that Spencer regarded as evolutionary progress may not always be worthwhile. A simple, good-hearted person, the honest uncomplicated soul can be far more admirable than the complex juvenile delinquent or devious politician. Even though complexity may be a later development in evolution, it is not necessarily better.

This last criticism brings us back full circle to the first, for it

---

5. Spencer also opposed various social measures to help the helpless, which seems oddly incongruous with his emphasis on mutual concern.

indicates that evolutionary developments are not always good; therefore conformity to the evolutionary process cannot be the criterion of good and bad. Every type of evolutionary theory of ethics runs afoul of this problem and is rendered highly dubious as a consequence. Not only Spencer but all advocates of evolutionism judge certain aspects of the evolutionary process beneficial and others harmful, and in doing so they must refer to some external standard of judgment.

NATURALISM BROADLY CONSIDERED

In a wider sense, it is naturalism itself that stands indicted for, as indicated previously, not everything natural is *ipso facto* good. Also, of all the theories of ethics, naturalism commits the naturalistic fallacy most blatantly and can be criticized on those grounds. For it asserts that conduct is right if it conforms to some natural fact, whether that fact is the character of nature, destiny, or the evolutionary process. But we cannot logically derive a value from a fact. Just because nature exhibits characteristic *X,* that does not mean, therefore, *X* is good. It would seem that we must look beyond nature if we are to find a sound basis for our ethical judgments.

Naturalism nevertheless holds considerable attraction because it places human conduct within the context of a larger world, linking it to the surrounding environment through which human beings move. Rather than viewing action as essentially individual, performed in solitude and unique isolation, naturalism offers a comprehensive view of the natural world that embraces human actions as part and parcel of itself. Human beings become integral to the organic whole of nature, not a foreign body outside its skin. Whether nature is regarded as a basic model in its varied aspects of animals, seasons, growth, children, or beauty; whether it is seen as a manifestation of the divine, in rational or irrational form; or whether it is conceived as a blind, inexorable process of evolutionary advancement, it holds a very elemental appeal for us. Human life is placed in relation to the natural world that envelops us; ethics becomes vitally connected to metaphysics.

One of the most insistent problems in ethics today is to demonstrate how such a linkage between human beings and nature or the larger cosmos can be justified. We would like to view our actions not just against a backdrop of history but as intrinsic to the natural order; the problem comes in showing the logic of that relation so we have good reasons for believing our wish for connectedness corresponds to some reality.

RECAPITULATION

Chapter 8 dealt with the third type of naturalism, evolutionary ethics. It was first described in its Darwinian version, and its challenge to religion was explained. The ethical inferences drawn from it were then discussed, first in the form of a rather crude interpretation of Darwin, and then in a more sophisticated version presented by Spencer. The strengths and weaknesses of both forms of evolutionism were indicated, and some general remarks were made about naturalism as seen in broad perspective.

▼ ▼ ▼

REVIEW QUESTIONS

1. *Explain why Darwin's theory of evolution undermined the teleological argument for the existence of God. Are evolutionism and theism compatible?*

2. *Present an assessment of the "survival of the fittest" doctrine as a theory of ethics.*

3. *What does Herbert Spencer mean by "breadth of life" and by "cooperation"? Why are they thought to be conducive to evolutionary survival and development?*

4. *In your view, does nature tend toward evolution or devolution, progress or entropy? Defend your position.*

5. *In what way can naturalism itself be criticized in all of its manifestations? Can ethics be grounded in the natural world?*

9

DUTY

Thus far we have examined three ethical theories concerning the good life: hedonism, self-realization, and naturalism, and one criticism we have discovered to be common to all of them is that a disparity can exist between the respective conceptions of good and conduct that is considered right. With regard to hedonism, we found that stealing can produce happiness for the thief, or, if he is a Robin Hood, the greatest happiness for the greatest number, but that does not legitimize taking other people's property; at best, it only romanticizes it. In the case of self-realization, we concluded that a tyrant, for example, may be realizing himself or expressing basic human nature, but the tyranny is not thereby justified. And in naturalism, even if rampant selfishness were found in nature, that would not make it right in human society.

In the theories that we will examine in this chapter and in

Chapter 10, the ethic of duty and religious ethics, the good and the right are combined in such a way that doing what is right becomes the definition of what is good. That is, a good life is conceived of as one in which people perform actions that are right. In this way, the disparity between the two is eliminated and the split is healed.

DEONTOLOGICAL THEORY

Both duty ethics and religious ethics are considered to fall within the category of formalism or deontological theories, which stress doing what is right precisely because it is right. As stated previously, formalistic ethics assert that rules or acts are right according to certain characteristics that they possess, and for that reason we must accept them as obligations in our lives. An act is not right by virtue of its outcome, that is, by the fact that it promotes some good end, but because of some innate and excellent features. And once we recognize these features we realize that our duty consists in carrying out these rules or actions regardless of whether good or bad is brought into being as a consequence. The term "deontology" comes from the Greek meaning "ought," and the emphasis is on the obligatory character of certain actions apart from their results. Our duty is to act, not necessarily to achieve, and we must act according to identifiable facts about the act itself. If we do so, our existence will be justified.

Obviously, deontological theories stand in diametric opposition to a teleological approach to ethics (although they can be compatible with intentionalism if the intentionalist favors wanting to do what is right). In teleologism, as previously described, the results of an action determine its moral worth, whereas deontological theories deny that the consequences are a moral criterion. Instead, the deontologist claims that the characteristics or nature of the act itself determine its rightness, apart from any good or evil that results.

The conflict today between environmentalists and industrialists is a prime example of deontologism versus teleologism. Environmentalists affirm certain principles they believe should be honored, often irrespective of the consequences. Respect for the natural environment is the prime principle. We should conceive of ourselves as stewards of the earth, God's shepherds entrusted with preserving the flora and fauna and maintaining the beauty of the world's landscape.

Rather than following the Biblical injunctions to take "dominion over the fish of the sea, and over the fowl of the air, and over the cattle, and over all the earth and over every creeping thing that creepeth upon the earth" (*Genesis*, Chapter 1, verse 26), we should conceive of our purpose as the English justice Matthew Hale rendered it in the seventeenth century: "The end of man's creation was, that he should be viceroy of the great God of heaven and earth . . . to correct and abridge the excesses and cruelties of the fiercer animals, to give protection and defense to the [tame] and useful, to preserve the species of divers vegetables . . . to preserve the face of the earth in beauty, usefulness, and fruitfulness."

The industrialist, on the other hand, takes a teleological viewpoint and considers the consequences of preserving the earth in its natural condition. Saving species such as the snail darter or the spotted owl means halting the development of our natural resources. For our industrial society to flourish, we need logging, coal mining, oil wells, natural gas pipelines, hydroelectric power, mills and factories, housing developments, shopping malls, cars, trucks, railroads, and roadways. None of this is possible if we subscribe to the environmentalist's values and keep the earth in pristine form. In fact, the opposite result will occur. We will lose our competitive edge in the world economy and many different types of jobs will be lost, leading to massive unemployment. Development produces widespread happiness for humankind; preservation, which gives priority to plants and animals, results in a deterioration in our standard of living.

From a teleological perspective, then, the choice must be development, whereas the formalist or deontologist sees the values of preservation as having overriding importance.

ACT- AND RULE-DEONTOLOGICAL THEORIES

Quite often a distinction is made between two kinds of deontologism. *Act-deontological theories* claim that reflection on particular situations will yield judgments as to which action is appropriate at that time and place. However, no general rules of conduct can be referred to in deciding how one should behave. Each situation is considered to be unique and distinct from every other; therefore, actions that are right in one case cannot be carried over to another. Judgments of obligation, then, must be particular rather than general in form, so that one cannot say, for example, "Human life should always be preserved," but only perhaps, "In these circumstances I ought to preserve this person's life."

Some act-deontologists, adopting a more moderate position, maintain that general principles can be constructed *post hoc* from particular judgments, but most believe that because each situation is essentially different no general rules can be made. In any event, judgments about particular situations occur first and always take precedence over any broad rules of conduct that may subsequently be formed. Specific judgments are always primary, both temporally and in order of priority. No rules can ever be invoked as the ultimate and decisive criterion of rightness in action, and, of course, the consequences of an action are considered morally irrelevant.[1]

Rule-deontologism maintains that general principles always take precedence over particular judgments and inform us as to which actions are appropriate in specific circumstances. We must reason from the general to the particular, deducing our obligations in various cases from the broad rules of conduct that cover them. The rule-deontologist contends that situations are not so individual and unique that they cannot be grouped according to type. Various

---

1. As a representative of act-deontologism, see E. F. Carritt, *Theory of Morals.* Also included under act-deontologists are situation moralists such as Rudolf Bultmann, John A. T. Robinson, and Joseph Fletcher, and most existentialists, especially Jean-Paul Sartre.

common denominators always exist that enable us to classify situations under the same heading and therefore enable us to judge them by the same rules. No two situations are identical, but they can be alike in all essential respects so that a moral judgment can be made that covers both situations.[2]

Moral rules, then, are considered to be possible and the best way to determine the mode of conduct we should follow. If an action can be seen as an instance of some general moral principle, then that act should be done, and adherence to these principles makes our behavior right regardless of whether a good or bad result occurs in consequence. The act- and rule-deontologist differ markedly regarding the question of whether the action or the moral rule should be referred to in determining our obligations, but they agree in maintaining that the recognition of certain moral features should govern our conduct rather than the desire to promote some good end.

The ethic of duty as espoused by Immanuel Kant is generally considered to be a major deontological theory, and we will examine it at some length, both as a prime example of deontologism and as a proposal for the good life. It will become apparent that Kant strongly advocated a rule- rather than an act-deontologism, and opposed all teleological systems of ethics.

KANTIANISM

Immanuel Kant (1724–1804) is considered among the world's most eminent philosophers, although his fame derives more from his *Critique of Pure Reason*, which deals with epistemology and metaphysics, than from his work in ethics. Nevertheless Kant did present a celebrated theory of ethics in his *Foundations of the Metaphysics of Morals* and the *Critique of Practical Reason*, and his speculations are worth considering at some length.

---

2. Among rule-deontologists could be listed R. H. Price, W. D. Ross, Samuel Clarke, Thomas Reid, and, of course, Immanuel Kant.

► **KANT'S INTENTIONALISM**. "Nothing in the world . . . can possibly be conceived which could be called good without qualification except a good will,"[3] Kant wrote at the beginning of the *Foundations of the Metaphysics of Morals*, and with that opening statement we know him to be an intentionalist rather than a teleologist. He was saying that the basis for evaluating conduct is not the consequences that follow from it but the will that lies behind it, that "good" does not stand for any end of action but can only be applied to the will of the agent performing the action. A person of good will, someone with a noble nature and high intentions, is praiseworthy regardless of whether his or her actions achieve some worthwhile result. Circumstances, chance, physical necessities, and so forth may prevent the accomplishment of that which a person wills, but such blockages are morally irrelevant. The significant factor is whether the motive of the moral agent is commendable. If so, then praise is appropriate, and if not, then no praise may be given regardless of whether the action proves to be ultimately beneficial.

For the will to be good, however, Kant stipulated that it must not operate from inclination but out of the recognition of a moral obligation. For example, if we were moved to help a blind person to cross the street out of a sudden rush of pity and compassion, that would not constitute a moral action, but if we offered our help because of a realization that we have a moral duty to do so, then the action would be moral. Kant distrusted the emotions, regarding them as fickle and unreliable as determinants of correct behavior. The emotions could impel us to acts of sympathy and generosity but they could also produce responses of cruelty, and destructiveness. Just because we feel certain emotions, that is no justification to act upon them. On the other hand, if we recognize certain actions as morally binding upon us, we have a more trustworthy basis for behavior. It is not that our sense of obligation informs us as to which emotions are trustworthy, but that obligation rather than emotion should be taken as the criterion of moral conduct.[4]

3. I. Kant, *Foundations of the Metaphysics of Morals* (New York: Bobbs-Merrill, 1959), p. 9. See also H. Paton, *The Moral Law; Kant's Groundwork of the Metaphysics of Morals* (London: Hutchinson University Library, 1965). Paton offers an excellent textual analysis.
4. One question that has been frequently raised in this connection is whether it would be preferable to have one behave well on principle or by inclination. Many

The next question addressed by Kant is how one is to know where one's obligation or duty, lies. We might accept the notion that obligations rather than feelings and emotions are the foundation of morality, but how is one to determine which actions are obligatory? Kant answered this question by saying that if our act can be subsumed under some general principle of conduct, then we know that we are in the realm of moral obligations. If we can say that a contemplated action is an instance of some general rule of behavior, we can feel confident in proceeding with it. For example, suppose we are contemplating the rightness of stealing food rather than obtaining it by working. In order to test the morality of the action, we must ask ourselves whether such an action can be advocated as a universal practice. Can we in good conscience recommend that everyone steal food instead of working for it? Obviously we cannot, which means that our action is not moral; it cannot be placed under a general moral principle and is, therefore, prohibited.

▶ **THE CATEGORICAL IMPERATIVE**. Kant sometimes described this standard of morality as a matter of respecting the moral law. By this he meant operating with deference to objective rules of rightness in contrast to behavior that springs from emotions or is based on the consequences of action. "Duty is the necessity of an action executed from respect for law . . . ," he wrote adamantly. "Now as an act from duty wholly excludes the influence of inclination and therewith every object of the will, nothing remains which can determine the will objectively except the law, and nothing subjectively except pure respect for this practical law. This subjective element is the maxim that I ought to follow such a law even if it thwarts all my inclinations."[5]

However, the most definitive formulation of Kant's views on duty and the core of his moral system is expressed in what he called the *categorical imperative*. Various descriptions of this are given by Kant but broadly speaking the categorical imperative can be stated

---

moralists conclude that they would be better off living among those who are naturally kind instead of those who are controlling their malice in accordance with proper rules of conduct.
5. Kant, *Foundations*, p. 17.

as follows: We should act in such a way that the principle for our actions could become a universal law. That is, in order for an action to qualify as moral we should always be able to affirm that all people at all times and all places should follow the same principle of conduct.

Kant stated the point as follows:

> But what kind of law can that be, the conception of which must determine the will without reference to the expected result? Under this condition alone the will can be called absolutely good without qualification. Since I have robbed the will of all impulses which could come to it from obedience to any law, nothing remains to serve as a principle of the will except universal conformity of its actions to law as such. That is, I should never act in such a way that I could not also will that my maxim should be a universal law.[6]

Kant elaborated his categorical imperative by saying that if we cannot declare that everyone ought to do the same as we have done, then we know our conduct is wrong. When we make an exception for ourselves, declaring that the action is wrong in general but we can do it nonetheless, that is a certain indication that our action is immoral. A genuine rule of conduct has no exceptions, so that if the rule covering our action has universal application, then we know the action is right.

Kant gives various examples of the operation of the categorical imperative that help us to understand its meaning. Suppose we are considering borrowing some money, but in order to obtain the loan we must promise to repay it—which we do not intend to do. Should we, Kant asked, make an insincere promise to repay the loan in order to obtain it? To decide this question in a moral way we must refer to the categorical imperative. Could we will that everyone should act according to the same principle, that whoever wants to borrow money is justified in making a false promise to return it? Obviously not, Kant said, for if everyone did this no one would ever lend money, which means that the conduct cannot be universalized

6. Ibid., p. 18.

and, therefore, cannot be right. Once we apply the test of the categorical imperative, we see that if everyone practiced this mode of conduct then the conduct would become impossible to practice; consequently, it must be immoral.

Another example is that of truth-telling. We may be tempted in various circumstances to tell a lie, perhaps to extricate ourselves from an awkward situation or to spare someone's feelings, but the acid test of the rightness of our behavior is whether it can be universalized. Can we will that lying should become a universal practice? Apart from any questions about the undesirability of a world operating that way, Kant maintained that lying would be impossible to universalize because if everyone said the opposite of what he or she believed to be the case, no one would ever be deceived. People would simply assume that the reverse of a statement is the truth. Universal lying, then, would be self-defeating, which means that lying cannot be universalized and, therefore, is wrong.

It is important to realize that Kant did not say that a maxim could be considered wrong if the results of universalizing it would be bad; rather Kant's point was that the wrongness could be determined by the inconsistency or self-contradiction that would be entailed if the maxim were universalized. To take still another example, to have as a rule that a contract can be broken whenever a person finds it inconvenient to keep would violate the nature of contracts, and this contradiction makes it impossible for such a rule to be universally practiced. It would be, Kant said, as though a contract with four clauses specifying the mutual obligations of the parties involved were to have a fifth clause stating that either party could break the contract whenever he or she wished. Such a contract would negate itself and cease to be a contract at all. In the same way, any principle that contradicts itself when universalized is thereby revealed as being outside the realm of reason and morality.

▶ **MEANS AND ENDS.** Kant formulated the categorical imperative in another way that seems to be quite different from the concept of universalizability, although Kant regarded it as essentially the same. He stated that we should "treat humanity, whether in thine own person or in that of any other, always as an end and never as a means only.''[7] Kant was here emphasizing respect for persons or, more specifically, rational beings, and affirming that people should not be used just as instruments or objects. Notice that Kant said "as a means only," thereby acknowledging the fact that people must regard each other as means to some extent, whether as employers, shopkeepers, mothers, or doctors; but human relationships ought to be more than that. We should, Kant asserted, have regard for people as worthy of respect in and of themselves, and, insofar as possible, treat them as the purpose of our actions, not as a means for achieving our ends.

This version of the categorical imperative provides a second reason for condemning lying and suicide. In both instances we are treating someone only as a means. In the case of lying to another person about our intentions to repay a loan, we are using them in order to obtain money. This is the reason why we feel insulted when we discover that someone has lied to us; we have been regarded as an obstacle and an object rather than as a person. In the case of suicide, we are treating ourselves as a means of avoiding difficult circumstances and ignoring the respect that should be accorded to all human beings, including ourselves. Kant's analysis may seem somewhat odd, but usually when suicide is prohibited, whether by the church or some other authority, the argument is made that the taking of human life is wrong, and that means one's own life as well as the lives of others.

Treating humanity as an end is an important element in Kant's ethics but his theory hinges mainly on the concept of universalizability; this is the main formulation of the categorical imperative. If we cannot claim that the rule authorizing an action is a universal one that should always be done, then the action cannot be considered moral. Kant, quite obviously, was an objectivist in ethics, one who maintained that certain actions or, in his analysis, certain moral principles governing actions are intrinsically and absolutely right; otherwise, they cannot be considered right at all. And if a principle is morally correct, then the actions that follow from it should always be done, without exception. To Kant, intrinsically right implies universalizable.

7. Ibid., p. 47.

► **HYPOTHETICAL VERSUS CATEGORICAL IMPERA-TIVES**. In order to clarify and develop his point still further, Kant differentiated between a hypothetical type of imperative and a categorical one, saying that hypothetical imperatives always contain conditions under which the imperative becomes obligatory, whereas categorical imperatives are absolutely obligatory regardless of circumstances. For example, if we are overweight and wish to have a healthier and more attractive body, we should exercise and watch our diet. This would be an example of a hypothetical imperative because it is conditional; if one wants X, then one is obliged to do Y. A categorical imperative would not be of an "if/then" type but would state that a certain principle is right and therefore should be done. For example, keeping promises might be declared categorically right and not just right provided that we want others to like or trust us in the future. According to Kant, the type of proposition that can be judged as moral is the categorical one in which there are no stipulations, provisions, or conditions made on our obligations. This led Kant to affirm the categorical imperative as the master rule of ethical conduct. By saying this, Kant was asserting that genuine moral principles have no exceptions. The categorical imperative is, therefore, the highest expression of categorical morality as opposed to a hypothetical approach, and the ultimate criterion for moral behavior.

► **A SUMMARY OF KANT'S ETHICAL THEORY**. Thus Kant advocated an approach to proper living in which we perform actions that can be placed under a universal rule of conduct. An act is not right because it leads to good results or because it flows from moral inclinations. A good will alone is praiseworthy and the will is good when it acts out of pure respect for moral law. We must treat people mainly as ends rather than means and, above all, we must be sure that our conduct falls under principles that can be advocated for all human beings, categorically and without exception. Kant was thus an intentionalist and a deontologist while rejecting teleologism as a criterion of morality.

▸ **A CRITICAL APPRAISAL.** But is the criterion of universalizability a viable one for determining moral conduct? In evaluating Kant's ethical theory, can we accept his central concept of the categorical imperative as the fundamental touchstone of morality?

The Conflict Between Universalizable Principles. Kant has been criticized for constructing a system in which two universalized principles can be in opposition, and for failing to provide a means of resolving the conflict. Suppose, for instance, we maintain as part of our absolute and inviolable principles that human life should be preserved and also that one should always tell the truth. Then one day we are asked by a Mafia killer where a friend of ours is living. In these circumstances we can either tell the truth and contribute indirectly to a murder or preserve a life by telling a lie. We are forced to make a choice between the two principles because in this case we cannot both preserve life and tell the truth simultaneously. Many moral principles will oppose each other in this way, and under Kant's system, in which genuine moral rules cannot be broken, we find ourselves faced with an irreconcilable dilemma.

It might be said that, in this case, we can decide which of the two principles takes precedence, and by examining a number of cases, set up a hierarchy of values with the most important on the top. Clearly, preserving life is more important than telling the truth, so the former must be given priority.

But that means only the top principle would be considered truly moral within the Kantian system since all the others would have to give way if they conflicted with it; they could not always be carried out and, therefore, would not qualify as genuine moral principles. A moral theory with only one principle seems rather odd. Furthermore, how is this foremost principle to be determined? The preservation of life does not seem to be the overriding rule of morals since situations could arise in which other values would take precedence. A doctor, for example, who is bound by the Hippocratic oath to preserve life and alleviate suffering may well be justified in ending life in a situation in which the patient is in an excruciating condition and death is imminent. For instance, in the case of a seriously injured accident victim, who is in extreme pain and who is expected to die within a brief period of time, a doctor could decide not to employ "exotic" or "heroic" measures to prolong the victim's life because that would also mean prolonging his or her suffering. In instances such as this, the quality of a person's life can be more significant than its quantity, which means that the preservation of life is not always of supreme importance.

The same problem, of finding a rule that cannot be overridden, plagues us whenever we try to set up a moral hierarchy leading to the highest principle. In some circumstances, principle *A* is more important than principle *B*; in other circumstances the reverse is true. To set up a strict scale of values, or to arrive at one superlative principle which transcends the rest and never gives way to any other, is difficult if not impossible to do.

The Lack of Universal Rules of Behavior. This leads to a second major criticism of Kant's ethic. Not only can universalized principles conflict, without the possibility of resolving the dilemma, but our preceding analysis has exposed the difficulty of finding any principle that can be applied without exception and can qualify as moral. Kant considered only universal rules as truly right, but we cannot find any rules that are universal. Each rule covers a certain number of cases, perhaps a majority, but none can be said to apply in all circumstances. It seems as though there are some situations in which we feel morally obliged to steal, lie, break promises, and so forth, even though in general we do not feel justified in committing any of these acts. By insisting that only principles without exceptions are moral, Kant created an ethical system which does not contain any genuine principles! The class of moral principles becomes a null class since none can satisfy Kant's criterion.

To remedy this situation, many deontologists endorse the concept of *prima facie* obligations (as discussed in Chapter 2). Most notably, the philosopher William David Ross (1877–1940) spoke of *prima facie* duties as those generally binding upon us unless other duties assume greater importance and supplant them.[8] According to Ross, we have a subjective awareness of our objective duties, but these are in no sense absolute. Rather, one duty takes precedence over another and vice versa, depending upon the circumstances.

Although Ross's proposal seems an improvement over the

8. W. D. Ross, *The Right and the Good* (Oxford, England: Clarendon Press, 1930).

rigidity of Kantian ethics, his theory fails to provide a reliable method of determining which actions are *prima facie* obligations. To Kant our duty was recognizable by its universalizable character but Ross gives us no such moral standard. In addition, Ross does not adequately explain how we know when one *prima facie* obligation transcends another. Therefore, he provides no basis for resolving conflicts.

The notion of *prima facie* obligations, although closer to common sense, still fails to solve many of the problems that plague deontological theories of ethics. How can objective moral principles be identified, and how are we to rank them in importance?

The Morality of Nonuniversalizable Principles. In addition to these embarrassing problems in Kantian ethics—irreconcilable moral dilemmas and an empty class of moral principles—a further criticism can be made that follows from the foregoing analysis. Kant does not seem correct in claiming that only universalizable principles are moral since some principles might be considered moral even though they are impossible to universalize. For example, self-sacrifice does seem commendable in various circumstances but it cannot be practiced by all people at all times. For if everyone were self-sacrificing, there would be no one left to accept the sacrifice. On Kantian grounds we would thus have to say that self-sacrifice is not a virtue, but it appears more reasonable to maintain that, although self-sacrifice cannot be practiced universally, nevertheless it is morally commendable and should sometimes be practiced. A principle need not be universal, then, in order to be judged as moral.

The Universality of Immoral Principles. A fourth criticism of Kant's ethics is that some principles can be universalized even though they are not moral. For example, the rule that we should exploit the weaknesses of other people for our own advantage does not contradict itself when it is universalized but it is hardly moral. In other words, it is certainly possible for everyone to behave according to this principle (in a way that it is impossible for everyone to make false promises to return borrowed money or to continue the practice of committing suicide). Society can operate by people taking advantage of each other's weaknesses, but we would not call it desirable. The fact that exploitation is capable of being universalized does not legitimize it as moral behavior.

Kant recognized this problem and tried to protect himself by involving the *criterion of reversibility* to differentiate between universalizable principles that are immoral and those that are moral. This criterion is similar to the golden rule, that one should do as one would wish to be done by. In Christianity, this is expressed as doing unto others as we would have them do unto us, whereas Confucianism and Judaism (both of which stress that avoiding harm is more important than doing good) state that we should not do unto others as we would not have them do unto us. The concept, however, is the same: Any action is moral only if we would want it done to us. Using this criterion Kant tells us that some conduct is immoral even though it can be universalized without logical contradiction. Only on condition that we would agree to have the same action done to us if positions were reversed can we declare a universalizable principle to be moral.

But there is something rather odd about the standard of universalizability not being universalizable—that it does not always hold true but is qualified by a condition, namely, that a universalizable principle must also satisfy the criterion of reversibility before it can be considered moral. In other words, it seems incongruous for Kant to claim that there is an exception to the rule that genuine moral principles are ones that have no exceptions. Passing over that difficulty, however, a further problem occurs with regard to the criterion of reversibility. At times it appears that Kant means by reversibility that we should not treat others in a way we would not like to be treated ourselves because we then run the risk of being treated that way in turn. If this was his meaning, he was appealing to consequences in determining the morality of conduct (and consequences of personal advantage to boot) rather than being a consistent intentionalist and formalist. Or to put the point differently, Kant seems to be saying that if we want to be treated well, then we should treat others the same way, which is a hypothetical rather than a categorical imperative in violation of his basic ethical approach. In order to be a consistent deontologist, Kant would have to base the criterion of reversibility not on consequences but on some more abstract ethical considerations, for instance, that putting oneself in someone else's shoes reveals the moral or immoral nature of an act. Kant did, however, refer to consequences, saying, for example, that we should desist from actions where we would not want to be paid back in "our own coin," and in this he was contradicting his fundamental deontological position.

Legitimate Qualifications of Universal Rules. Kant has also been criticized for failing to distinguish between qualifying a rule and making exceptions to it. That is to say, it seems legitimate for Kant to claim that we should not make an exception for ourselves in promulgating a universal rule, but he falsely assumed that this means no qualifications can be built into such a rule. Granted that it would be wrong to argue, for example, that "No one may break a promise except myself," nevertheless, that is not the same as qualifying promise-keeping by saying that "No one may break a promise unless a person's life would be endangered by keeping it." In the latter case, the qualified rule might be universalized without exceptions, which would satisfy the criterion of the categorical imperative. By failing to make this distinction, Kant was led to insist that moral rules be stricter and narrower than they need be.

It might be added that Kant failed to make a proper distinction between two separate concepts: He claimed that the criteria of universalizability and treating people as ends were versions of a single categorical imperative. They are actually different moral standards, for actions that are not universalizable could be performed for the sake of treating people as ends. For example, an individual might steal food for the purpose of alleviating the hunger of his or her family but that action might not be capable of being universalized. Kant had, in fact, several "versions" of the categorical imperative (H. J. Paton in his book *The Categorical Imperative* identified as many as five), and at least some of these are separate principles rather than formulations of a single doctrine.

▶ **CONCLUDING REMARKS.** In conclusion, we find that Kant's ethical theory, although seriously flawed, is a tantalizing and persuasive one nonetheless, perhaps because of its deontological purity. In some basic way, it seems appropriate to say that an action that is intrinsically right should always be done, and whatever we can endorse as universal behavior is thereby shown to be right behavior.

A criterion of conduct of this kind seems to make sense and to be in accordance with our moral understanding. And living in terms of what is right appears superior to goals of maximizing our pleasure, developing our abilities, or living naturally; the latter seems almost trivial and self-indulgent by comparison.[9]

Nevertheless, if we are to accept a deontological system of the type that Kant prescribed, the various criticisms of that system must be met. Kant would be the last one to advise us to accept an ethical theory on the basis of emotional inclination. He would want any system of ethics to satisfy canons of rationality—including his own deontological scheme.

Deontologism in general has the same appeal as Kant's specific version of it, and it suffers from many of the same defects. We would like to regard certain principles as right and binding, either as universal or *prima facie* obligations, but we have difficulty in identifying these principles. Peoples' moral "sense" differs, and an insistence on one's own insights too often leads to a dogmatic position, unarguable and self-righteous. Furthermore, consequences do seem important in determining the justification of actions. Whether we adopt a rule- or an act-deontologism, it would seem foolish to ignore the results of our behavior in judging the moral worth of our conduct.

RECAPITULATION

We began this chapter by describing deontological theories of ethics and by showing how they resolved the frequent conflict between the right and the good. Then we differentiated between act- and rule-deontologism and explored the areas of agreement and disagreement between them.

---

9. Both Socrates and Plato endorsed this sentiment and have strong deontological elements in their ethics. Cf. the *Crito*, which is generally considered to express the ideas of Socrates, and the *Republic* (especially Book II), which is thought to be almost entirely Platonic, in Plato, *The Works of Plato*, trans. B. Jowett (New York: Dial Press, 1936).

The rule-deontologism of Immanuel Kant was then discussed as an ethic of duty. His concept of a good will was developed and the question of how one's duty is known was examined. This led to an explanation of the categorical imperative, mainly in terms of universalizability but also as a principle of treating people as ends. To clarify Kant's position further, the distinction was made between hypothetical and categorical imperatives as types of ethical prescriptions.

Kant's theory was then criticized for not being capable of resolving ethical conflicts, which led to a discussion about hierarchies of values. Another problem noted in Kant's theory was the difficulty in finding any moral principles that satisfy his criterion of universalizability; in this connection the notion of *prima facie* obligations was mentioned. Two final criticisms were made concerning the relationship between genuine ethical principles and universalizability, and this entailed a reference to Kant's criterion of reversibility.

▼ ▼ ▼

REVIEW QUESTIONS

1. *Differentiate between act-deontologism and rule-deontologism. Which do you judge superior? Why?*

2. *Explain what Immanuel Kant means by a good will and respect for the moral law.*

3. *Describe the "categorical imperative" and provide illustrations of the way in which it functions to determine moral action.*

4. *Explain what Kant means by saying we should "treat humanity . . . always as an end and never as a means only." Why would you affirm or reject this principle?*

5. *Explain the criticism that, in the Kantian system, two universalized principles can conflict. How could such a conflict be resolved?*

10

RELIGIOUS ETHICS

ccording to Western religious ethics, we should commit ourselves to a particular type of existence as pleasing to God. Scripture has revealed that we should live in a special relation to our fellow human beings on earth and to the divine being who created and sustains us. A good life is one in which we believe in the reality of God and accept his word as authoritative. We should regard ourselves as the agents of God's will, here to fulfill his design for humanity, which is one part of the grand scheme of the universe.

Since a good life consists in doing what is right, and the right is found by following the spirit and intentions of God, religious ethics fall into the category of deontologism. In the Kantian ethic our duty consists in carrying out certain types of behavior because we recognize them to be intrinsically and objectively right. In religious ethics we are called upon to perform actions that possess the feature of being willed by God. Both theories are deontological because they affirm that certain characteristics of conduct confer a moral obligation upon us, and both deny that acts are made moral by their results. Furthermore, both Kantian and religious ethics are examples of rule-deontologism because it is principles or maxims that are considered inherently right; the recent theological movement of situation ethics is an exception, for it shades from an act-deontologism to an outright teleologism.

Religious ethics, then, are deontological ethics, finding justification for actions in the divine will. The fact that God has commanded an act indicates that it is right and becomes the *sine qua non* or indispensable condition for asserting it to be obligatory for us to do. It is not consequences that determine the rightness of an action but the fact that is a divine command. We must recognize obedience to God as our primary duty, which we are morally obligated to fulfill above all other considerations.

With regard to the issue of abortion, for example, as discussed in Chapter 2, those who oppose it on religious grounds will often argue that God alone can decide when life shall occur, or that we have a religious obligation to be compassionate and self-sacrificing toward the weak and defenseless, or that the unborn have a God-given right to life. To those who adopt a position of this kind, abortion is judged to be wrong regardless of the beneficial consequences that may ensue to society or to the parents if abortion were permitted. Right-to-life advocates will be unmoved by counterarguments concerning overpopulation or the fact that having another child will overburden an impoverished mother of eight, or even that the woman's physical or mental health will be severely damaged by the pregnancy. These are all teleological considerations concerning the harmful results of prohibiting abortion, and consequences are considered morally extraneous to the deontological religious thinker. Only those obligations imposed upon human beings by God are regarded as binding and authoritative, not the worldly benefits an action may achieve. Only that which is commanded by God can be considered as having moral force.

In Western religion the Bible is considered these source of knowledge as to what God requires of human beings, and these sacred works, together with the theological interpretations that have been made of them within the field of hermeneutics, gives us our theory of religious ethics. There is certainly room for theological interpretation, for although most devout Jews and Christians regard Scripture as infallible, that does not mean human beings possess infallible knowledge of the meaning of Scripture. And whether God's word was transmitted through the automatic writing of scribes or the inspired transcriptions of saints and prophets, we must allow for human error in conveying or comprehending God's message.[1]

THE OLD TESTAMENT

In the Old Testament, which consists of a series of sacred books produced by Hebrew writers over a period of four hundred years, a deontological ethic is presented in which certain acts are judged as right principally because they are commanded by God. In contrast to the view of Socrates and the Greeks in general, wrongdoing in the Old Testament was not thought the result of ignorance but of disobedience to God's laws. To the Greeks, knowledge of the good was paramount, whereas to the Hebrews it was the will that mattered—an obedient will that accepted the word of God (Yahweh).

▶ **OBEDIENCE TO GOD'S COMMANDS**. Beginning with *Genesis* and running throughout the Old Testament, primary emphasis is placed on the human duty to obey God and not question his commands. In the story of the Fall, for example, in which Adam and Eve were banished from the Garden of Eden, the sin they committed lay in disobeying the explicit word of God. They had been told not to eat the forbidden fruit but they succumbed to the temptations of the devil (in the form of a snake) and were punished

---

1. It has often been pointed out that the earliest Gospels, *Matthew* and *Mark*, were written about A.D. 75, some forty-five years after the death of Christ, and the latest, *John*, around A.D. 95. A gap of time of this magnitude would necessarily produce inaccuracies; it therefore seems unwise to treat the Bible as literal truth or to insist on one true interpretation.

accordingly. "Ye shall not eat . . . of the fruit of the tree which is in the midst of the garden," God had said, warning that death would follow if they did. However, "when the woman saw that the tree was good for food, and that it was pleasant to the eyes, and a tree to be desired to make one wise, she took of the fruit thereof, and did eat, and gave also unto her husband with her; and he did eat" (*Genesis*, Chapter 3, verses 3–6).

Various interpretations have been offered as to what the fruit symbolizes: knowledge (perhaps of good and evil), sexual gratification, genuine choice (which is an indispensable condition for humanness), property, the succulent fruit as a symbol of beauty, sensual experience, and so forth. And it matters whether one thinks of Eve as tempted by the snake or by the apple; the snake, for example, could be a phallic symbol. But the wrongdoing of Adam and Eve consisted in their rebelling against God's authority and in defying his wishes. As a consequence, they lost paradise for themselves and their descendants, so that now human beings must live in a world of natural calamities and disease, suffering and death. We question whether anything the fruit might symbolize should be forbidden to man, or whether one should dangle forbidden fruit, or whether subsequent generations of human beings should be punished for the original sin of their forebears, but this would have been blasphemous to the ancient Hebrew mind. In their view, God's commands cannot be questioned. It is sheer presumption for finite humans to doubt the infinite God, for human beings of limited power and intelligence to do anything but obey the absolute will of Yahweh, the omniscient and omnipotent God.

Other Biblical incidents reinforce the same lesson. The Flood occurred because people were living sinfully in violation of God's laws (*Genesis* Chapter 6, verse 5, through Chapter 7, verse 10), and Sodom and Gomorrah were destroyed for the same reason (*Genesis* Chapter 19, verses 16–28). When the Hebrew people worshiped Baals, the nature symbols of fertility, they were rebuked by the prophets Hosea, Elisha, and Elijah for disobeying God's commandment to Moses that "you shall worship no other God, for the Lord . . . is a jealous God" (*Exodus* Chapter 34, verse 14); Moses condemned the worship of the Golden Calf on the same grounds. And when Uzza tried to steady the Ark of the Covenant so that it would not fall from an ox-cart on which it was being carried, he was struck dead because God had ordained that only the priests could touch the Ark (*1 Chronicles* Chapter 13, verse 10). Similarly, in a war with the Amalekites, Saul violated God's instruction to destroy all men, women, children, and animals. He spared the king, Agag, along with various animals to be used as sacrificial offerings; but he was denounced by the prophet Samuel, who said that "to obey is better than sacrifice, and to hearken than the fat of rams" (*1 Samuel* Chapter 15, verse 23). The acts of some of these Hebrews seem justified to us, others appear unjustified, but the common failing is that they disobeyed God's commands and for that reason alone they were thought to have acted wrongly and to deserve punishment.

In this same connection a great deal is made within Judaism of the covenant relation with God, which it is sacrilegious to break. In the Jewish tradition a special and personal relationship was established between the Hebrew peoples and God whereby they entered upon a solemn agreement to obey the holy laws and, in return, were given a privileged status as God's chosen people. In later Christianity the chosen-people concept was enlarged to include all of humanity as beloved creatures of God, but the point is that the covenant was considered inviolable. Unrighteousness was viewed as violating the compact with Yahweh as well as transgressing specific divine commands.

▶ **THE PROPHETIC TRADITION.** It should be emphasized that although the main tenor of the Old Testament is to define rightness in terms of formal obedience, the Hebrews did advance from this conception, particularly through what is termed the *prophetic tradition.* There is a common tendency among early faiths to emphasize a strict adherence to rules and the ritual of worship above more substantive religious requirements. The ancient Hebrews were no exception, but they did begin to see a certain justice in God's demands and to follow his will not just as obedient children but as morally responsible adults.

In parts of the Hebrew Bible, God is viewed as commanding adherence to moral principles rather than being a stern judgmental and wrathful father, perpetually jealous of his authority. His commands are no longer arbitrary and he does not exact vengeance for transgressions quite so readily. Mercy and forgiveness appear, paternal love becomes more prominent, and the actions he commands are seen to have a moral base. Sin still consists in disobedience, but God's laws can be followed out of respect for their exalted character and not just through blind obedience and the fear of punishment. This advance is seen best, perhaps, in the later interpretation of the Ten Commandments as moral principles of a high order. To be sure, God requires that we follow these commandments in a legalistic way, but they are in no sense a mere expression of his will.

THE NEW TESTAMENT

A basic legalism thus lies at the heart of Hebrew ethics, a strict adherence to rules and principles because they issue from God. Sin lies essentially in disobedience to divine commands, and goodness consists in fulfilling one's duty to our heavenly Father.

In contrast to this conception of religious obligations, the New Testament stresses not loyalty to God so much as love of him. The Christian emphasis is always placed on the spirit rather than on the letter of the law, the cultivation of our hearts more than our wills, proper attitudes, intentions, and beliefs instead of correctness, deference, and ritualistic observance.[2] Hope should replace fear, according to Christianity, the hope of salvation through free divine grace, and rather than cowering from God's wrath we should trust him to be merciful, compassionate, and forgiving toward the repentant soul. Feelings of brotherhood and kindness are regarded as important virtues, particularly toward the poor and lowly, and in place of a special-people idea the Christian considers all human beings as having equal worth. Possessing the right motives of love toward all humankind is more significant than performing particular acts, although social morality is important as the emulation of God's concern for humanity. To love our neighbor and forgive our enemy (rather than loving just our own family and retaliating against

2. For an interesting contrast between the ethics of Jesus and Hebrew legalism compare *Numbers* Chapter 15, verses 32–36 and *John* Chapter 5, verses 5–19.

our foe) is a reflection of God's treatment of human beings and the actual worship of God through the spirit of love and mercy.

This transformed ethic as presented in the New Testament is preached, of course, by Jesus, who is accepted as the Christ or Son of God. He is considered by Christians to be divine, the promised Messiah, sent to redeem the human race from sin—both the original sin inherited from Adam and Eve and the subsequent weight of sin acquired through evil actions.

Christians divide over the question of which way is best to serve Christ: through faith, whereby we believe in his divinity and accept certain dogmas of Christianity such as the trinity, the resurrection, and the day of judgment, or through works, which means living as closely as possible to the perfect moral life of Christ, following in his footsteps with regard to our treatment of humanity. Both ways are often thought to bring salvation for there are many mansions in heaven (*John* 14:2) but the debate is ongoing as to which way is best; saints of both persuasions, however, have been canonized in the Catholic Church.

▶ **CHRISTIAN ETHICS**. The ethical approach of Christianity concerns us most, and the principles of the Christian life are best expressed by Jesus in the Sermon on the Mount (*Matthew* 4:25). Here Jesus presented the main statement of Christian ethics, which centers around the concept of love.

Agape Love. The various forms of love that are identified and distinguished in our Western tradition stem mainly from Greek concepts and include sexual love ("lust"), *philia* ("brotherly love"), eros ("possessive love"), and *agape* or *caritas* ("selfless love").

It is the agape type of love that is endorsed by the Christian moralist, who contrasts it most sharply with eros, which is characterized by a desire to possess the person (or object) that is beloved. In erotic love we want the person to belong to us, to assert our right to ownership—oftentimes in romantic relationships, exclusive ownership. It is essentially a selfish form of love because we are concerned with satisfying our own desire for the person rather than wanting to satisfy the other person's need for us. In some way we wish to incorporate others, to be personally enriched by appropriating them or assimilating their excellence. By making another our own, absorbing him or her within ourselves, we experience an expansion of our being even though it may mean the other's diminution. We do not exist for the other person but rather he or she exists for us, and we maintain the relationship just so long as we continue to benefit from it. Sacrificing our own good for the sake of the other person is anathema to erotic love, for we do not desire what is best for another but only what is best for ourselves.[3]

In agape love our feelings for another individual are so strong and genuine that we desire his or her good even above our own. Our love impels us to dedicate ourselves to the other person's welfare, and that may entail the extreme act of withdrawing from the relationship rather than wanting to possess the other. That is, if we accept an agape ideal and feel that authentic love for others means acting selflessly instead of selfishly toward them, we will remain in a relationship just so long as we believe that the other person is benefited by having us there. If that point is passed, and the relationship is not good for the person we love, then, regardless of whether it is good for us, we will sever the relationship. The depth of our love for the other person would make us unwilling to be possessive if that worked to his or her detriment. We would also not be jealous or resentful of the happiness that he or she found with another person since our primary concern is the other's well being. If in these circumstances we refused to let go of the person we loved, or felt bitterness about his or her happiness, this would indicate that we placed our own feelings above the other person's and that the relationship was essentially a selfish one throughout. In brief, "real" love is considered by the advocates of the agape ideal to consist of dedication to the other person more than to ourselves, and this implies a willingness to allow the person we love to find happiness with someone else if that happened to be greater than the happiness we could provide.

A love relationship, then, is not regarded as a business transaction in which each party seeks the utmost advantage but a com-

---

3. Erotic love is sometimes regarded favorably because possessiveness can be creative or procreative if a new reality is produced through the fusion of two elements. Eros was also treated positively by Freud, who contrasted it with *thanatos*, the death drive.

mitment to the other person's good. In the words of the philosopher Martin Buber (1878–1965), we regard the other as "thou" rather than "it,"[4] and involve ourselves in a personal way, which means care, tenderness, and a self-denying generosity. And the agape love that we give does not have to be earned by the other person because it is not based on merit or deserts; in the same way it will not be withdrawn if the person we love disappoints us. It is not what the person does but what he or she is that matters. People are lovable because of their nature not their accomplishments, and we forgive them their sins while maintaining a constant love for the individual.

The Christian moralist who affirms agapeistic rather than erotic love is concerned that this mode of relatedness be applied not just to romantic attachments but to our attitudes and conduct toward all humankind. We are told to love our neighbors as ourselves, which is interpreted to mean that we should treat all our fellow human beings with the degree of concern that we evince toward ourselves; now we must place their needs even higher than our own. Charity, as St. Thomas Aquinas said, is "the mother and root of all the virtues" (*"caritas est mater omnium virtutum, et radix"*),[5] and to be charitable means loving humanity, our brothers, without reservation as God the Father intended and Christ exemplified. We may not be able to feel the same affection for all people or judge them of equal worth, but we can carry an identical love for them in our hearts and behave toward them with self-transcending charity. Agape love should typify all personal relations and replace envy, malice, spite, greed, lust, hate, and selfishness as our dominant attitude toward humanity. Fellowship and brotherhood should supplant individualism and pride, especially in relation to the poor, lowly, and downtrodden. All souls are equally precious, and humble people in particular should elicit our compassion.

The supreme prototype of agapeistic love, of course, is God's love for humankind, which is not awarded because of any particular merit in people (or any covenant) but is a constant blessing upon

---

4. See M. Buber, *I and Thou* (New York: Charles Scribner's Sons, 1958).
5. St. Thomas Aquinas, *Summa Theologica*, trans. the English Dominican Fathers (London: Burns, Oates, and Washbourne, Ltd., 1912–1936), First Part of the Second Part, A.62, A.4.

the human race.[6] Divine love does not grace humankind because people have earned the right to it but because pure love is of an unqualified character, an unreserved giving without necessarily receiving. God loves humanity for its own sake and human beings should love God in the same way, not for the good he can do us by granting our prayers or guaranteeing us heaven but solely because he is God. And our caring attitude toward our fellow human beings should be prompted by a sense of our common relationship to God in agape love: "This is my commandment, that you love one another as I have loved you" (*John* Chapter 15, verse 12), and "Let no man seek his own but each his neighbor's good" (*1 Corinthians* Chapter 10, verse 24).

Paradoxically enough, as we give so do we receive, in both a reciprocal sense and because virtue is its own reward. When we subordinate our egos in agape love, deferring to our Maker and our fellow human beings, we become infinitely richer within; as we lose ourselves we gain ourselves. Rather than being absorbed by the other we experience a profound fulfillment in our dedication. Instead of feeling self-alienated and riddled with anxiety, dissatisfied and isolated because of our selfishness, we arrive at a state of peace, reconciled with God and our own inner being.

Divine Justice. The agape ideal leads to a special conception of justice, which also distinguishes Old and New Testament thinking. Unlike the Hebrews who believed in giving a person his just deserts, the Christian wants to give a person what he needs. Starting with the metaphysical belief in the law of *Talion*, according to which people can expect to have done to them whatever they do to others, the ancient Hebrews conceived of justice as balancing the scales, as giving a person exactly what he or she deserves. This meant either evening out accounts or "getting even," that is, either equalizing the scales of justice or avenging a wrong to the degree appropriate to the crime. In any case, the doctrine of "an eye for an eye and a tooth for a tooth" pertained, and this was thought to be just treatment.

---

6. Although God's love is freely given to human beings, the Christian view is that a person can only come into relation with that love through faith in Christ. In this way humanity's sinful nature is redeemed and people are drawn into the realm of divine grace.

In contrast, Christian ethics tries to cater to a person's needs regardless of what that person's conduct might merit. Instead of getting revenge in kind, or rewarding or punishing people in proportion to what they deserve, the New Testament stresses support of individuals so that they may improve, with their sins used as an index of their need for love and care. No thought is given to people paying for their crimes or being paid back for them, but only to providing the person with what we recognize to be their fundamental needs. As mentioned in the discussion of the utilitarian theory of punishment (in Chapter 2), we do not want to make people pay, but to make them better, and that means focusing on how people can be helped rather than on what they have done.[7]

Divine justice, as the New Testament theory is called, thus concentrates on needs rather than deserts, redemption of the person rather than compensation for the crime. For example, a child who is caught stealing cookies from the cookie jar may deserve a spanking or ostracism in his or her room for a time or loss of some privilege. But the child might need more affection (for which eating was a substitute), or be genuinely hungry for more food, or want attention and prefer negative attention in the form of punishment to personal neglect. In this situation, the Christian approach would be to give the child love, nourishment, or attention—whatever was required rather than meting out the punishment that the wrongdoing merits. In the same way, murderers might be said to deserve capital punishment but they might need prison sentences during which time they can reform and be rehabilitated. The Old Testament approach would be to punish the killer severely enough so the debt to society would be paid, whereas the New Testament approach would favor forgiveness and salvation of the person. Obviously, the case of the child and the murderer are at two extremes but the principle of justice would be the same, and to the Christian mind

---

7. The Christian idea of eternal damnation in Hell has sometimes caused considerable embarrassment to theologians because of the difficulty in reconciling this idea with the general concept of forgiveness. The notion of a temporary Hell has been proposed and Catholic theology includes belief in Purgatory, which is an intermediary stage where souls are punished and purified of sin; but even these milder ideas appear to contradict a nonretaliatory system. If Christians are obliged to help even unrepentant sinners, it is difficult to see why God would exact punishment, giving them what they deserve.

that means responding to human needs with genuine love. Sometimes people need love most when they deserve it least.

The Christian view of violence is a natural outgrowth of the divine concept of justice and, more ultimately, the agapeistic ideal. In the New Testament Christ commands us to "turn the other cheek" if we are struck, to offer a man our cloak if he demands our coat. We are not to return evil for evil but good for evil (fighting fire with water rather than fire), responding not in a reciprocal or retributive way but with the kindness and caring that the other person lacks. Christ preached a gospel of understanding and forgiveness, peace and compassion rather than aggression and violence. God has ordained that harming others is wrong; therefore, it should not be done even if the other person harms us.[8] We must not return injury for injury but love our fellow human beings enough not to hurt them despite the fact that we may have suffered at their hands. "Forgive them for they know not what they do" is Christ's cry when he himself is being tortured and crucified. The people who destroyed Christ are behaving sinfully, in ignorance of the word of God, and he would be guilty of betraying divine principles if he copied their cruelty.[9] In *Matthew* Chapter 5, verse 44 Christ declared, "Love your enemies and pray for those who persecute you."

Christians hope that by the example of their courage and fidelity to God's commands, as well as through preaching the Gospel, others will realize the virtue of a Christian way of life. By precept and example, the Christian hopes to lead people away from a self-centered life in which personal pride provokes us to retaliatory measures, to an other-centered existence where devotion and service to humanity becomes our primary focus.

---

8. Socrates predated Jesus in this idea, for Plato reported Socrates as saying "we ought not to retaliate or render evil for evil to anyone, whatever evil we may have suffered from him," and again, "a man ought to do what he admits to be right . . . neither injury nor retaliation nor warding off evil by evil is ever right." Plato, *The Works of Plato*, trans. B. Jowett (New York: Dial Press, 1936), Vol. 3, pp. 150–51.
9. Christians have differed in their adherence to a pacifist view. Some, such as Leo Tolstoy in *A Confession, The Gospel in Brief*, and *What I Believe*, trans. Maude, Aylmer (Oxford, England: Oxford University Press, 1948), have taken nonviolence as a primary Christian principle, whereas others have accepted the "church militant" and justified the Inquisition and the Crusades. There is Biblical precedent for both views, for Christ not only advocated turning the other cheek but he also whipped the money lenders out of the temple.

► **SITUATION ETHICS**. A great deal more could be said about Christian ethics, especially as it has been interpreted and developed by the Catholic theologians St. Augustine (354–430), St. Anselm [1033(4)–1109], and St. Thomas Aquinas (1225?–1274), the Reformation leaders Martin Luther (1483–1546) and John Calvin (1509–1564), and modern Protestant theologians, such as Reinhold Niebuhr (1892–1971), Karl Barth (1886–1968), Emil Brunner (1889–1966), D. Bonhoeffer (1906–1945), and Paul Tillich (1886–1965). But to discuss the particular contributions of these theologians would take us too far afield. Before leaving Christianity, however, mention should be made of a contemporary ethical movement that has attracted a considerable following and some notoriety. This is "situation ethics," "contextual ethics," or the "new morality," which has come to be associated with the theologians Rudolf Bultmann (1884–1976), John A. T. Robinson (1919–1983), and Joseph Fletcher (1934–1984).

These contemporary theologians share certain ideas with the "God is dead" movement, which maintains that the archaic Biblical conception of God is no longer applicable to the modern experience. But their main emphasis is on the primacy of love as the guiding principle for society. They are more concerned with the ethics than the metaphysics of Christian thought, and even if religious belief entirely disappeared they would still want to salvage the ethic of love and not throw out the baby with the bath water. These theologians want God redefined in a more adequate way, so that we abandon the archaic concept of a lawgiver, a righteous God who gives us codes engraved on stone tablets and specific dictums for the governance of our lives. Whether the laws are Old Testament ones concerning stealing and coveting our neighbor's wife (or husband), or New Testament principles concerning divine justice and nonresistance to evil, they do not furnish us with a basic ethic. We can no longer affirm the notion of a God who dictates specific principles or accept those principles as absolute and inviolable.

To these contemporary theologians, ethics are situational, that is, the context determines whether or not a particular principle or value should be applied. Contrary to Kant, situation ethics would not necessarily condemn suicide or lying since the circumstances may mandate them, and fidelity, honor, loyalty, even life itself may have to be forfeited for the sake of some practical moral good. No ethical principle is universally right to practice but each gains sanction within some specific context that validates its use and makes it lawful. We must "tailor our ethical cloth to fit the back of each occasion."[10]

The only norm of conduct that the situationist accepts is not a law at all but the spirit of agape love, which seeks only one's neighbor's good. Instead of being governed by specific rules, the Christian ideal of love should be taken as the sole criterion for action. To the situationist, it does not matter which principle or value is chosen provided that our choice is motivated by altruistic sentiments. In some contexts, force will be appropriate, whereas in others, pacifism will be indicated, and both can be correct if some good is achieved for the people affected by the actions. In this manner, the Christian can justify the crusades against the Muslims in the twelfth and thirteenth centuries at the same time that St. Francis of Assisi (1182?-1226) taught gentleness and was preaching a sermon to birds. Sometimes honesty will be called for, at other times deceit, in certain circumstances humility is best, in another situation self-assertion should be expressed, all according to the requirements of love. There are no absolutes for the situationist, only an attitude of loving concern for humanity that can legitimize the acceptance or rejection of any principles as the situation and love demand.

The situationist goes so far as to say that, contrary to traditional Christian teaching, any action may be justified by the results, that is, by the human welfare that is achieved. Joseph Fletcher has stated unequivocally that the end does justify the means and that nothing else can. Fletcher claimed that we should operate according to "agapeistic expediency," adopting any means that love requires to bring about good for humanity. As St. Paul (died c. 67) said, it is not lawfulness that makes an act worthwhile but rather whether it is expedient, constructive, and edifying. If, in certain contexts, divorce, abortion, euthanasia, birth control measures, and the like would effect some beneficial end, then agape love would dictate their employment.[11]

10. Joseph Fletcher, "Six Propositions: The New Look in Christian Ethics," *Harvard Divinity Bulletin* (October 1959), p. 17.
11. Ibid., p. 14.

To the situationist, then, the advantageousness of actions is what counts, and love impels us to perform these acts regardless of religious laws. As Fletcher wrote, Christian ethics is not "living according to a code but a continuous effort to relate love to a world of relativities . . . ; its constant task is to work out the strategy and tactics of love, for Christ's sake."[12]

Situation ethics can easily be related to orthodox Christian theory mainly through the common denominator of agape love. It does diverge radically from traditional teachings by relying wholly upon love and the ends of action as moral criteria, but in reacting against legalism and centering on the primacy of love it follows the main thrust of the New Testament.

FEMINIST THEOLOGY

The feminist movement in theology should also be mentioned as centered around the virtues of love as well as related feelings of compassion, mercy, communion, and tenderness. Feminist theologians stress the female nature of God, sometimes conceiving of the divine being as a goddess, sometimes emphasizing the feminine aspects of the godhead and the nature of the women that are depicted in the Bible. Above all, they deplore the supermasculine image of God as just, stern, and lawful—a being of wrath, power, and judgment. To the feminists, Christianity should present more maternal and womanly ideals, an all-forgiving love in place of principles and righteousness. And this love should embrace every type of person equally—men and women, black and white, heterosexual and homosexual. The feminists see love as encompassing not exclusionary, and they want the female aspects of human nature and the divine nature to come to the forefront.

12. Joseph Fletcher, *Situation Ethics: The New Morality* (Philadelphia: Westminster Press, 1964), p. 158.

A CRITICAL APPRAISAL

▸ **RELIGIOUS ETHICS AND THE DEMAND FOR EM-PIRICAL PROOF**. One obvious problem in basing an ethic upon the word of God is that the reality of that God can be called into question. Many people today are skeptics rather than believers, not having had the religious experiences on which belief depends. They demand empirical proof and rational arguments which religion, perhaps by its very nature, is not readily able to supply. Somehow it seems irrelevant for theologians to point out that the existence of God cannot be disproven, for this is also true of the Norse, Icelandic, Greek, Roman, and Egyptian deities; they too might exist but that bare possibility is not sufficient to induce in modern man an attitude of worship. The contemporary mind requires something positive in the way of evidence and cannot believe simply because there is no disproof of God's existence.

Similarly, the appeal to blind faith leaves us unmoved today. Faith should not consist of belief without adequate proof but should be an affirmation beyond the point at which the evidence leaves off. In the present age a significant number of people believe that this springboard of evidence, which is necessary for the leap of faith, appears lacking, and without belief in God the ethic based upon divine authority is eroded.

This problem does not arise for the devout persons, for whom God remains a living force, revealed through Scripture, and made manifest in innumerable experiences throughout their lives; God remains the author of the moral code by which they conduct themselves.

▸ **THE INDEPENDENCE OF ETHICS AND GOD**. A further problem arises, however, for the believer who regards God as the source of ethics.[13] As mentioned in Chapter 1, an act does not

---

13. Emil Brunner, who may be taken as representative of this approach, has written that whatever God wills becomes good or right. "God's will controls absolutely

become right because God wills it but rather God would will an act because it is right. That is, ethical value is not derived from God's approval but God approves of that which is, in fact, valuable. Ethics, therefore, is independent of God rather than being based on his authority. He cannot make that which is wrong right by endorsing it, or that which is right wrong by disapproving of it. If gratuitous torture is immoral, it cannot be made moral by God's condoning it, and if compassion toward the helpless is moral, it cannot be made immoral by God's changing his mind about its virtue.

Another way of putting the point is to say that God does not approve of actions capriciously but for good reason, which means that he recognizes the inherent value in certain modes of conduct and for that reason commands that human beings behave accordingly. And we, on our part, can appreciate the moral worth of his commands and see them not as the expression of his arbitrary will but as ethically sound judgments that are worthy of praise.

The force of this criticism, therefore, is that no theory of deity can provide the basis for a system of ethics. God prescribes certain actions because of some moral quality that they possess, and it is this quality that makes these actions right rather than God's approval. The existence of God is, therefore, irrelevant to the rightness of actions for they would remain right even if there were no God.

With regard to the Old Testament notion of God, it is precisely because he often appears tyrannous rather than fair-minded that questions are raised about the adequacy of deriving ethical principles from his authority. A God might be acceptable who is less than omnipotent—in fact, the American philosopher William James (1842–1910) suggested that God may lack the power to prevent natural evils from occurring, and in this way attempted to solve the problem of evil while saving the character of God. In the same way, God could be regarded as less than omniscient; he might, for example, be thought of as deficient in foresight and unable to foretell all the ramifications of creation. But a God who is not wholly good can hardly be considered a God at all. Our contemporary under-

everything," he wrote, and "What God does and wills is good; all that opposes the will of God is bad." E. Brunner, *The Divine Imperative, A Study in Christian Ethics,* trans. Olive Wyon (Philadelphia: Westminster Press, 1947), p. 119 and p. 53, respectively.

standing of the nature of God would make an evil God a contradiction in terms and a God who is deficient in goodness an inadequate conception of the supreme being. Ideally, we would want to consider God omnipotent, omniscient, and "omni-good," but even if we were forced to abandon a belief in his total perfection, perhaps as a result of the problem of evil or uncertainty as to whether or not prayers are answered, we would be most reluctant to dispense with the attribute of goodness.

The Old Testament concept of God has therefore been criticized as portraying a supernatural paternal authority rather than a benevolent deity whose commands can be understood as having an ethical base. And the virtue of obeying these commands simply because they issue from God rather than because they are right can also be questioned. We do not have an obligation to obey orders simply because they come from an authority; the authority must show itself worthy of being obeyed and the orders must be in keeping with our moral values. Otherwise there is no way of preventing such heinous actions as human sacrifice among the Incas, the cult of stranglers in Bombay, or the torture and burning of heretics during the Inquisition, all of which were done in the name of obeying God's will.

Religious people today would say that these actions did not express the genuine will of God but were a distorted perception of it, that God would never command conduct that is cruel. In saying this they are affirming the belief that the "real" God is good and wills only actions that are genuinely moral. It is significant to notice here that God is thought to issue commands and we to obey them for the same reason, namely, because they are right.

▸ **THE IMPRACTICALITY OF CHRISTIAN ETHICS**. Although the ethical ideals of the New Testament do not stress the notion of blind obedience, they can be criticized on other grounds. For example, Christian ethics has encountered objections with regard to its practicality. The principle of agape love and responding to human needs is certainly a high ideal, but the person who operates a business on this basis is doomed to bankruptcy. A banker, for example, cannot follow the maxim of "Give to him that asketh thee, and from him that would borrow of thee turn not thou away"

(*Matthew* Chapter 5, verse 42). And in international relations, Christians who treat their enemies as brothers and act for their welfare would endanger themselves, their families, and their nation. A totalitarian dictator, for instance, would like nothing better than an attitude of nonresistance; Christian pacifism will thus only help the advance of evil by default, that is, by not opposing it. To effect positive changes in world conditions, the approach of universal love simply is not feasible. If everyone adopted the ideal of agape love in their relations, then the Christian approach would work. But in a world where only some operate selflessly and the rest selfishly, altruistic people become casualties and victims in the power struggle. Little good is achieved, and a great deal of suffering can occur.

Christian theologians recognize the practical difficulties involved in applying the agape ideal, and they make various concessions to the business economy and *realpolitik*. These compromises are more or less successful but they stray very far from the pure ethics of Christianity. The American Protestant theologian Reinhold Niebuhr, for example, concluded that we must abandon the law of love and engage in evil actions if we are to improve the world politically. Individuals may behave in just and loving ways toward one another but "all human groups tend to be more predatory than the individuals which compose them . . . they take for themselves whatever their power can command." Therefore, we cannot expect to make widespread moral progress through withdrawal or pacifism but only through employing the evil tactics of racial, economic, and national groups. We must get our hands dirty, and "if we repent, Christ will forgive and receive us."[14] Niebuhr may be correct in his assessment, but his theory does point up the impracticality of utilizing Christian ethics in real social contexts.

▶ **THE SPIRIT OF LOVE VERSUS ETHICAL LAWS**. A second major problem with the agape concept has to do with the conflict that can occur between the spirit of love and the ethical laws that are listed in the Old and New Testaments. It appears right to choose Christian love over the letter of the law, and to adopt the

14. R. Niebuhr, *Moral Man and Immoral Society* (New York: C. Scribner's Sons, 1953).

viewpoint of situation ethics that love is all important, but can moral rules always be violated in the name of love?

It seems odd to be able to set aside principles regarding killing and stealing, respect for persons, the alleviation of suffering, and the avoidance of destruction—to disregard, in fact, the Ten Commandments and the Sermon on the Mount insofar as they offer codes of ethical conduct. Agape love is certainly a vital part of Christian ethics, but perhaps its role is being overemphasized if it can always override any moral principle. Furthermore, in operating this way we are left without firm moral guidelines, with too great a burden placed upon our consciences to decide which action best expresses the spirit of love. Surely a loving attitude toward humanity would naturally lead to the formulation of certain principles as the embodiment of that love, and that is what we have in the tradition of Christian ethics. By ignoring this body of ethical principles, we only condemn ourselves to repeat its development.

Thus, principles cannot simply be sacrificed to an attitude of love. Both elements must be considered, and this creates a tension within Christian ethics as to which should take priority in various circumstances. Old Testament legalism sins in one direction and situation ethics sins in another, so that we are left with an ongoing dilemma with regard to love and principles that Christians have difficulty in resolving.

▶ **CONCLUDING REMARKS**. As in the case of the ethics of duty, religious ethics, in general, present a deontological theory that is admirable in concept but fraught with very substantial flaws upon analysis. Kantian ethics can be classified under rule-deontologism, and religious ethics range from rule- to act-deontologism as we move from Old Testament ethics through New Testament ethics to situation ethics (which even approaches teleologism in its emphasis on the ends of action). But in all forms of religious ethics, practical and theoretical difficulties arise that make us question its worth even though we still respect the nobility of its sentiments. As has been noted, religious ethics can be criticized in terms of its foundation in the belief that God exists, a belief which not everyone shares, and the illogicality of deriving values from the will of God. The Old Testament notion of God was found deficient in moral qualities and the virtue of obedience to this God became dubious as a consequence, while the New Testament ethic was criticized for its impracticality and the disparity that can occur between Christian principles and the spirit of agape love. For these reasons we are led to wonder about using religious ethics as our basic reason for living. Humility dictates, however, that we should carefully consider any theory that has been maintained for several thousand years.[15]

RECAPITULATION

This chapter began with a general description of religious ethics within the Western tradition and continued with an explanation of the fundamental thrust of the Old Testament concept of God and human obligations in terms of divine commandments. The Christian ethic was then described in reference to the New Testament God, and the central motif of agape love was discussed in contrast to eros and in relation to divine justice and the attitude toward violence. The contemporary Christian position of situation ethics was briefly presented, and the chapter concluded with a critical assessment of religious ethics in their general and specific forms.

▼ ▼ ▼

REVIEW QUESTIONS

1. *Describe the principal characteristics of the religious ethic advocated in the Old Testament.*

2. *Explain the ideal in Christian ethics of* agape *as contrasted with* eros *love. What criticisms can be offered of it?*

15. For a good contemporary discussion of religious ethics see R. Adams, *The Virtue of Faith* (Oxford, England: Oxford University Press, 1987).

3. *Compare and contrast the concepts of divine and human justice. Which do you think is ethically more defensible?*

4. *Explain the ways in which situation ethics differs from the more conventional religious ethics. Why would you consider it better or worse?*

5. *In Christian ethics, how can a conflict occur between the spirit of love and the ethical laws? Which is preferable?*

11

EXISTENTIALISM

he philosophy of existentialism has had a stormy history, from the time of its inception in the nineteenth century to its flowering (like a thistle) in the midtwentieth century. Critics have excoriated the movement as promoting moral anarchy and rampant individualism, for justifying social alienation, inaction, and ennui, and for wallowing in the sordid and perverse aspects of human life. One writer has called existentialism "a blend of Nordic melancholy and Parisienne pornography." Yet despite frequent criticisms from church pulpits and college lecterns, existentialism has persisted in its appeal and must be considered as one of the major philosophic movements of the modern age. Perhaps the American pragmatist William James was right when he described the classic stages of a theory's career: "First . . . a new theory is attacked as absurd; then it is admitted to be true, but obvious and insignificant; finally it is seen to be so important that its adversaries claim that they themselves discovered it."[1] Existentialism seems to have undergone each of these stages, and has now been absorbed by a number of theories and has colored the fabric of contemporary thought.

The Danish philosopher Sören Kierkegaard (1813–1855) is usually taken as the founder of theistic existentialism, although Blaise Pascal (1623–1662) prefigured a number of his preoccupations,[2] and the German philosopher Friedrich Nietzsche (1844–1900) is generally regarded as the founding father of the atheistic branch. In the twentieth century, the list of existential philosophers includes Martin Heidegger (1889–1976), Karl Jaspers (1883–1969), Gabriel Marcel (1889–1973), and, of course, Jean-Paul Sartre (1905–1980).[3] The expression of existential ideas in literary form has always been an integral part of the movement, and numbered among writers with strong existential themes are Franz Kafka (1883–1924), Fedor Dostoyevski (1821–1881), Rainer Maria Rilke (1875–1926), André Gide (1869–1951), Jean Genet (1910–1986), and Albert Camus (1913–1960). Together, these thinkers and writers have appreciably influenced our modern concept of man and the way in which a meaningful existence should be lived.

THE STARTING POINT

Rather than beginning at the level of some abstract theory and then deriving a concept of the role of human beings in the total scheme of things, the existentialist prefers to start philosophizing from the perspective of the concrete, individual human being in the here-and-now. What does it mean to be in existence as a human being, the existentialist asks, or, more specifically, what is

1. W. James, *Essays in Pragmatism* (New York: Haffner Publishing Co., 1948), p. 159.
2. B. Pascal, *Thoughts*, trans. W. F. Trotter (New York: P. F. Collier, 1910).
3. Also numbered among the existentialists are Nicholas Berdyaev (1874–1948), Miguel de Unamuno (1864–1936), José Ortega y Gasset (1883–1955), Jacques Maritain (1882–1973), Martin Buber (1878–1965), Paul Tillich (1886–1965), and Simone de Beauvoir (1908–1986).

it to experience oneself as a person at this particular time and place? We are thrown into the world, and once we become conscious of existing, we must ask ourselves about the nature of the human condition in which we find ourselves. This is the proper starting point for understanding human beings, not via a materialistic Marxist system, or through Freudian lenses that see Oedipus complexes and symptoms of repressed feelings, or by means of a Platonic theory which regards the ideal of a human being as more real than the actual person. To the existentialist, ideas are reflections of physical reality; the physical world is not the shadow or imperfect copy of a system of ideas. We must begin with our experience of existence as it presents itself to our awareness, and not regard ourselves as detached observers, comprehending life from some objective vantage point outside life itself. "Existence is not something which can be thought from a distance," Sartre wrote; "it overwhelms you brusquely . . . it weighs heavily on your heart like a fat, loathsome beast."[4]

Once we become conscious of ourselves as existent beings, we realize that certain psychological states are present which have philosophic significance, for they are endemic to the human condition. These states bulk large in existential thought, and include anxiety, anguish (angst), dread, forlornness, boredom, alienation, estrangement, despair, and melancholy, along with many others derivative from them. Each of these feelings is abhorrent and agonizing to bear, yet they are unavoidable and form part of the predicament of man on earth, who has been cursed and blessed with consciousness. These feeling states cannot be eliminated, but it is possible to overcome their debilitating effects, and in this sense they can function as catalysts, enlivening human beings to the possibilities of existence. Although they make people uncomfortable, these psychological states can prove beneficial, arousing individuals from their customary stupor and challenging them to mobilize their energies toward a lucid and full existence.

▶ __ANXIETY__. The psychological phenomenon of anxiety may be used to illustrate this point, and explanations of it are a common feature of existentialism. To understand anxiety, both Kierkegaard

4. J.-P. Sartre, *Nausea*, trans. L. Alexander (Norfolk, CT: New Directions, 1964).

and Heidegger contrasted it with the more easily definable emotion of fear. When we are afraid, some specific source of our fear can be identified, a definite and localizable object; we can be afraid of a gun, lightning, a deadly disease, or a fall. "In fear we are always in the presence of this or that determinate being which threatens us in this or that determinate manner," Kierkegaard wrote. Once we are able to name the threat, we gain a certain degree of control and can take the appropriate measures to combat it. In anxiety, however, nothing can be specified as the cause. There does not seem to be any particular reason why we are anxious, yet we feel profoundly uneasy as though a shadow were cast over us, some impending doom. Heidegger said that if we are asked what we are anxious about we usually reply that it is really nothing.

▶ **NOTHINGNESS**. But this answer is revealing; we are exposing the truth that our anxiety is really about nothingness, that is, the possibility of our no longer being in the world.[5] In the phenomenon of anxiety we confront the sensation of utter terror at the threat of annihilation, realizing that the world offers no protection against the void awaiting us. It is the state, as Tillich described it, of a being "aware of its possible non-being,"[6] and feeling wholly bereft, abandoned, and helpless to avert the ultimate extinction of consciousness. We are aware of the absence of awareness that preceded our birth and that also constitutes the meaning of our death, and we know that our being is thus transitory and finite, enclosed by infinitudes of nonbeing.

In facing nothingness (rather than pretending to ourselves that we will live forever), the individual comes to terms with his or her actual state of mortality. Instead of being self-deceived and living in "bad faith," people can choose to exist in an authentic way. Although we may lie to others (for their own good), we ought never to lie to ourselves; the cardinal sin to the existentialist is to deny the truth of our extinction, for then we deprive ourselves of the chance to be fully alive.

5. Martin Heidegger, "What is Metaphysics," in *Existence and Being* (Chicago: H. Regnery Co., 1949), pp. 141ff.
6. P. Tillich, *The Courage to Be* (New Haven, CT: Yale University Press, 1952).

Most human beings live as though they were going to live forever. The confrontation with nonexistence can jolt people from their slumbers and make them aware of their finite state; they can then utilize the time available to them to become something before they are nothing. Nonbeing can impel people to maximize their beings within the temporal constraints that reality has imposed. Anxiety, nothingness, and existence are, therefore, intimately connected, for as Camus wrote, "There is no sun without shadow, and it is essential to know the night."[7]

The analysis of each of these psychological states yields similar insights concerning the human condition, and the existentialist explores their ramifications, not to wallow in depressing truths but to stimulate people to lead an intense and rich existence.

EXISTENCE PRECEDES ESSENCE

By beginning at the level of human beings in the world and understanding what we confront as part of our psychological reality, we are led to a central tenet of existential philosophy. Since man's mode of being is such that he is aware of his eventual nonbeing, he is then in a position to act to fulfill himself. In fact, he must act because he will not become a human being unless he does; failing to make a choice means failing to achieve humanness. That which makes human beings what they essentially are comes about as a result of their concrete choices. We are "the sum of our actions" and "none of our non-actions" as Sartre said, and we create ourselves through the commitments we make. Our actions do not follow from any innate character but our character is the product of our actions. In choosing, we define ourselves and bear responsibility for the type of person we become.

Sartre developed this point by contrasting the mode of being of objects with that of human beings. Objects possess their essential

7. A. Camus, *The Myth of Sisyphus* (New York: Alfred A. Knopf, Inc., 1955), p. 91.

characteristics when they come into being; their essence, or set of qualities that identify them, is fully formed at the moment of existence, and the objects will not become anything further or different during their lifespan. A paper knife, to use Sartre's example, must be in the craftsman's mind before it is brought into existence, and once it exists it will never develop into anything other than what is meant by paper knife. Human beings, however, first exist and then fill out their essence by their choices and actions. People do not possess an essence prior to their existence but become specific individuals (and collectively define humankind) by what they do once they are in being. Once can think of the characteristics of a paper knife without its existing, but one cannot conceive of a person's characteristics until he or she exists and acts to become someone.[8]

In making these assertions, the existentialist presupposes that people have the power to decide about their lives, that human beings are creatures with free will who can choose the kind of person they want to be and can become the person they choose. They therefore oppose all forms of determinism as applied to human beings, preferring to apply causal thinking only to objects that have fixed characteristics. Existentialists also reject all theories of human nature, for to regard man as possessing some specific nature when he comes into being would render him an object whose essence preceded its existence. Human beings are nothing other than the ensemble of their actions and do not manifest the working out of any inherent nature. "Man is the future of man," Sartre said, and history does not teach us anything about the human race since man is constantly creating himself anew in every age; whatever generalization one attempts to make about humankind is contradicted by the "choice of themselves" of the next generation. Sartre even based his atheism on these grounds, arguing that if God created man then human beings would resemble paper knives with their essence already conceived of in the mind of God. (In Christianity, in fact, man is believed to be born with a sinful nature.) It is only without the notion of God that existence precedes essence, and man can be regarded as truly human.

To the existentialist, then, existence precedes essence, and

8. J.-P. Sartre, *Existentialism*, trans. B. Frechtman (New York: Philosophical Library, 1947).

being human is not a biological fact but a task that is accomplished through decisions and commitments. We achieve humanness by appropriating the freedom to choose our identity and acting to create our individual selves.

THE EXISTENTIAL METHOD

In attempting to understand the human situation, and to resolve the various tensions of existence, the existentialist gravely distrusts the methods of empiricism and rationalism as well as the conventional morality that is based upon them. The empiricist, using the techniques of scientific method, is thought to reside outside the events and objects that are being investigated, remaining a detached observer who never penetrates the heart of the subject. External attributes are all that can be ascertained through empirical research and even then, only those external phenomena that can be quantified. The existentialist prefers the searcher to the researcher and regards that searcher as participating in the subject of the inquiry in a sympathetic and empathetic way. With this approach one can enter into the *eidos* or quiddity of whatever experience presents itself to consciousness.

▸ __PHENOMENOLOGY__. The formal name given to this method is phenomenology, and Edmund Husserl (1859–1938) is generally credited as its founder. The various existentialists have formulated its meaning in different ways, Gabriel Marcel, for example, regarding it as concentration on the primacy of experience over pure thought,[9] and Heidegger defining it as the analysis of the way being manifests itself to consciousness.[10] In general, the phenome-

9. G. Marcel, *The Existential Background of Human Dignity* (Cambridge, MA: Harvard University Press, 1963), p. 96.
10. M. Heidegger, *Being and Time*, trans. J. Macquarrie and E. Robinson (New York: Harper and Bros., 1962), p. 62.

nological method seems to mean the intuitive apprehension of the fundamental being of whatever is encountered by our consciousness. Instead of entertaining dogmatic assumptions as to the nature of the objects we experience, or categorizing them according to their practical function, historical associations, or scientific classification, we plunge directly to the center of phenomena and achieve understanding from within. The inessential layers of utility, historicity, and so forth must be set aside (bracketed) so that the reality of the thing-in-itself is revealed. A landscape, for instance, is not real estate, the site of a decisive battle, or an igneous lava intrusion, but that experiential reality that appears to our consciousness as a self-enclosed phenomenon with its own inner being.

Sartre, in his novel *Nausea*,[11] described the principal character Roquentin entering a room and feeling something cold and hard in his hand. It is the doorknob, an object that we normally do not notice because we treat it strictly as a means for opening a door. But Roquentin regards it suddenly as an entity in itself, and cannot simply dismiss or make use of it. He experiences the same reaction to a glass, which is usually disregarded, being merely a vessel for conveying liquid to one's lips, and to a skimming stone, which we customarily attend to only for its practical characteristics of shape and weight, not that gritty, dense, moist object that it unexpectedly appears to be to Roquentin. All of these objects suddenly demand attention and recognition as though they were in picture frames; they are phenomena in themselves with unique and essential modes of being.

Various insights are thought to accrue from the employment of the phenomenological method. In moral philosophy, for example, the phenomenon of contrition was analyzed, and it was found that to be contrite meant more than being sorry for the wrong one had done, for even after one repented and compensated for the harm, the feeling of contrition remained. More deeply understood, contrition means not being sorry for the action but regretting that one is the kind of person who could perform the awful action. In a similar manner, Max Scheler (1874–1928) concluded with regard to human goals that actions are never directed toward pleasure but

---

11. J.-P. Sartre, *Nausea*, pp. 7–20.

toward values; we recognize values in the world and pursue them with pleasure as the emotional accompaniment of our striving. Dietrich von Hildebrand (1889–1977), in his examination of the idea of sexual purity, claimed that a phenomenological investigation reveals purity to be something achieved through sensitivity to sexual attraction since insensitivity to sex is a defect in itself. People who are not especially moved by sexual desire cannot then claim to be pure even if they have not had sexual relations. In all of these cases the phenomenologists attempted to understand experience from within rather than from without. As the poet Gerard Manley Hopkins wrote, we should always try to comprehend the "inscape" of things.

▶ **UNDERSTANDING THE HUMAN CONDITION**. The existentialist uses the phenomenological method to understand the human condition and the various attendant phenomena of nothingness, being, freedom, authenticity, commitment, and the like. The empirical approach to knowledge, by contrast, does not descend within the phenomenological object and fails to engage the inquirer who is neutral, alienated, and frozen toward both the object of inquiry and his or her own subjective self; for this reason it remains superficial. Likewise, rationalist epistemology is thought to suffer from the same defects and to be specifically opposed to emotion as a genuine channel of understanding. The existentialists regard emotion, feeling, and the affective states, in general, as being superior to reason, and thus do not attempt to demonstrate the truth of their ideas in syllogisms like a "poor definition cutter with logical scissors," but try to provoke personal responses by their poetic style. This is also why so much of existentialism is cast in literary form, and why existentialists feel such contempt for contemporary academic philosophies such as linguistic analysis, which regards the clarification of language as the proper function of philosophers. A professor, Sartre has said, is someone who professes that someone else suffered. In place of rational objectivity the existentialist wants to stimulate our subjective, emotional grasp of truths, through an immediate and direct arousal of our feelings.

If we are ruled by reason, we also relinquish our freedom, for then we cannot think or do as we please but only as reason dictates. We become intimidated by the requirements for consistency, reasonableness, and coherent thinking, and must justify our behavior and ideas before some imaginary, rational tribunal sitting in judgment inside us. The existentialist believes that we must liberate ourselves from the straitjacket of reason if we are to lead a full existence; we should be free to behave rationally or irrationally, just as we like. To contradict yourself is a great relief, so refreshing, as Camus wrote in his play *Caligula*. And as Dostoyevski wrote in *Notes from the Underground:* "What sort of free will is left when we come to tables and arithmetic, when it will all be a case of two times two makes four? Two times two makes four even without my will. As if free will meant that!"[12] Reason must always be subordinate to freedom because it is through freely chosen actions that human beings develop their essence and live a full life. If we defer to logic, we are machines not people.

▶ **THE GRATUITOUS ACT.** The existential novelist André Gide went so far in his championing of emotion as to advocate unpremeditated, spontaneous action as the highest kind. The "gratuitous act," as Gide called it, is truest to the person and expressive of the real self, because it does not arise from intellectual considerations as to which alternative is most advantageous, which offers the smallest risk, or what consequences may follow from each possibility. Whenever we deliberate, Gide maintained, weighing the pros and cons judiciously, then factors that do not form part of our selves begin to dominate our thinking and make the decision for us. Our education, social conventions and prejudices, family beliefs, books we have read, technical skills, and so forth are brought into play and become the basis for our choice. For an act to come from us, it must be impulsive and spontaneous, without any time for second thoughts, almost without thinking at all; only then are outside influences eliminated. According to Gide, "the quickest, the most sudden action seemed to me to be the best. It appeared to me that my action was all the more sincere in that I was sweeping away before it all those considerations with which I attempted to justify it at first. Henceforward, acting haphazardly and without giving myself

12. F. Dostoyevski, *Notes from the Underground*, trans. R. E. Matlaw (New York: E. P. Dutton, 1960).

time to reflect, my slightest actions appear to be more significant since they are no longer reasoned out.''[13]

The idea of gratuitous actions is illustrated best, perhaps, in *The Vatican Cellars*, where Gide portrayed a character named Lafcadio who, on an impulse of irritation, hurls a fellow passenger out the door of his train compartment. To Gide, even criminal actions are permissible in order to be oneself; he would not want us to deliberate over the morality of actions any more than we should pause for any rational considerations. This would be the extreme position within existentialism, although Dostoyevski was drawn toward that ultimate assertion of freedom in *Crime and Punishment*, and Nietzsche has told us that ''the greatest fruitfulness and the greatest enjoyment of existence is: to live dangerously!''[14] By and large, however, the antiintellectualism of the existentialists would not be carried that far. Camus' existentialism has a strong humanistic component, Rilke has been compared to St. Francis, and Sartre maintained that we should share our freedom with other people. The existentialists do assert the primacy of emotion over reason but relatively few would be in favor of total spontaneity, particularly in situations where harm would result.

▶ **SUMMARY**. The general existential emphasis on the emotions relates to the conviction that the affective part of human beings is the major part, and rationality is the tip of the iceberg; in this the existentialists agree with Freud. The emotions are also thought to be the medium through which the most essential human communication takes place. It is the way we understand each other, expressing our mutual terrors and most profound hopes, and the means by which we project ourselves into the innermost nature of all experience and intuitively grasp its ''inscape.''

The existentialist, then, favors emotion over reason, subjectivity over objectivity, phenomenology rather than empiricism or

13. A. Gide, *Prometheus Illbound*, trans. L. Rothermere (London: Chatto and Windus, 1919).
14. F. Nietzsche, *The Gay Science*, in *The Portable Nietzsche*, ed. W. Kaufmann (New York: Viking Press, 1954), p. 97. See also F. Dostoyevski, *Crime and Punishment*, trans. S. Monas (New York: Signet, 1968), especially Part 3, Chapter 5, pp. 255ff, and Part 8, Chapter 4, pp. 400ff.

rationalism, and the direct experience of human existence instead of abstract theories through which we deduce man's place in the universe. And the existentialist affirms that through these means we come to an understanding of the human condition, which is an anguished one, lived in the realization of our impending nonbeing and charged with the necessity to make commitments and thereby achieve humanness and individuality. The confrontation with nothingness should galvanize us into asserting our freedom and thereby maximize our being within the finite limits imposed upon human existence.

VERSIONS OF EXISTENTIALISM

To deepen and elaborate the existentialist position, we now examine the particular versions of existentialism that have been propounded by three of its leading exponents: Friedrich Nietzsche, Sören Kierkegaard, and Jean-Paul Sartre. We cannot cover their entire philosophies but an exposition of some of their major ideas should prove helpful in understanding existentialism more fully.

▶ **FRIEDRICH NIETZSCHE.** Nietzsche, like Marx, was an iconoclast who wanted to destroy many of the values in his nineteenth century world in order to allow human beings a rich and complete existence. He deplored mass society, which in his view suppresses the spirit of individuals striving for greater fullness in life, and regarded it as a leveling force, imposing common and mediocre standards upon all people. The tendency in modern social life, Nietzsche believed, is toward producing an amorphous mass of anonymous individuals, "one flock and no shepherd," for all independent thought is crushed by the weight of public opinion. The outstanding person does not dare to assume leadership or even speak his or her mind, but is reduced to an internal rebelliousness and ineffectuality by the numerical opposition of the masses. Rather than valuing individual accomplishment, society always prizes conformity to the norm, which necessarily means mediocrity and adjustment to the status quo. The goal of mass society is thus to make all the sheep equal rather than free, and anyone who differs or excels or asserts himself is stifled in his progress, and along with him the development of the human race. If innovative and outstanding individuals were allowed to be heard, society would be lifted to new heights and the human race would surpass itself. But as it is, there exist only stagnation and deadness.

The Forces of Oppression. Nietzsche singled out democracy, socialism, and Christianity as oppressive forces. He regarded democracy and socialism as enemies of the vital spirit of humanity because they maintain that all people are equal and should have the same proportion of the world's goods and an equal voice in government; the idea of someone being superior and entitled to greater consideration is anathema to their values. Everything must be decided by majority rule, which means that bourgeois morality will carry the day. We do not take a vote in order to decide the merits of a work of art or a scientific theory, but oddly enough we allow the masses to decide the social morality under which we live daily; the norms of mediocrity are allowed to rule our social existence.

Nietzsche criticized Christianity on similar grounds, for it seems in league with everything that is common and timid. To Nietzsche's mind, Christianity favors humility and self-denial, pacifism, conservatism, and mutual helpfulness. This is a manifestation of "herd morality," which Christianity reflects and supports, and it is founded on weakness rather than strength. Christians are merely extolling their own inadequacies and transforming them into virtues because they do not have the courage to assert themselves. They believe the meek shall inherit the earth because they lack the strength of will to master the earth. "Christianity is the religion of pity," Nietzsche wrote, and

> . . . pity stands opposed to the tonic emotions which heighten our vitality; it has a depressing effect . . . (and) makes suffering contagious. . . . In Christianity the instincts of the subjugated and oppressed come to the fore: here the lowest classes seek

> their salvation. . . . Christian too is mortal enmity against the lords of the earth, against the "noble"—along with a sly, secret rivalry (one leaves them the "body," one wants only the "soul"). Christian, finally, is the hatred of the spirit, of pride, courage, freedom, liberty of the spirit; Christian is the hatred of the senses, of joy in the senses, of joy itself.[15]

Nietzsche thought Christianity is not only antivital but distracting in that it draws people's attention away from real issues of human progress and personal growth. Like Marx, he did not want to understand the world so much as to change it, and Christianity stood in the way as a conservative force that persuades people to pin their hopes on the life to come and to control their earthly longings.

Nietzsche's "Master Morality." In place of the "herd" or "slave morality" promoted by democracy, socialism, and Christianity, Nietzsche advocated a "master morality"—at least for the outstanding individuals who have the courage to adopt it. Slave virtues may be fine for the masses who endorse their own mediocre and obsequious state but these virtues must not be allowed to govern the strong, decisive, daring, and creative individuals whom Nietzsche called the "masters." They must have a new ethic founded on the will to power rather than on safety and conformity, one that brings about a "transvaluation of all values" or is "beyond good and evil." The masters can transcend conventional morality and, creating their own code, assume leadership of the world, guiding it out of the lethargy and stagnation into which slave morality has plunged it.

Nietzsche advocated a dualistic theory of morals, with one set of principles for masters and another for slaves, although he hoped for the eventual dispersion of the mass of slaves as they achieved progressive self-awareness. For no man is a slave or a master by nature, but only through cowardice or courage. The master asserts his will and uses his capacity for free action to escape the abject state; he takes the risk of freedom to create himself according to his own lights and raise humanity to a new level. Master morality was obviously Nietzsche's ideal and he affirmed it even though social turmoil

---

15. F. Nietzsche, *The Anti-Christ*, in *The Portable Nietzsche*, pp. 572–573, 589.

would result. In *The Gay Science* (also translated as *The Joyful Wisdom*) Nietzsche wrote:

> The strongest and most evil spirits have so far advanced humanity the most: they have always rekindled the drowsing passions—all ordered society puts the passions to sleep; they have always reawakened the sense of comparison, of contradiction, of joy in the new, the daring, and the untried. . . . I welcome all signs that a more manly, a warlike, age is about to begin, an age which, above all, will give honor to valor once again. For this age shall prepare the way for one yet higher. . . . To this end we now need many preparatory valorous men who cannot leap into being out of nothing—any more than out of the sand and slime of our present civilization and metropolitanism: men who are bent on seeking for that aspect in all things in which must be overcome; men characterized by cheerfulness, patience, unpretentiousness, and contempt for all great vanities . . . men who have their own festivals, their own weekdays, their own periods of mourning, who are accustomed to command with assurance and are no less ready to obey when necessary, in both cases equally proud and serving their own cause; men who are in greater danger, more fruitful, and happier![16]

Nietzsche used the term "*Übermensch*," or "overman," for the perfect master, the true lord of the earth who has overcome his lower self and created meaning for his existence. He has drawn strength from man's most basic drive, the will to power, and succeeded in reaching a superior, more powerful state of being. The overman is able to elevate humanity to a higher destiny than all previous eras, which had leaden, superstitious belief in gods. We

16. F. Nietzsche, *The Gay Science*, in *The Portable Nietzsche*, pp. 93, 97. Passages such as these have left Nietzsche open to the charge that his doctrines support fascism, and the Nazi party did make use of some of his ideas. By and large, Nietzsche's meaning was distorted by the Nazis, as when he wrote about the ideal of the "blonde beast," by which he meant the lion but which was taken to mean the "Aryan" race. Nevertheless, there are parts of Nietzsche's writings that easily lend themselves to a fascist interpretation even though that may not be the main thrust of his philosophy.

have killed God, Nietzsche declared in an enigmatic metaphor, and now man must fill the void created by his absence and assume responsibility for his own future. "God is dead. God remains dead. And we have killed him. How shall we, the murderers of all murderers, comfort ourselves? What was holiest and most powerful of all that the world has yet owned has bled to death under our knives. . . . Is not the greatness of this deed too great for us? Must not we ourselves become gods simply to seem worthy of it?"[17]

▶ SÖREN KIERKEGAARD. The theistic existentialism of Kierkegaard should stand in strong contrast to Nietzsche's atheism, but oddly enough the similarities between these two men are more impressive than their differences. Nietzsche's writing, like that of Kierkegaard, has a decidedly religious tone, especially his *Thus Spake Zarathustra*;[18] and Kierkegaard too criticized his society for its lethargy and inauthentic mode of living, although Kierkegaard thought the remedy lay in genuine Christian faith rather than in its repudiation.

Kierkegaard's diatribes were directed specifically against the smugness and complacency of his native Denmark in the nineteenth century, which he conceived as a microcosm of the modern world. The religious observance of the people consisted of prosperous membership in an institution, "conventional Churchmanship," as he regarded it, rather than an encounter with the living God. The people had substituted the church for religion, and the sense of challenge that Christianity should provoke had been lost, for the church itself had become secularized and social with little relation to God. Kierkegaard had some harsh words for the bishop, wearing orders on his chest, who told his parishioners to renounce the pomp and glory of the world. With this type of example, according to Kierkegaard, the people no longer realized that God was the reality behind the church, that he was the fundamental being on whom our lives depend. We are all in the "inescapable presence of God," Kierkegaard wrote, and to confront that fact forces us to a decision

17. Ibid, pp. 95, 96.
18. F. Nietzsche, *Thus Spake Zarathustra*, trans. M. Cowan (Chicago: H. Regnery Co., 1957).

as to whether or not we will lead an authentically Christian life. Being a Christian does not come about automatically at birth or through childhood baptism or by church attendance; it is a conscious choice and a lifelong task that calls for extreme spiritual heroism.

Kierkegaard also denounced rational theology as tepid and objective, having nothing of the commanding passion of the Gospels. Theology transforms the spiritual impact of Scripture into a system of ideas and demonstrations of logical arguments, thereby substituting a detached, technical approach to God for a personal relationship with him. This allows people to evade their responsibility of deciding for or against God; it intellectualizes the question and leaves it suspended. To Kierkegaard, human beings should live with the constant awareness that they are face to face with their maker, naked, guilty, blind, and awaiting judgment. Only then will they come to live an authentic existence.

The Three Stages of Human Development. A central part of Kierkegaard's philosophy was his description of the three stages through which human beings can pass in their ascent toward God. The aesthetic stage comes first and many people remain there all their lives, for it means to Kierkegaard the usual life in which we savor a variety of the world's pleasures. We want to enjoy ourselves and we invent a continually changing array of activities as entertainment. To distract ourselves, we adopt what Kierkegaard called the "method of repetition" in which we change our jobs, our residences, our friends, our appearance, and the like in an endless round of pleasure-seeking. The pace becomes frenetic as we look for greater variety, and as our immunity to pleasure increases, we derive less and less satisfaction from every activity. We sustain ourselves, Kierkegaard said, like a stone skipping across the water that must sink beneath the waves when the dance is done.

At this point, Kierkegaard maintained, we descend into despair, and the future character of our life is determined by the way in which we despair. If we redouble our efforts for enjoyable experiences, we will inevitably sink into states of despair again and again and this cycle will become the pattern of our existence. However, we can leap upward from this level and attain the ethical stage of being. Here we abandon the attitude of selfishness and detachment and commit ourselves to the well being of others. We join causes and are interested in human progress, the improvement of ourselves, and the establishment of justice, freedom, and equality for our fellow human beings. We endorse moral principles and believe in human perfectibility, investing our energies in organizations that aim toward achieving that perfection.

Gradually, however, our energies wane as we encounter the resistance of the human race to being improved as well as the perverseness inside ourselves that balks at a life of selfless dedication. In short, we come to realize the depth of evil in humanity that makes the moral ideal impossible to attain, and with this realization we experience the debilitating states of penitence, remorse, and guilt that, Kierkegaard said, take the heart out of a person. Again, everything depends on whether we then throw ourselves into ethical programs with even greater dedication or whether we decide to risk existing at the religious stage. The first is doomed to repeated failure, the second constitutes our salvation.

In the religious stage ethical considerations are left behind and our trust is placed wholly in God. We no longer look to justify or explain our actions in terms of moral standards but desire to come into direct relationship with God and follow his will without qualification. In seeking understanding of God, we do not consult the established church or the interpretations of theologians but try to experience his presence in our lives. And once we hear the voice of God, it becomes absolutely authoritative, transcending our concern for a personally enjoyable life or our obligation to promote the good of humanity. This is the commitment of faith that surpasses the demands of rationality or morality. To Kierkegaard, it is an either/or situation; either we trust in God or we rely upon the standards of man.

The Paradigm of the Truly Religious Life. Kierkegaard used the Abraham and Isaac story as his exemplar of the truly religious life. According to the Biblical account, Abraham is ordered by God to sacrifice his son Isaac on Mount Moriah, and without faltering, Abraham is prepared to carry out the command. He does not ask himself whether God's command is correct and rational, or whether it is a genuine divine command or an imaginary voice: He simply acts in accordance with his primary response to the word of God.

Rather than circumscribing God by logic and saying that he cannot command an irrational act, or limiting God in terms of morality by claiming that he cannot order anything immoral, Abraham accepts the supremacy of God without question.

This, to Kierkegaard, represents the paradoxical nature of faith, that it demands complete trust even in the face of absurdity. For the infinite to come into being in time through the person of Christ is also a paradox, as is the doctrine of three persons in one of the trinity, but each must be accepted. To question them would be to place reason over religion and to betray our faith in God. To be a "knight of faith" in the manner of Abraham, we must risk everything and experience the anguish of our commitment, for in this way we overcome despair and penitence and lead the fullest existence possible for human beings.

▸ JEAN-PAUL SARTRE. Kierkegaard's philosophy is articulated most completely in his work *Concluding Unscientific Postscript*[19] and that of Sartre is best expressed in *Being and Nothingness*. These two books, together with Nietzsche's *Thus Spake Zarathustra* and Heidegger's *Being and Time*, sound the principal themes of existentialism. The conclusions and recommendations of these existentialists can be markedly different (as we have seen with Nietzsche and Kierkegaard) but their style, concerns, and criticisms are much the same. Sartre's views are expressed through plays and novels as well as in his philosophic works, and we will examine some of his main ideas although we cannot do justice to the full range of his thought.

The Completeness of Objects versus the Incompleteness of Human Beings. As mentioned previously, Sartre distinguished between the mode of being of objects and that of human beings by claiming that the essence of objects precedes their existence, whereas for man the reverse is true. He also distinguished the two by saying that things exist in an *en-soi* (in itself) state and human existence is always *pour-soi* (for itself). By these concepts Sartre meant that objects are dense and integrated, packed and whole; they are

19. S. Kierkegaard, *Concluding Unscientific Postscript*, trans. D. F. Swenson and W. Lowrie (Princeton, NJ: Princeton University Press, 1941).

complete in themselves and lack nothing. We can never say that an object should be more than it is, that a rock ought to be a better rock, or that a frog lacks something as a frog. However, this can always be said of a human being in the *pour-soi* state because people always have gaps in their being and are less than they could be. Man always exists for himself in that he is perpetually striving to become complete.

The main gap within human beings lies between their selves and their awareness of themselves—that is, between the person as subject and the person as the object of his or her own awareness, the "I" and the "me." Nothing really separates us but it is an everlasting nothing that can never be bridged. There is the self, and the self contemplating the self, and, even worse, the self that is aware of the self which contemplates the self, and so on ad infinitum, so that the schisms inside the human being increase in direct proportion to the individual's awareness. The only way in which this fundamental division can be healed is through loss of awareness, but since that type of consciousness is the main constituent of humanness, a person can only become complete by becoming less than human. Therefore, people will always have fundamental gaps in their being unless they consent to be unconscious objects; man *qua* man remains perpetually incomplete.

In a sense, human beings are a "futile passion" ("*passion inutile*"), for they long for the impossible and spend their time pursing it. They want to have complete being and at the same time to retain their human consciousness; that is, they basically desire to be *en-soi-pour-soi*, and all their projects are ultimately aimed at this self-contradictory goal. Human life is, therefore, tragic by the very logic of man's metaphysical position.

Man must of live out his life, then, in a state inferior to the wholeness of objects, yearning for a completeness that his "ontological status," as it is technically called, necessarily precludes him from attaining. But at the same time that his consciousness makes him inferior to objects, it also constitutes his superiority, for consciousness enables man to choose the character of his life, to project meaning into what is otherwise just a meaningless proliferation of life forms. "Man's freedom is the result of his ontological inferiority," Sartre said. We are less than objects but also more, for at least we can decide what we will become as individuals

EXISTENTIALISM

and our lives can gain significance by the striving to attain greater fullness of being.

Investing Life with Meaning. To Sartre's mind, there is no reason for the existence of humans or objects. All forms of matter burgeon, multiply, and blossom, ooze and secrete themselves into being without any purpose for existing. There is a "thatness" to everything but no "why." If there were a God, then life would have meaning, but since, to Sartre, the universe is empty, all existence is *de trop*, that is, pointless, unnecessary, excessive, and superfluous. However, at least human beings are aware of the senselessness of their existence, and that understanding enables people to invest their lives with meaning even though life in itself is inherently meaningless. Matter has become self-conscious in human beings only to realize the pointlessness of matter, but people can use this knowledge to fill their lives with purpose. "Before you come alive," Sartre wrote, "life is nothing; it's up to you to give it a meaning, and value is nothing else but the meaning you choose."[20]

Our efforts to lead a full and meaningful life of our own choice naturally produce conflict because each person is striving to do likewise. Sartre devoted considerable space to the analysis of "the other" and the blockages and frustrations that human beings present to one another; in his play *No Exit*, in fact, he declared that Hell is other people. But we must learn to share our freedom with others and not thwart their projects since we are all in the same situation of trying to invent a personally meaningful existence. We also have an obligation, Sartre felt, to assume responsibility for our actions because they have been freely chosen by us, in the void and without compulsion. Furthermore, we are nothing but the totality of our actions, so to deny any act means denying part of ourselves.

Sartre also maintained that we must realize the full extent of our responsibility, for in choosing to act in certain ways and becoming a particular type of person we are also choosing for others in that we are presenting a model for all mankind: ". . . if I want to marry, to have children; even if this marriage depends solely on my own circumstances or passion or wish, I am involving all humanity in monogamy and not merely myself. Therefore, I am responsible for

20. J.-P. Sartre, *Existentialism*, p. 58.

myself and for everyone else. I am creating a certain image of man of my own choosing. In choosing myself, I choose man."[21] In order to be human we must act, but we do so without any objective foundation in values now that God has disappeared, and we experience anguish and forlornness in the realization that our actions "fashion an image" that is "valid for everybody and for our whole age."

To exist as a human being, then, meant to Sartre acting in good faith with a clear awareness of our existential condition. The completeness of objects is impossible for human as beings as well as undesirable, for we would then lose consciousness (which is the condition for choosing our lives), but we must commit ourselves to courses of action so as to fulfill ourselves to the greatest extent. Man's capacity for freely chosen action must be engaged for the maximization of his being, and in acting we should not interfere with other people's freedom or evade the full responsibility for our own actions. Without illusions, with a lucid recognition of our solitary state, we must decide upon the meaning of our lives and thereby achieve authentic existence.

A CRITICAL APPRAISAL

▶ **THE EXISTENTIALIST STRESS ON SUBJECTIVITY.**
The subjective and personal tone of a great deal of existential writing is extremely worrisome to a number of critics. The existentialists are thought to rely much too heavily on their private emotions and feeling states to the exclusion of the more general experience of humankind. As Bertrand Russell (1872–1970) remarked, "Subjective certainty is inversely proportional to objective certainty." The fact that we have strong feelings, therefore, cannot be taken as a criterion for truth. Quite often the preoccupation with

---

21. J.-P. Sartre, *The Humanism of Existentialism,* in *Essays in Existentialism* (New York: Citadel Press, 1968), p. 37. This is the same essay as in footnote 16, but under a different title and in a newer edition.

such conditions as anxiety, dread, forlornness, and alienation also borders on the pathological. The existentialists claim they are actually uncovering those psychological states that are endemic to the human condition, but perhaps they are merely reflecting their own, rather morbid personalities.

By stressing subjectivity so strongly, the existentialists are also led to a wholesale rejection of reason and empiricism; personal emotions alone are considered to be valid means of knowing. This position is extremely dangerous, for then no one's subjective impressions can be challenged by rational arguments or sense data. For example, there is no way to adjudicate between an existentialists's claim that existence precedes essence and an essentialist's contention (such as Plato's) that essence precedes existence. Both cannot be right, but there is no way of resolving the issue once reason is disqualified. Similarly, Heidegger's support for Nazism becomes as defensible as does the humanistic existentialism of Camus since each is founded on private sentiments. And if the empirical findings of science do not square with existential notions, these results would be rejected by existentialists even though they are publicly verifiable. A position of this kind does not have sufficient safeguards against error and lacks appropriate means of distinguishing between truth and self-delusion.

▶ **HUMAN NATURE AND FREEDOM**. Another set of criticisms has to do with the existential view of man's mode of being. The existentialist claims that there is no such thing as human nature, that man creates his essence through his actions. But this is contradicted by the existentialist claim that man possesses an innate capacity for free actions: Freedom, then, must be part of his essential nature. Furthermore, theistic existentialists such as Kierkegaard have contended that an inherent depravity characterizes human beings, and Marcel and Jaspers spoke about the human need to establish social communication. Surely these are assertions about human nature. All of the existentialists appear to have some concept of man apart from what human beings make of themselves, if only the assumption that we strive to maximize our being.

The existentialist also seems to carry the concept of human

freedom too far in maintaining that people are wholly responsible for their lives and their character; common sense tells us that circumstances do affect what we become, at least to some extent. To hold people responsible for what others do as a consequence of their example also seems an extreme and indefensible position. On the other hand, the existentialist limits freedom unduly by saying that man is compelled to activate his freedom in order to be human; apparently human beings are not free to refrain from the exercise of their freedom. The term "freedom," like many other key existentialist concepts, is used in such an ambiguous way that it is often difficult to determine what the existentialist means by it.

▶ **EXISTENTIALIST VALUES**. Another difficulty with the existentialist position has to do with values. Nietzsche's hard code of master morality is certainly open to question insofar as it makes a virtue of warlike behavior (if not war itself) and condemns Christian pity and compassion. And Gide carried gratuitous action to the point where he approved of unpremeditated murder. Kierkegaard for his part would have us kill our children if we thought we heard God telling us to do so, which makes one wonder whether people should not stop at the ethical stage rather than go on to the religious one.

Apart from specific criticisms that can be made, the existentialists generally have maintained that values are created, not discovered, and that an action becomes valuable by virtue of the fact that we choose it. Sartre, perhaps as the prime example, quoted with approval Dostoyevski's statement that "If God did not exist, everything would be permitted," and since Sartre himself rejected a belief in God he could not see any ultimate justification for ideals. We have previously seen that the loss of God need not entail the loss of values, but passing over that difficulty for the moment, it hardly seems correct to say that whatever type of life we lead is valuable because we freely elect it. Mass murderers or political despots cannot escape blame for their actions or character simply because they chose that particular way of life. And there do seem to be better and worse ways to live, otherwise the existentialists would not be trying to persuade us to adopt their philosophy. Yet Sartre wrote that "all human activities are equivalent ... Thus it amounts to the same thing whether one gets drunk alone or is a leader of nations."[22] This seems to carry subjectivism to the point of absurdity.

Despite these criticisms, existentialism does challenge us to confront the basic terms of our lives and to decide how to exist most fully. It enlivens us to the necessity for choice, to the large degree of responsibility that we bear for the person we are, and to our temporary position on earth. In all of these ways it has a beneficial effect on our existence because it forces us to account for ourselves and, hopefully, lead more intense and meaningful lives than we would have done otherwise.

RECAPITULATION

Chapter 11 has dealt with the principal features and representatives of the existentialist movement. We began with a description of the existentialist approach to philosophy in contrast to previous starting points for philosophizing, and, in this connection, we analyzed the phenomenon of anxiety in relation to nothingness. The implications of the existential maxim that existence precedes essence was then developed with regard to the concepts of freedom and human nature, and the existentialist's use of phenomenology rather than empiricism as the primary epistemological method was discussed; the role of the emotions was also treated in relation to reason.

The atheistic existentialism of Nietzsche was elaborated in terms of its opposition to democracy, socialism, and Christianity, and its endorsement of master morality, and the theistic existential position of Kierkegaard was discussed, highlighting the targets of his criticisms and his description of the three stages of human life. Sartre's contemporary existentialism was then developed principally through his *en-soi* and *pour-soi* distinction, and we explored the implications of it for freedom, responsibility, and an authentic exis-

---

22. J.-P. Sartre, *Being and Nothingness*, trans. Hazel Barnes (New York: Philosophical Library, 1956), p. 627.

tence. The chapter ended with three criticisms of the existentialist position.

▼ ▼ ▼

REVIEW QUESTIONS

1. *Describe the starting point of existential philosophy, and illustrate it by citing various psychological states.*

2. *Explain the meaning of "existence precedes essence" and the way in which it impacts on the existential ethic.*

3. *What did Nietzsche mean by master and slave morality, and by "God is dead"?*

4. *Describe the three stages through which human beings can pass in their ascent toward God according to Soren Kierkegaard. What are the dangers in the religious stage?*

5. *Explain Jean-Paul Sartre's distinction between the "en-soi" and the "pour-soi" and his concept of acting in "good faith."*

AFTERWORD

e have now examined two basic problems in ethics, determinism and relativism, and explored a variety of theories concerning the good life.

We found that hedonism is a popular theory of the good with a long tradition and a common-sense appeal. If we endorse this view, we must decide between an individualistic version (either Cyrenaic or Epicurean) and a universalistic one (either the utilitarianism of Jeremy Bentham or of John Stuart Mill). Furthermore, criticisms such as the hedonistic paradox, must be addressed, and we need to consider whether happiness is a sufficiently high goal for human existence.

We divided self-realization into the development of selfhood or humanness, and we explored Aristotle's special type of self-realization ethic. The doctrine is appealing in its concern with actualizing our potentialities, but we must contend with the possibility that our tendencies and interests could be destructive. Aristotle's version, which champions moderation, seems safe and wise but lacking, perhaps, in verve and joy.

We found naturalism to be persuasive in that it grounds our ideals in the natural order of things, whether as a "be natural" ethic, as transcendentalism or as Stoicism. If only everything natural were worthwhile, we could endorse naturalism without reservation. As it stands, however, we must select from among natural phenomena those that should be emulated and those that should be avoided.

Evolutionism likewise bound us to the universe by declaring that we should aim to support evolutionary development. This took the form of Darwin's ethic of survival of the fittest or Spencer's more humane interpretation of evolution as including cooperation, pleasure, and breadth of life. We found social Darwinism rather brutal; also, Spencer combined elements that are not necessarily compatible.

The Kantian theory of duty seemed rigorous and pure, a commitment to moral principles that could be universalized. According to Kant, the benefits of action, to others or oneself, are beside the point; dedication to moral law is all important. Such an ethic is challenging, but we also found it placed principles over people. Furthermore, most (if not all) principles do not qualify as moral under the standard of the categorical imperative.

Religious ethics placed us in a rich Western tradition from which many of our basic values are derived. We did, however, see problems with the obedience exacted in Old Testament prescriptions, and with the impracticality of agape love and divine justice advocated in the New Testament.

Existentialism has great emotional resonance and recalls us to the fundamental question of how best to live. Nietzsche, Kierkegaard, and Sartre each proposed a different way of maximizing existence. They were united, however, in claiming that we must exercise our freedom in the here and now, even if that means trampling reason and morality underfoot. We found it an exhilarating philosophy but rather dangerous and without stringent reasoning.

At this point, having reviewed the various alternatives and the strengths and weaknesses of each, we are in a position to form our own theory of the good life. It could trade heavily on one theory or be an amalgam of several, but we know the alternatives and the considerations that apply in forming an ideal for our own lives. We realize that whatever theory of the good life we create, it must meet standards of reasonableness, especially the criterion of consistency.

And having come this far, we can now arrive at an ideal for our own lives that is both personally satisfying and philosophically sound.

Absolutism. The affirmation of absolute moral principles that are universally binding. For example: Never treat people as a means only, but as an end as well (Kant).

Act-deontologism. The theory that we should choose those actions that are right in themselves. *Compare with Rule-deontologism.*

Act-utilitarianism. The theory that we should choose those actions that will produce the greatest good or happiness for the greatest number of people. *Compare with Rule-utilitarianism.*

Aesthetics. That branch of philosophy dealing with taste and standards in judging art and nature, especially the canons of beauty.

Agape. Selfless love, as endorsed by Christian ethics, in which one is dedicated to what is best for the object beloved rather than for oneself.

Akrasia. Knowing what is right but lacking the will to do it; a weakness in self-control. The presence of a moral struggle indicated to Aristotle an imperfection in character.

Altruism. The position that one should always act for the welfare of others. *Compare with Egoism.*

Antithesis. An opposing or contrasting idea. In the Marxist and Hegelian dialectic, a contradictory proposition that is equally assertible. *Compare with Thesis* and *Synthesis.*

Anxiety. Acute apprehension and distress due to impending danger. In existentialism, a basic dread of our ultimate nonbeing.

Apatheia. A Stoic state of tranquility and emotional detachment regarding external events, including disasters and misfortunes. The Stoic will play his part in human affairs but will remain aloof and untouched by them.

Arete. Excellence or virtue. In Aristotle's system, the arete of our function of rationality would be to reason well, choosing appropriate means and ends.

Argumentum ad hominem. An argument to the person whereby the character or status of the individual is attacked rather than the position presented.

Aristotelianism. The philosophic position advocated by Aristotle. In ethics, Aristotle emphasized using our function of reason to choose moderate virtuous actions.

Atheism. The doctrine or belief that God does not exist.

Aurea mediocritas (meden agan). The so-called golden mean of Aristotle's ethics, whereby virtue consists in acting and feeling neither too much nor too little but just the right amount in all circumstances.

Axiology. A division of philosophy dealing with value in ethics, aesthetics, politics, and religion.

Behaviorism. The theory that human (or animal) psychology can only be studied scientifically through objectively observable and quantifiable events.

"Be natural" theory. The view that the good life consists in living naturally, emulating primitive and animal ways that are elemental and harmonious with the natural order.

Biographical fallacy. The mistake of assuming that the value of a person's actions or creations can be determined by understanding the person's life.

Calculus of pleasures. *See Hedonic calculus.*

Calvinism. The doctrine of John Calvin that emphasizes predestination, the authority of Scriptures, the supremacy of grace over works, and the sovereignty of God.

Caritas. Charity, dearness, love, affection, or esteem. Equivalent to the Greek *agape*, meaning selfless love that desires the other's well being above one's own.

Carpe diem philosophy. Seize the day. The philosophic view that stresses the enjoyment of the present moment without regard for the future.

Categorical imperative. Immanuel Kant's formulation of the unconditional moral rule, usually expressed as only acting on those principles that we could make universal law.

Censor. Sigmund Freud's concept of a psychic force that guards the gateway to consciousness, prohibiting entry to traumatic thoughts or emotions.

Christian ethics. The position that divine commands should furnish the basis for human conduct, especially the principles of love, forgiveness, brotherhood, and mercy contained in the teachings of Christ.

Christian Science. A religion, founded by Mary Baker Eddy, that strongly emphasizes spiritual healing based on Scriptures.

Communism. A political system based on Marxism that favors common ownership of property, a classless society, and the ultimate "withering away" of the state.

Confucianism. A religious and philosophic tradition, beginning in the sixth century B.C., with Confucius, that emphasizes love for humanity, reverence for parents and ancestors, and the moral perfection of the individual.

Consequentialism. The ethical view that the result or outcome of actions is most important in judging their value.

Contextual ethics. *See Situation ethics.*

Cost-benefit analysis. An approach to economics in which the ratio of costs to benefits is used to determine the desirability of business decisions.

Cultural relativism. The view that ethical judgments are relative to society; right actions are those approved of by the culture.

Cyrenaic. An ethical view, originating in Cyrene in ancient Greece, that pleasure alone should be sought.

Daimon. A spirit, supernatural power, "genius" of a family, or "demon" said by Socrates to stop him from wrongdoing. It has been interpreted as a divine voice or sign, perhaps the prohibitions of conscience.

Deconstructionism. A critical movement, originating in France in the 1960s, that questions the ability of language to diagram reality.

Deduction. Along with induction, one of the two main forms of logic; in deduction, the conclusion follows necessarily from the premises.

Deontological theory. The ethical position (also called *formalism*) that actions are inherently right or wrong.

Determinism. The doctrine that all events and actions which occur are the result of natural law, so that causal conditions necessitate the occurrence of every happening exactly as it happened.

Dialectic. In Plato, a process of question and answer to elicit a fundamental philosophic idea. In G. W. F. Hegel and Karl Marx, a process of reaching a higher truth through the confrontation between a thesis and its antithesis.

Divine justice. the notion in Christian ethics that, following Christ's example, people should be given what they need, not what they deserve.

Duration. One of the seven "marks" in Jeremy Bentham's hedonic calculus, referring to the length of time that a pleasurable experience continues.

Eidos. A metaphysical concept referring to the essence or core of a phenomenon.

Ego. An energy system in Freudian psychology that is the conscious, rational component of the psyche, mediating between the id and superego.

Egoism. The doctrine that one ought always to act for one's own self-interest above all else.

Empiricism. The epistemological view that all knowledge is based on sense-perception.

En-soi. A concept used by Jean-Paul Sartre to indicate the unity and completeness of objects as compared to the dividedness of human existence. *Compare with Pour-soi.*

Epicureanism. The ethical view of Epicurus and his disciples that mental happiness or the absence of pain is the goal in living, far surpassing physical pleasure in value. *Compare with Cyrenaics.*

Epistemology. A branch of philosophy concerned with the nature, scope, origins, and limits of the valid ways of knowing, with the definition of truth, and with knowledge.

Eros. In Christian ethics, a form of love that desires possession of the object beloved for the sake of personal enrichment; it is contrasted unfavorably with agape.

Ethical hedonism. The ethical theory that happiness or pleasure, for the individual or society, is the aim of life.

Ethics. The branch of philosophy that investigates ideals in living (a good life), and morally correct conduct (right actions).

Eudaimonia. Vital well being or happiness, which for Aristotle consists in using the unique function of reason to choose the mean and to engage in contemplation.

Evolutionary ethics. The theory that a good life is one in which we support and further the evolutionary development of nature.

Existentialism. A twentieth-century philosophic theory with roots in the nineteenth century that stresses the maximization of human existence in a fortuitous world in which the exercise of our freedom provides meaning.

Extent. One of Jeremy Bentham's seven "marks" in his hedonic calculus, referring to the number of people to whom an act extends.

Fallacy of composition. An informal fallacy of assuming that what is true of the part is true of the whole; for example, since a feather is light, a truckload of feathers is light.

Fecundity. Another of Jeremy Bentham's "marks" in his hedonic calculus, referring to the tendency of a pleasure to be followed by similar pleasures.

Feminist theology. A revisionist theological movement that stresses the importance of the goddess in religious history, the feminine aspects of the godhead, and the role of women within institutional religion.

Formalism. *See Deontologism.*

Formal logic. The rules and application of strict, rigorous, and systematic reasoning in argumentation.

Free will. The doctrine that human decisions are not causally determined by prior factors but emanate from an autonomous self.

Freudian psychology. The theory of personality and psychoanalytic view of Sigmund Freud that emphasize the force of the unconscious in motivating behavior.

Function. The philosophic notion, originating with Aristotle and often called *teleologism,* that every object including human beings has a unique or distinctive function in being.

Genetic fallacy. Also called the *fallacy of origins* and *biographical fallacy,* the mistake of assuming that the source of an idea is the measure of its worth. For example, since Nietzsche went insane, his ideas can be dismissed.

Golden mean. *See Aurea mediocritas.*

Good. That which is postulated as the ideal goal, end, aim, or purpose in human existence.

Grace. In Christian theology, the freely given, undeserved favor and love of God.

Gratuitous act. In existentialism and in the writings of André Gide in particular, the unmotivated act that arises spontaneously from the individual.

Hard determinism. The view that, since every event is caused in accordance with natural law, people are not responsible for their actions. *Compare with Soft determinism.*

Hedon. A pleasure unit in Jeremy Bentham's hedonic calculus.

Hedonic calculus. The system devised by Jeremy Bentham to measure scientifically the number of hedons to be derived from any given action.

Hedonism. The ethical theory that pleasure or happiness alone is the only intrinsic good, and pain or unpleasant consciousness the only intrinsic evil. Pleasure is therefore the goal in life, and pain should be avoided.

Hedonistic paradox. The apparent contradiction that when we pursue pleasure, we are least likely to attain it; but when we seek some other goal, pleasure can occur as a byproduct, accompaniment, or result.

Hermeneutics. The science of interpretation, especially of Scripture, as in Biblical exegesis.

Highest good (summum bonum). Often synonymous with "the good," it is the ultimate end or aim of life.

Homeostasis. The tendency of a system, whether animal, institutional, or cosmic, to maintain its equilibrium and internal stability.

Human nature. The psychological, physical, and social qualities that constitute the essence of human beings.

Hypothetical imperative. A moral prescription of a conditional kind; for example, treat people with respect if you want to be treated with respect in turn. Usually contrasted with categorical imperatives, which state unconditional moral duties; for example, treat human beings as worthy of respect.

Id. The basic energy system in the Freudian theory of psychology, standing, above all, for constant and inextinguishable sexual desire.

Inchallah. The Moslem notion that all events are preordained by Allah.

Individualistic hedonism. A variety of ethical hedonism which recommends that each individual should pursue his or her own pleasure.

Induction. Along with deduction, one of the two main forms of logic; in induction, the premises provide proof of the probability of the conclusion.

Intensity. One of Jeremy Bentham's factors in his hedonic calculus, referring to the strength of the pleasure to be derived from an experience.

Intentionalism. The view that the intention or motive of the agent is the most important factor in judging the ethical worth of action.

Kantianism. The philosophic position advocated by Immanuel Kant. In ethics, Kant stressed our obligation to act in accordance with universal principles.

Karma. In Hinduism and Buddhism, actions that incur inevitable rewards or punishment in this life or in a reincarnation.

Kismet. The Islamic concept of fate or destiny.

Laissez-faire. The economic doctrine that the market should operate freely, without government regulation.

Law of noncontradiction. The basic law in logic, first articulated by Aristotle, that two contradictory propositions cannot both be true.

Law of parsimony. A rule of thought, first presented by William of Occam (and sometimes called *Occam's razor*), that the simplest explanation is best or that explanations should not be compounded beyond what is required.

Lazy argument. A standard criticism against Stoicism that if all events are inevitable, then human effort is futile and laziness is justified.

Libertarian. In ethics, an individual who affirms a free-will position.

Linguistic analysis. A twentieth-century movement maintaining that the clarifying analysis of language can solve, resolve, or dissolve many philosophic problems.

Logic. One of the main branches of philosophy, concerned with the principles governing correct inference in deductive and inductive reasoning.

Logos. Reason, proportion, word, definition, or faculty. Socrates used *logos* to mean a distinguishing characteristic; Plato, to mean a true account; and Aristotle to mean rationality, right, reason, or ratio. To the Stoic, it was the bond of the universe or the mind of God.

Major premise. In logic, the first premise in a deductive syllogism, usually the most general statement in the argument.

Marxism. The philosophy of Karl Marx and Friedrich Engels. *See Communism.*

Meden agan. *See Aurea mediocritas.*

Metaphysics. One of the major branches of philosophy, concerned with the nature of ultimate reality, its features, processes, and structure.

Method of repetition. In the philosophy of Kierkegaard, the futile process of varying one's occupations, entertainments, residences, etc., in an effort to escape boredom and despair.

Moira. The Greek concept of fate or destiny that circumscribed even the will of the gods.

Multiculturalism. The modern movement to recognize and include the diverse array of world cultures when deciding political, social, religious, educational, psychological, and intellectual questions.

Naturalism. In ethics, the view that we should conform to the natural order in living the good life, whether as the "be natural" movement, transcendentalism, Stoicism, or even evolutionism.

Naturalistic fallacy. The logical mistake of deriving values from facts, the evaluative from the descriptive, ought from is.

Natural selection. A key feature of Darwin's theory of evolution whereby those creatures possessing the requisite attributes called for by the environment survive and produce offspring, whereas the unfavored creatures perish in the struggle for survival.

New morality. Situation ethics that rejects general moral principles and affirms the uniqueness of each circumstance and a particular morality appropriate to it.

Objectivism. The ethical position which maintains that moral principles can have objective validity whereby certain actions are right or wrong in themselves. *Contrast with Relativism.*

Occam's razor. *See Law of parsimony.*

Oedipus complex. The Freudian notion that a complex can develop from the developmental phenomenon whereby boys desire union with their mothers and the death of their fathers.

Overman. Friedrich Nietzsche's ideal of the perfect master, who is courageous, innovative, strong-willed, joyful, and powerful.

Phenomenology. A twentieth-century Continental philosophic movement that attempts to describe scientifically the structure of phenomena as they appear to consciousness.

Philia. The Greek prefix meaning *love of*; philosophy, therefore, is literally, the love of wisdom.

Philosophy. The field of knowledge that tries to understand the nature of human existence at its most fundamental level.

Phronesis. Practical wisdom in conduct that, in Aristotle's system, enabled an individual to choose virtuous actions prior to virtue becoming habitual common sense.

Political philosophy. The study of the ideal form of government, the grounds for the authority of the state, the concepts of justice, freedom, and equality, and the rights and obligations of citizens.

Post hoc, ergo propter hoc. Literally, after this, therefore caused by this. The mistake in thinking that because event *A* preceded event *B*, event *A* is necessarily the cause of *B*.

Pour-soi. Jean-Paul Sartre's notion of the "for itself," the mode of being of humans whereby consciousness enables them to choose the type of life they want to live. *Compare with En-soi.*

Predeterminism. In contrast to social scientific determinism, predeterminism is the theory that a cosmic destiny controls all physical events.

Prima facie obligations. Duties that are apparent, perhaps self-evident, and that we ought to honor unless overridden by another *prima facie* duty.

Principle of entropy. The view that energy is constantly being transformed into unusable forms or that it is being progressively lost to human beings or less available for use.

Principle of utility. In utilitarianism, the moral principle that we should seek the greatest amount of happiness for the greatest number of people.

Projection. A defense mechanism in Freudian psychology in which the psyche protects itself from guilt by assigning blame for shameful conduct onto outside forces or other people.

Prophetic tradition. The series of Hebrew prophets, in the second of the three divisions of the Old Testament, who are believed to speak for God or to prophesy by divine inspiration.

Psychoanalysis. The method of treating psychological disorders, devised by Sigmund Freud, that seeks to draw repressed material to the level of consciousness and thereby effect a cure.

Psychological egoism. The view that all people seek their own advantage or self-interest, whether they acknowledge it or not.

Psychological hedonism. The view that everyone pursues his or her own pleasure in life; sometimes referred to as the *pleasure principle.*

Psychology. The study of the human mind, and mental states and processes, or the study of human and animal behavior for the sake of deriving principles of understanding and methods of control.

Purity. Another of the "marks" in Jeremy Bentham's hedonic calculus, referring to the degree of pleasure and pain in a given action.

Quiddity. The core, essence, or *eidos* of a phenomenon.

Rationalization. A term sometimes used as synonymous with reasoning but more properly, finding a plausible excuse for what we want to do anyway.

Realpolitik. Political realism or practicality in public affairs, especially the belief that power, not ideals, always proves decisive.

Relativism. *See Cultural relativism.*

Religious ethics. Ethical theories in which the basic principles are grounded in divine commands, usually as contained in sacred writings and interpreted by institutions.

Retributive theory of justice. The doctrine that justice should be meted out according to people's deserts, not their needs, that a system of proportionality should operate whereby rewards or punishment are commensurate with the individual's praiseworthiness or blameworthiness.

Right. Morally correct conduct, actions, or behavior.

Rule-deontologism. The theory that we should choose those moral principles that are right in themselves. *Compare with Act-deontologism.*

Rule-utilitarianism. The theory that we should choose those rules that would promote the greatest good (especially happiness) for the majority. *Compare with Act-utilitarianism.*

Sadism. The view, associated with the Marquis de Sade, that advocates sexual gratification through inflicting pain or causing degradation to others.

Sadomasochism. Sexual gratification through inflicting pain or receiving pain or psychological humiliation.

Sapir-Whorf hypothesis. The sociological theory that language determines thought much more than thought determines language.

Second law of thermodynamics. *See Principle of entropy.*

Self. The individual person that exists as the same continuous being from birth to death, underlying consciousness and experience.

Self-realization. The ethical theory that advocates the maximum development of one's self or one's humanness.

Sine qua non. A necessary or indispensable condition or factor; for example, freedom as a *sine qua non* of democracy.

Situation ethics. *See New morality.*

Social Darwinism. The doctrine, prominent in the nineteenth century, that wealthy and prominent people have shown by their success that they are the fittest to survive.

Soft determinism. The view that, although events occur according to natural law, rational beings are responsible for their actions insofar as they act voluntarily. *Compare with Hard determinism.*

Stoicism. The philosophic theory that advocates the acceptance of the natural and inevitable order of events as a way of achieving independence and tranquility.

Subjectivism. The ethical view that moral judgments simply reflect the personal beliefs, attitudes, or feelings of the person rendering the judgment. *Contrast with Objectivism.*

Sublimation. The Freudian concept of diverting sexual energy from an unacceptable goal to one that is socially approved.

Summum bonum. *See Highest good.*

Superego. In Freudian psychology, the energy system that embodies social rules and prohibitions as instilled in us by our parents acting as society's agents.

Syllogism. A formally structured argument in deductive logic containing a major premise, a minor premise, and a conclusion.

Synthesis. In the philosophies of G. W. F. Hegel and Karl Marx, a new and higher level of development of an idea, institution, or phenomenon produced by the reconciliation of a thesis and its antithesis.

Talion. The Hebrew law of talion whereby one reaps what one sows; people receive what they deserve in a universe governed by a just God.

Teleological argument. One of the principal proofs for the existence of God, which argues that since the world exhibits evidence of design, there must be an intelligent cosmic designer.

Teleologism. The view that the universe and human existence is purposive in nature and contains ends and goals rather than being random and purposeless. *See Function.*

Theistic existentialism. The branch of existential philosophy that assumes human existence can only be maximized through nonrational devotion to God.

Theology. The study of the nature of God, his attributes, and his relation to human beings.

Theoria. Aristotle's concept of the highest employment of reason, which is pure contemplation.

Thesis. In the Marxist and Hegelian systems, an ascertainable proposition that is opposed by an apparent opposite, and is reconciled in the higher unity of a synthesis. *See Antithesis and Synthesis.*

Transcendentalism. The American philosophic movement that affirms the intuitive and spiritual realm above or within the natural world.

Übermensch. *See Overman.*

Universalistic hedonism. The hedonistic view that pleasure or happiness should be sought not just for oneself but for humankind. The individual agent is to count for one and only one in the moral equation. *Compare with Individualistic hedonism.*

Utilitarianism. The form of universalistic hedonism that seeks the greatest happiness for the greatest number.

Utilitarian theory of justice. The doctrine that justice consists in giving people what they need, not what they deserve. Punishment therefore should be forward-looking, designed to improve the individual, deter potential wrongdoers, and protect society. *Compare with Retributive theory of justice.*

Valid argument. A train of reasoning that is formally correct, such that the conclusion is entailed by the premises.

Weltanschauung. A world view that encompasses a conception of the universe and humanity's relation to it.

Zen Buddhism. A form of Chinese Buddhism that later spread to Japan and Korea in which meditation and intuition, rather than sacred writings or rational teaching, are used to receive enlightenment.

INDEX

A

Abortion controversy, 58–59, 232
Absolutism, 84
Act-deontologism, 216. *See also* Rule-deontologism
Actions, evaluating, 39–48. *See also* Right
Act-utilitarianism, 135
Aesthetics, 29–31
Agape love, 237–40, 248–50
Aim, in Aristotelianism, 156
Akrasia, 5
Altruism
  egoism and, 11, 13
  hedonism and, 110
  utilitarianism and, 123
American transcendentalism, 169, 180–83, 280
Anselm, St., 243
Anthropology, 85–89
Antithesis, 94
Anxiety, 255–56
Apatheia, 186
Aquinas, St. Thomas, 20, 163, 196, 239, 243
Arete, 158, 164
Argument from design, 196–97
Argumentum ad hominem, 18
Aristippus, 115–16
Aristotelianism, 155–62, 279
  critique of, 162–66
  function in, 157
  good in, 156–57
  reason in, 157–62
Aristotle, 5, 24, 109, 138, 155–57
  on ignorance-responsibility, 40–41
  on reality of future events, 189*n*
Art, 29–31
Atheism
  of Nietzsche, 264–68
  of Sartre, 258
Augustine, St., 3, 243
Aurea mediocritas, 158–61
Aurelius, Marcus, 183
Authoritarian personality, 191
Autobiography (Mill), 136
Axiology, 29

B

Barth, Karl, 243
Behaviorism, 72–73
Being and Nothingness (Sartre), 271
Being and Time (Heidegger), 271
"Be natural" movement, 169–74, 280
  critique of, 175–79
  country living, 175–76
  natural state, 176–77
  nature as model for conduct, 177–79
  nature and the good, 179
  history of, 170–74
Benedict, Ruth, 70, 88–89
Bentham, Jeremy, 122, 123–24
Biographical fallacy, 18
Blanshard, Brand, 22
Boethius, 185–86*n*
Bonhoeffer, D., 243
Bonum faciendum, 48
Bradley, F. H., 139
Brunner, Emil, 243
Buber, Martin, 239
Bultmann, Rudolf, 243
Butler, Joseph, 136
Byron, George Gordon, Lord, 172

C

Calculus of pleasures, 124
Caligula (Camus), 262
Calvin, John, 243
Calvinism, 95
Camus, Albert, 52, 97, 254, 257, 262, 263
Caritas, 237
Carpe diem philosophy, 116
Categorical imperative, 219–21
  hypothetical imperative vs., 223
Categorical Imperative, The (Paton), 228
Censor, 91
Certainty, in hedonic calculus, 125
Christian ethics
  agape love in, 237–40
  divine justice in, 240–42

Christian ethics (*cont.*)
    impracticality of, 248–49
    spirit of love vs. ethical laws in, 249–50
Christian Science, 19
Chronicles, 1 (Old Testament), 235
Chrysippus, 183
Climate, determinism and, 68–69
Communism, 45–46. *See also* Marxism
Composition, fallacy of, 188–89
Concluding Unscientific Postscript (Kierkegaard), 271
Confucianism, 184*n*
Consequentialism, 43
Consistency, 3–5
Consolation of Philosophy, The (Boethius), 185–86*n*
Contextual ethics, 243–45
Corinthians, 1 (New Testament), 240
Cost-benefit analysis, utilitarianism and, 129
Crime and Punishment (Dostoyevski), 263
Criterion of reversibility, 227
Critique of Practical Reason (Kant), 217
Critique of Pure Reason (Kant), 217
Cultural relativism, 61, 62, 82–106
    contemporary trends in, 84–85
    moral experience and, 100–101
    moral progress and, 101–2
    multiculturalism and, 105–6
    objectivist position vs., 102–4
    self-contradiction of, 96–99
    subjectivism and, 99–100
    theoretical sources of, 85–96
        Freudian psychology, 90–92
        Marxism, 92–96
        sociology/anthropology, 85–89
Cyrenaic doctrine, 115–16
    critique of, 116–18

D

Daimon, 183
Darwin, Charles, 194–96
Darwinism, 194–203, 280
    ethics and, 199–203
    religion and, 196–99
Deconstructionism, 84
Deductive logic, 28
Deontological theory, 46, 214–16. *See also* Kantianism
De Rerem Natura (Lucretius), 182
Descartes, René, 157
Design, argument from, 196–97

Determinism, 61–80
    climate/geography and, 68–69
    contemporary, 66–73
    genetic endowment and, 67–68
    hard, 63–64
    illusion of freedom and, 62–63
    libertarian rebuttal to, 73–80
    predeterminism as early form of, 64–66
    psychology and, 72–73
    society/culture and, 70–72
    soft, 63–64
Dialectic, 94
Divine justice, 240–42
Dostoyevski, Fedor, 254, 262, 263, 276
Dryden, John, 188
Duration, in hedonic calculus, 124–25
Duty ethics, 214–30
    act-deontologism and, 216
    deontological theory and, 214–15
    Kantianism and, 217–23
        critique of, 224–29
    rule-deontologism and, 216–17

E

Earnestness of purpose, 41–42
Eddy, Mary Baker, 19
Ego, 91
Egoism. *See* psychological egoism
Eidos, 259
Emerson, Ralph Waldo, 181, 182
Empiricism, 2, 3, 7–8
    existentialism vs., 259
Engels, Friedrich, 92
En-soi, 271–73
Entropy, principle of, 208
Epictetus, 183, 185
Epicurianism, 118–21
    critique of, 121–22
Epicurus, 118–21
Epistemology, 25–27
Eros, 237–38
Ethical egoist, 12
Ethical hedonism, 112
Ethics. *See also* specific doctrines, theories
    as branch of philosophy, 23–31
    justification of values and, 1–3
    psychology contrasted with, 17–19
    religion and, 19–23
    science contrasted with, 2, 3, 7–8, 10–17
    scope of, 31–32
    standard of reasonableness in, 3–8

on nature, 178
on utilitarianism, 122, 131–34
Minor premise, 28
Moderation, in Aristotelianism, 158–61
  critique of, 164–65
Moira, 64
Moore, G. E., 15
Mortality, 6n
Motives, 39–40
Multiculturalism, 84, 105–6

N

Naturalism, 168–92, 280. *See also* Evolutionism
  American transcendentalism and, 169, 180, 181–83
  "be natural" movement and, 169–74
  critique of, 175–79
  in broad perspective, 210–11
  meanings of, 168–69
Naturalistic fallacy, 15–17
  hedonic calculus and, 129–30
Natural selection, 195
Nausea (Sartre), 260
Neoplatonism, 181
New Morality, 243–45
New Testament, 236–45
  Christian ethics and, 237–42
  situation ethics and, 243–45
Nicomachean Ethics (Aristotle), 31, 156
Niebuhr, Reinhold, 243, 249
Nietzsche, Friedrich, 19, 254, 263, 268, 276, 280
  atheistic existentialism of, 264–68
  "master morality," 266–68
  oppressive forces, 265–66
No Exit (Sartre), 273
Noncontradiction, law of, 98
Noncontradiction of facts, 5–6
Notes from the Underground (Dostoyevski), 262
Nothingness, 256–57

O

Objectivism, 47, 84
  relativism vs., 102–4
  scientific view and, 104–5
Obscenity, 29–30

Occam's razor, 198
Oedipus complex, 255
Old Testament, 233–36
Origin of Species, The (Darwin), 194
Ought, 38–39
Outcomes, 43–44

P

Pacifism, 242n
Paley, William, 197
Pareto, Vilfredo, 87
Parsimony, law of, 198
Pascal, Blaise, 191, 254
Paton, H. J., 228
Pavlov, Ivan, 72
Phenomenology, 259–61
Philia, 237
Philosophy, branches of. *See also* Political philosophy
  aesthetics, 29–31
  epistemology, 25–27
  ethics, 23–31
  logic, 27–29
  metaphysics, 24–25
Phronesis, 165
Plato, 5, 98, 158
Pleasure. *See* Hedonism
Political philosophy, 30
Post hoc, ergo propter hoc, 77
Pour-soi, 271–73
Predestination. *See* Predeterminism
Predeterminism, 64–66
  in Stoicism, 184
  critique of, 188–90
Prima facie obligations, 38, 225, 226, 229
Principle of utility, 123
Probability of interpretation, 6–7
Projection, 91
Prophetic tradition, 235–36
Propinquity, in hedonic calculus, 125
Psychoanalysis, 5
Psychological egoism, 11–13, 56, 130
Psychological hedonism, 110–11
  critique of, 111–12
  hedonic calculus and, 129–30
Psychology
  determinism and, 72–73
  ethics contrasted with, 17–19
  Freudian, 19, 90–92
  and self-realization, 139
Purity, in hedonic calculus, 126

R

S

Syllogism, 28–29
Synthesis, 94

T

Tabula rasa, 151
Talion, 240
Teleological argument, 196–97
    Darwinism and, 197–99
Teleologism. *See also* Intentionalism
    Aristotle and, 39, 43–46, 163
    deontological theory vs., 214–15
    formalism contrasted with, 48–52
    outcomes and, 43–44
    weaknesses of, 44–46
Theaetetus (Plato), 98
Theistic existentialism, 254
Theoria, 161
Theory of types, 97n
Thesis, 94
Thoreau, Henry David, 169, 170–71
Thus Spake Zarathustra (Nietzsche), 268,
    271
Tillich, Paul, 243, 256
Toynbee, Arnold, 68–69
Transcendentalism. *See* American tran-
    scendentalism
Types, theory of, 97n

U

Übermensch, 267
Unconscious mind, 90

Universalistic hedonism, 113–14, 113–15,
    279
Utilitarianism, 122–34
    Bentham on, 124–27
        critique of, 127–31
    historical background of, 122–24
    Mill on, 131–32, 134n
        critique of, 132–34
Utilitarianism (Mill), 131
Utilitarian justice, 50–52
Utility, principle of, 123

V

Value theory, 29
Vatican Cellars, The (Gide), 263

W

Walden (Thoreau), 170
Watson, John B., 72
Weltanschauung, 199
Wesley, John, 48
Wilde, Oscar, 147
William of Occam, 198
Wittgenstein, Ludwig, 71
Wordsworth, William, 171–72, 173–74

Z

Zeno of Citium, 183